RHETORIC RETOLD

RHETORIC RETOLD

REGENDERING THE TRADITION FROM ANTIQUITY THROUGH THE RENAISSANCE

Cheryl Glenn

SOUTHERN ILLINOIS UNIVERSITY PRESS

Carbondale and Edwardsville

Library of Congress Cataloging-in-Publication Data

Glenn, Cheryl.

Rhetoric retold : regendering the tradition from antiquity through

the Renaissance / Cheryl Glenn.

p. cm.

Includes bibliographical references and index.

1. Rhetoric—History. 2. Feminism and literature. 3. Women

authors. 4. Women and literature. I. Title.

PN183.G54 1997

808'.08209—dc21

ISBN 0-8093-1929-2 (alk. paper). —   97-7051

ISBN 0-8093-2137-8 (pbk. : alk. paper)   CIP

Frontispiece: *Socrates Seeking Alcibiades at the House of Aspasia* by
Jean Léon Gérôme. Private collection, New York.

The paper used in this publication meets the minimum require-
ments of American National Standard for Information Sciences—
Permanence of Paper for Printed Library Materials, ANSI
Z39.48-1984. ♾

FOR ANNA

The entire history of women's struggle for self-determination has been muffled in silence over and over. . . . Each feminist work has tended to be received as if it emerged from nowhere; as if each of us had lived, thought, and worked without any historical past or contextual present.
—Adrienne Rich, "Foreword,"
Lies

What would happen to logocentrism, to the great philosophical systems, to the world order in general if the rock upon which they founded this church should crumble?

If some fine day it suddenly came out that the logocentric plan had always, inadmissibly, been to create a foundation for (to found and fund) phallocentrism, to guarantee the masculine order a rationale equal to history itself?

So all the history, all the stories would be there to retell differently; the future would be incalculable; the historic forces would and will change hands and change body—another thought which is yet unthinkable—will transform the functioning of all society. We are living in an age where the conceptual foundation of an ancient culture is in the process of being undermined by millions of species of mole (Topoi, ground mines) never known before.
—Hélène Cixous and Catherine Clément, "Sorties,"
The Newly Born Woman

CONTENTS

PREFACE

Rhetoric Retold: Regendering the Tradition from Antiquity Through the Renaissance encompasses antiquity through the Renaissance for several important reasons, not the least of which is that the Enlightenment saw the end of classical rhetoric as the dominant and most influential system of education and communication. But equally important to this study, the Enlightenment brought about the end of the one-sex model of humanity that centered on the telos of perfect maleness, with women and all children being perceived as undeveloped men. What the pre-Enlightenment one-sex model provides *Rhetoric Retold* is a cultural—rather than a "scientific"—foundation for femaleness and maleness that accounts for the movement females and males have made along and across the range of gendered performances.

Using the schemes of periodization commonly referred to as antiquity, the Middle Ages, and the Renaissance, *Rhetoric Retold* charts women's inscriptions and contributions to rhetorical history and theory, beginning with Sappho, the tenth Muse. The thread connecting the women in this study may well be no more than John Donne's "gold to airy thinness beat," yet, in each of the following chapters, this thread is strong enough to weave women into the same networks of language, to bind them with the same cultural restrictions and literary stereotypes. Thus, the contributions of Greek and Roman women comprise chapter 2, "Classical Rhetoric Conceptualized, or Vocal Men and Muted Women." The Pythagorean women, Plato's Diotima, and Aspasia of Miletus all contributed to the philosophical thinking that evolved into rhetoric. In 42 BCE, Hortensia represented all the women of her class when she addressed the Roman triumvirs; other Roman women to speak publicly were Fulvia, Amasia Sentia, Gaia Afrania, and Sempronia. Chapter 3, "Medieval Rhetoric: Pagan Roots, Christian Flowering, or Veiled Voices in the Medieval Rhetorical Tradition," focuses on the writings of Julian of Norwich and Margery Kempe, two of a number of medieval women (Perpetua, Dhouda, Hrotsvitha, Héloïse, and Hildegard von Bingen) who demonstrate rhetorical sophistication believed to be inaccessible to women at the time. The Renaissance advanced to the margins the written works of Margaret More Roper, Anne Askew, Lady Jane Grey, Catherine Parr, Anne Dowriche, Elizabeth Cooke Russell, Anne Cooke Bacon, Mary Sidney Herbert, Mary Sidney Wroth, Elizabeth Faulkland Cary, Catherine of Aragon, and Elizabeth I. The contributions to rhetorical technique and literary rhetoric of Margaret More Roper, Anne Askew, and Elizabeth I are calibrated in chapter 4, "Inscribed in the Margins: Renaissance Women and Rhetorical Culture." The work of these Renaissance women has important implications for discourse theory, especially in terms of gender and gendered performance: what did it take—what were the criteria—for these women to rise in the social order to play an active, public role?

Beyond the recovery work of describing the performances and contributions of overlooked women rhetoricians, *Rhetoric Retold* brings selected subjects within fixed historical and geographical parameters. To locate women practicing within and outside of the Western rhetorical tradition, I follow the migration of our intellectual tradition from its inception in classical antiquity and its confrontation with and ultimate appropriation by evangelical Christianity to its force in the medieval Church and in Tudor arts and politics. Hence the site of this study not only permits narrative coherence, it also provides the rationale for subject selection. Alongside Plato, Pericles, Aristotle, Cicero, Augustine, and Thomas Wilson, this book locates Sappho, Aspasia, Diotima, Hortensia, Fulvia, Julian of Norwich, Margery Kempe, Margaret More Roper, Anne Askew, and Elizabeth I, providing a fully gendered rather than only a women's history of rhetoric. *Rhetoric Retold* describes women's resistance to and negotiations within the rigidly dichotomized social order, as well as within their educational boundaries. Finally, chapter 5, "The Implications of a Regendered, Retold Rhetoric, or Against Conclusions," discusses the research and teaching opportunities that grow out of a convergence of rhetoric and feminism, opportunities that continue to challenge our community of rhetorical scholars.

ACKNOWLEDGMENTS

This project could not have been accomplished without the substantial support of my teachers, colleagues, funding agencies, friends, and family. Back in graduate school at The Ohio State University, I became indebted to Edward P. J. Corbett, Andrea A. Lunsford, Frank O'Hare, the late Rolf Soellner, and the late Stanley J. Kahrl, all of whom gave me tough-minded suggestions and supportive criticism as a small part of this project was taking root. Andrea insisted that my project continue to its teleology; she wavered in neither her expectations nor her support. Although this book addresses broader issues and a broader audience and shows little resemblance to that initial research, those teachers have always been the invoked audience of this scholarly effort.

During my years at Oregon State University, I benefited from the support and interest of colleagues, who responded to my drafts, sent me relevant articles and books, wrote grant recommendations for me, invited my contributions to their collections or conference panels, and, most important, set professional examples for me of "good people speaking well": Chris Anderson, Jamie Barlowe, Walter Beale, Ann Berthoff, Suzanne Clark, Vicki Collins, Bob Connors, Lisa Ede, Rich Enos, Theresa Enos, Toby Fulwiler, Anita Helle, Win Horner, Susan Hunter, Susan Jarratt, Joyce Middleton, Beverly Moss, Roxanne Mountford, Jon Olson, Kris Ratcliffe, Sandy Spanier, Pat Sullivan, Jan Swearingen, John Trimbur, and Kathleen Welch.

During the work of this book, I was blessed by release time and financial support from various granting agencies. But most grant applications depended on the generosity of my department chairs, Bob Frank and Bob Schwartz, who consistently demonstrated their support of this project by signing off on my various grant applications when the last thing either of them needed was to lose a professor for a term—or two. Oregon State University awarded me College of Liberal Arts Research Award Grants, Research Council Grants, an L. L. Stewart Grant, and Library Research Travel Grants. The OSU Center for the Humanities provided me a resident fellowship, where I enjoyed a term of uninterrupted research and thus managed to lay out the methodology that I explain in the first chapter. The OSU Burlington Resources Foundation Faculty Achievement Award for teaching enabled me to make a long-overdue purchase of a computer and printer.

A National Endowment for the Humanities Summer Stipend together with two Oregon Council for the Humanities Summer Research Grants provided three summers of supported research and writing. And a National Endowment for the Humanities Fellowship for College Teachers allowed me a full year of composing, revising, proofreading, and copyediting—and rewriting. Finally, the OSU Elizabeth P. Ritchie Distinguished Professor Award afforded me the

Acknowledgments

time and resources to spend with my husband—and celebrate the completion of this book.

My great debt is, of course, to my family and friends, whose support makes my life better in every imaginable way: Anna Seitz, Darrin Quillen, Krysta Olson, Virginia Lehman, Terry Campbell, Meghan Campbell, Jane Berry, Gene Glenn, and Dorinda Glenn; Cindy Cox, Carole Crateau, Vreneli Farber, Debbie Fox, Angeletta Gourdine, Heather Brodie Graves, Roger Graves, Dianne Hart, Charlotte Headrick, Babette DuSang Jones, Sebastian Knowles, Kathryn Liggett, Marianne Makman, Marilyn Moller, Kathy Moore, Ray Muessig, Jerry Nelms, Bob Nye, Kay Schaffer, Diane Slywczuk, Judy Stockton, Molly Travis, and Becky Warner. I am deeply and forever indebted to the research assistance of Danielle Mitchell, whose library skills rank her among the finest, most valiant, and most promising of scholar-adventurers. I also want to thank Tracey Sobol-Hill, from Southern Illinois University Press, for her attention to both detail and unity, Kathryn Koldehoff for her keen eye, and Carol Burns for keeping us all on track.

Finally, my gratitude envelops Jon Olson: in general, for his kindliness, dignity, and judiciousness, and in specific, for his generous and thoughtful response to my work-in-progress. A fellow rhetorician, he read every word, gently but firmly giving me advice—especially when I needed it most but wanted it least.

For permission to reprint certain material, I gratefully acknowledge the following:

From *Sappho: Poems and Fragments*, translated by Josephine Balmer. Copyright © 1984 by Josephine Balmer. Published by arrangement with Carol Publishing Group.

From *Sappho: A New Translation*, translated by Mary Barnard. Copyright 1958. University of California Press.

From *Sappho's Lyre: Archaic Lyric and Women Poets of Ancient Greece*, translated by Diane Raynor. Copyright 1991. University of California Press.

From *Sappho and Alcaeus: An Introduction to the Study of Ancient Lesbian Poetry*, by Denys Page. Copyright 1955. By permission of Oxford University Press.

From "Dame Sirith," *Early Middle English Verse and Prose*, edited by J. A. W. Bennett and G. V. Smithers. Copyright 1968. By permission of Oxford University Press.

From "Judith" and "The Banished Wife's Complaint," *Select Translations from Old English Poetry*, edited by Albert S. Cook and Chauncey B. Tinker. Copyright 1935. Harvard University Press.

From *Annales*, by William Camden (SIC 4501). 1635. The Houghton Library, Harvard University.

From Elizabeth I's A.L.S. to Edward VI (pfMS Typ 686). Department of Printing and Graphic Arts, The Houghton Library, Harvard University.

RHETORIC RETOLD

ONE

Mapping the Silences, or Remapping Rhetorical Territory

INTRODUCTION

Alcibiades and Aspasia, the nineteenth-century print that serves as the frontispiece for this book, was depicted in beautiful detail by French artist J.-L. Gérôme, best known for transfusing his journeys to the East with an exotic and erotic charm. Gérôme presents us Aspasia of Miletus reclining seductively on Alcibiades, her hand cupping his breast, her head suspiciously near his stomach and wide-spread legs, while Alcibiades looks away from her and reaches out to clasp Socrates's hand. Thus, Aspasia comes down to us an odalisque, while Alcibiades, the object of Aspasia's attention, comes to us wreathed in laurel. According to Gérôme, then, the woman I refigure as Our Mother of Rhetoric, lifelong companion of Pericles and influential colleague of famous men, is the harem girl to Alcibiades, the arrogant, dissolute, untrustworthy love object of Socrates.

For the past twenty-five hundred years in Western culture, the ideal woman has been disciplined by cultural codes that require a closed mouth (silence), a closed body (chastity), and an enclosed life (domestic confinement) (Stallybrass 127). Little wonder, then, that women have been closed out of the rhetorical tradition, a tradition of vocal, virile, public—and therefore privileged— men. Men have acted in the polis, in the public light of rhetorical discourse, determining philosophic truth, civic good, the literary canon, and the theories and praxes of rhetoric. Meanwhile, women have been circumscribed within the seldom-examined *idios*, the private domain; women have been designated *idiots* who sustain family, friendships, and their public-discoursing men from within the *oikos*, the household. As enclosed bodies, the female sex has been both excluded from and appropriated by the patriarchal territory of rhetorical practices and displays.

Rhetoric always inscribes the relation of language and power at a particular moment (including who may speak, who may listen or who will agree to listen,

1

and what can be said); therefore, canonical rhetorical history has represented the experience of males, powerful males, with no provision or allowance for females. In short, rhetorical history has replicated the power politics of gender, with men in the highest cultural role and social rank. And our view of rhetoric has remained one of a gendered landscape, with no female rhetoricians (theoreticians) clearly in sight.

Only in the light of recent feminist scholarship recovering and recuperating women's contributions in the broad history of culture making—in philosophy, literature, language, writing, societal structure, religion, history, education, reading, psychology, and gender—have we begun to view rhetorical history differently, have we begun to regender it. Fading away is rhetoric as we have known it—*exclusively* upper-class, male, agonistic, and public, yet seemingly universal. Coming into view, albeit still dimly, are the inclusionary rhetorics of the future, rhetorics that will account for the regendered rhetorical terrain on which feminist archaeologists and researchers have already begun to identify women's bodies.[1]

Rhetoric Retold identifies women's bodies, explores their contributions to and participation within the rhetorical tradition, and writes them into an expanded, inclusive tradition, for this regendered history of rhetoric neither reproduces nor reduces the power politics of that concept we refer to as *gender*. After all, *gender* is merely a concept borrowed from grammar that connotes "a socially agreed upon system of distinction rather than an objective description of inherent traits" (J. Scott 29). So instead of working with gender as a hierarchical category, *Rhetoric Retold* examines and explores gender as a relationship among distributions of power, a relationship that plays itself out within cultural constraints and demands.

Except for rhetoric, no intellectual endeavor—not even the male bastion of philosophy—has so consciously rendered women invisible and silent.[2] But invisible and silent are not the same as absent, as this study shows. Silence is a fertile field of investigation: indeed, some women are silenced by others, but some use silence to their own ends, a delivery of silence that I interrogate in chapter 5. To enrich and complicate the concept of silence, Adrienne Rich writes that silence itself has a presence and a form that should never be confused with absence ("Cartographies" 17). To the connectedness of silence and safety, Audre Lorde implores all women to articulate their silences and to war against the "tyrannies of silence" (41). Thus, the feminist challenge is vital to locating invisible and silenced women and restoring them and their voices to rhetorical history.[3]

Until recently, few of us had heard of Aspasia; fewer still had connected her with rhetorical practice. But when her rhetorical colony is located within its larger context, when we examine the borders along which she defined herself— the writings of the men she influenced, for instance—we can better map out how Aspasia was perceived by those men and, perhaps, how she perceived her estate within the surrounding geography. Yet Aspasia's intellectual estate still seems to be off-limits, except as a morality tale for women who insist on entering the rhetorical arena: they will be used, misappropriated, and long ignored. Or worse, they will be disfigured, inscribed with masculine fantasy and curiosity, like Gérôme's idyllic (unfair and inaccurate) rendition of Aspasia and Alcibiades. The example of his print brings to the fore the whole notion of women's place in rhetoric. Where on the landscape we call rhetorical history should we look for women? How many women are hidden in the shadows of monumental rhetoricians? How many others remain misidentified as holes and bulges on out-of-the-way territories?

Therefore, because of and despite the feminist challenge to rhetorical history, the rhetorical landscape is proving to be the hardest history to remap. Fredric Jameson admonishes us that "history is *not* a text, not a narrative, master or otherwise, but . . . it is inaccessible to us except in textual form, and that our approach to it and to the Real itself necessarily passes through its prior textualization, its narrativization" (35). Still, we want to story rhetorical history, particularly a history inclusive of women. And such restorying entails our rethinking texts, approaches, narrative—and history itself. The writing of women into history "necessarily involves redefining and enlarging traditional notions of historical significance, to encompass personal, subjective experience as well as public and political activities" (Gordon, Buhle, and Dye 89). Such a methodology implies not only a new history of women but also a new rhetorical history, in short, an entirely new map of rhetoric.

REMAPPING RHETORICAL TERRITORY

Not long ago, we could pull a neatly folded history of rhetoric out of our glove compartment, unfold it, and navigate our course through the web of lines that connected the principal centers of rhetoric. Whether using Edward P. J. Corbett's, George A. Kennedy's, James L. Kinneavy's, or James J. Murphy's map, we followed an aristocratic blue line, a master narrative that started with Corax and Tisias and led directly to Plato and Aristotle, then Cicero, Quintilian, and St. Augustine, and eventually to Richard Weaver, I. A. Richards, Chaim Perelman, and Kenneth Burke—each rhetorician preparing us for the next, like Burma Shave signs. For years, we ignored the borders of our map, the shadowy regions where roads run off the edge of the paper and drop away at sharp angles. We assumed that some areas were barren territories devoid of scenic routes, historic events, influential people (i.e., influential men). Other regions were off-limits, like those murky territories on Renaissance charts that bore warnings of monsters beyond the sea.

The map we were using did exactly what we wanted it to do: it met our professional, intellectual, and social needs. That canonized, masculinized map embodied and reflected our institutional focus on great, powerful men whose texts, lives, and actions surely transcended the particularities of history and circumstance. Resonating with the rest of our intellectual traditions—

literary, poetic, scientific, historical, political—all of which focused on masculine power, that map both "expresse[d] and transcend[ed] the values, conventions, and circumstances of a discipline at a particular moment" (Atwill 91). But most important, perhaps, that map served us well "at a time when rhetoric's legitimacy as a field of scholarly inquiry was contested," for, as Takis Poulakos tells us, "a narrative account of rhetoric's stable subject matter across time proved to be an effective response to charges of illegitimacy . . . [as well as] a successful way of resisting pressures . . . to turn the study of rhetoric into a positivistic investigation" ("Introduction" 1).

Yet we all acknowledge that rhetorical history is not and has never been neutral territory and that our new map or, rather, our partially completed map*s* reflect and coordinate our current institutional, intellectual, political, and personal values, all of which have become markedly more diverse and elastic in terms of gender, race, and class. Over the past ten years alone, the cartographic achievements of James Berlin, Patricia Bizzell, William Covino, Sharon Crowley, Richard Leo Enos, Bruce Herzberg, Susan Jarratt, Nan Johnson, Susan Miller, Jasper Neel, Krista Ratcliffe, Edward Schiappa, C. Jan Swearingen, Victor Vitanza, Kathleen Welch, W. Ross Winterowd, and many others have encouraged us in our mapmaking. We all seem to agree that our new maps are "doing" differently what maps do: they are taking us more places, introducing us to more people, complicating our understanding in more ways than did the traditional map.

The Heritage Turnpike featured no communities of women, the places many of us want to visit. So, for several years now, my work has been to trace the routes to those settlements and to resurvey the territory to locate and position women rhetoricians on the map—rarely an easy task. But using particular reference points, I could plot my project (1) with resistant readings by women, as well as by men, of the paternal narrative; (2) with consideration of female-authored rhetorical works comparable to male-authored works; and (3) with broad definitions of *rhetoric* that move it from an *ex*clusionary to an *in*clusionary enterprise (Bizzell, "Opportunities").

It is beyond the scope of an introductory chapter to provide a thorough overview of those three methodologies, but I want to call to mind the broad scope of their application in the light of three angles: *historiography* (which informs the entire enterprise of feminist remappings); *feminism* (which specifically works to situate female rhetorical figures); and *gender studies* (which refigure gender as a category for historiographical analysis). I have viewed the terrain from these three angles throughout my project, but in this introduction, I will use Aspasia to illustrate just how these three angles inform my work. Of course, any such set of methodological categories overlap when used purposefully to advance a feminist project like *Rhetoric Retold*, and such categories also take a postmodern slant when used deliberately to reveal multiple and different *angles* from which to map rhetorical terrain.

LINES AND ANGLES ON THE RHETORICAL MAP

Postmodernism influences our resistant readings of the paternal narrative, particularly since it demands our awareness of situatedness, our angle (in my case, reading as a feminist, as a woman).[4] Resistant postmodernism, as opposed to ludic postmodernism, for instance, reveals various angles of meaning, the results of various social and material struggles over power and knowledge (Ebert 886–87). These angles help us identify previously unseen and unconsidered problems of "foundational" knowledge, in this case the tradition of rhetorical history. Therefore, "*The* History of Rhetoric" is quickly displaced by questions. *Whose* history? *Whose* rhetoric? *Which* rhetoric? All necessary challenges to a canon that continues to be so unrelentingly elite and male.

Forcing us to admit that we each have an angle, resistant postmodernism has made us skeptical about the procedures that legitimized and mapped out "the" history of rhetoric in the first place. No wonder, then, that historians of rhetoric no longer rely exclusively on *linear* plotting to connect one rhetorician to the "next." Instead, we have taken to measuring and charting territory by means of *angles*. By constructing our map by means of angular as well as linear measurements, we can chart and account for previously unseen and unmeasured contours of the landscape. Through angular lenses, we catch fragmentary glimpses of the previously unconsidered "irregularities" that had been smoothed over by the flat surface of received knowledge.

I began writing about Aspasia only when I began resisting the paternal narrative that assured me she was either apocryphal or a glorified prostitute, that she could not be legitimized because her words appeared only in secondary sources, that she could not and did not represent an entire community of rhetorical women in classical Greece. How could I write a map of rhetorical history if I did not have "proof," if I had instead only an angle, if Aspasia provided only a fragmentary view rather than a panoramic vision of rhetoric? Before I could publish anything, I had to come to an understanding of what I wanted my map, my history, to *do*. I wanted to challenge the male-dominated story of rhetoric by telling a story of Aspasia that illustrated just how the various renditions of her configure an emblem of Woman (and women) in rhetorical history. I wanted to tap many of the same secondary sources that have validated Socrates, for whom we have no primary sources.

Those of us charting historical maps know that we cannot tell the "truth," that no single map can ever tell the truth, that our traditional foundations are shaky, that maps are neither stable nor entirely coherent, and that the notion of capturing any "reality" rings of empiricism, positivism, and naïveté. Yet we cannot completely separate ourselves from writing or from reading these histories, these stories. Carroll Smith-Rosenberg insists that, despite any postmodern complications, we just continue to read and write such stories, for if we "relinquish our grasp on the world behind words," if we "deny the knowability of the world, we lose that aspect of the world we are . . . committed to knowing" (32)—in my case, women's use of rhetoric. Disagreeing with Smith-Rosenberg's argument for contextualized histories, Michelle Ballif writes that "efforts to make women legitimate by situating them in patronymic narratives does nothing to enfranchise them—because it does nothing to the phallogocentric [sic] economy which disenfrachised them" (95). *Rhetoric Retold* recognizes and addresses both Smith-Rosenberg's and Ballif's concerns by critiquing the regendered history it contextualizes. Indeed, *Rhetoric Retold* tells a story, one that identifies and evaluates women's rhetorical accomplishments, for "it is the power of story . . . that can make people change, and . . . such stories will . . . feature heroes" (Kellner, "Afterword" 249).

Maybe the story of fifth-century Aspasia will make some people change their view of rhetorical history, their opinion of women's participation in the theory and practice of rhetoric, even their research agendas. Maybe the story of a heroic Aspasia will open the door, just a crack, to a fuller understanding of the intellectual, non-Athenian, noncitizen woman in Periclean Athens, to a broader view of how Periclean Athens might look when it includes a woman. And maybe the resistances inherent in the postmodern critique (especially those resistances that play out in current historiography, feminism, gender studies) can influence and interrogate our traditional historiographic projects—our mappings—so that they survey many more women's settlements.

HISTORIOGRAPHY AND FEMINIST REMAPPINGS

As we write our histories of rhetoric, especially as we write women into the tradition, we, like historians in other fields, must continue to resist received notions both of history and of writing history (Certeau 21, 309). The task of historiography is one of connecting the real and the discourse, and at the point where this link cannot be imagined, historiography must work *as if* the real and discourse were actually being joined (Certeau xxvii). As we resist the paternal narrative of rhetorical history, we are all working as if the real and discourse were actually being joined in our texts, on our maps. We have no choice, for how can we know the world except through the words, ideas, beliefs it constructs?

The text of history writing, then, initiates a play between the object under study and the discourse performing the analysis. And even the most conscientious history writers play the game. Fredric Jameson defines *history* as nothing more than an "ideologeme," a construct that is susceptible to both a conceptual description and a narrative manifestation all at once (87). Hayden White writes that "a historical narrative is . . . at once a representation that is an interpretation and an interpretation that passes for an explanation of the whole process mirrored in the narrative" (51), echoing Richard Rorty, who, nearly twenty years ago, rotated the argument of Thomas Kuhn and convinced us that we simply cannot "mirror" any reality in any narrative—scientific, historical, or otherwise. And Nancy F. Partner describes history as "the definitive human audacity imposed on formless time and meaningless event with the human meaning-maker: language" and calls history writing "the silent shared conspiracy of all historians (who otherwise agree on nothing these days)," who "talk about the past as though it were really 'there' " (97).

The "terministic screen," of each history writer's language, then, is a *reflection* of reality; but by its very nature, it must be a *selection* of reality; and to this extent, it must function also as a *deflection* of reality (Burke, *Language* 45). Consequently, all historical accounts, even the most seemingly objective historical records are stories. And even these stories are selected and arranged according to the selector's frame of reference. Why, then, should we continue to write histories of rhetoric when both writing and history are suspect? when our language is our terministic screen? when the past was not really "there"? and when we agree that there was a past but not what the past really was? It is too late to do otherwise.

Historiographic practices are now so firmly situated in the postmodern critique of rhetoric that we already take for granted that histories *do* (or *should do*) something, that they fulfill our needs at a particular time and place, including our need for those familiar constructs referred to as historical *periods*. But even before that critique, Douglas Ehninger's 1967 "On Rhetoric and Rhetorics" inaugurated the call for revisionary histories of rhetoric (R. Scott; Berlin, "Revisionary History"). Since then, the proliferation of new rhetorical maps, as well as new ways of interpreting any rhetorical map—often conflicting, necessarily fragmented, never final—have allowed us to see that historiographic rhetorical maps never reflect a neutral reality. In choosing what to show and how to represent it, in choosing to refer to historical periods, these maps *do* something: they subtly shape our perceptions of a rhetoric englobed.

Because these mappings do something, we must keep on mapping. Learning to write new histories, histories worthy of the remarkable revival of rhetorical consciousness at the present moment, means, above all, devising new ways of reading, which will look at the texts as texts, which will look for the "other" sources of historical discourse in constant tension with the evidence (Kellner, "After" 32). We must risk, then, getting the story crooked. We must look crookedly, a bit out of focus, into the various strands of meaning in a text in such a way as to make the categories, trends, and reliable identities of history a little less inevitable, less familiar. In short, we need to see what is familiar in a different way, in many different ways, as well as to see beyond the familiar to the unfamiliar, to the unseen (32–33).

Narratives are no longer unquestioned or overarching; therefore, historiographers study the shape of each narrative to determine how "form outlines the contour of a loss, an absence, a voice, a silence, which in turn is assumed to be the ground of history" (Conley 8). And those contours have become more prevalent on our maps, as we continue to explore and chart those once-murky regions along the edges of our maps, particularly those regions occupied by women and other disenfranchised groups. The recent prominence of the Sophists is a case in point.

As soon as the Sophists were determined to be a conspicuous absence on our rhetorical map, historiographers began practicing the crafts of resurrection, animation, and even ventriloquism to re-present them. Following the influential work of G. B. Kerferd, recent books (Barrett; R. Enos, *Greek*; Jarratt, *Rereading*) and recent journals (*Pre/Text*, *Rhetoric Review*, and *Rhetoric Society Quarterly*) have featured various rehabilitations and promotions of the Sophists—specifically of Gorgias, Protagoras, and Isocrates. Such historiographic work enables us to move toward a broader understanding of the Sophists, their political and rhetorical influences, "their theoretical coherence and practical validity" (McComiskey 79). The idea of "sophistic rhetoric" has become so familiar (and therefore acceptable) in the works of Sharon Crowley, Roger Moss, Jasper Neel, and John Poulakos, for instance, that Edward Schiappa has argued that " 'sophistic rhetoric' is, for the most part, a mirage—something we see because we want and need to see it" ("Sophistic" 5).

So far as my own work is concerned, I wanted and needed to see sophistic rhetoric so that I could see beyond it, beyond the Sophists, beyond the scraps of texts that have insufficiently represented them. Until I crookedly read, to see how sophistic texts connected with other sources of historical discourse, I could not make my way past the configurations of Aspasia as intellectual joke or harlot. When I realized how closely connected Aspasia of Miletus was with the Sophists, both in proximity and ideology (a connection also made by Jan Swearingen and by Susan Jarratt and Rory Ong at the time), I could write about how that connection contributed to her erasure from rhetorical history.

Just because Aspasia was erased was no reason to stop looking for her trace. I could make the unfamiliar familiar and the familiar unfamiliar. After all, she was effaced in much the same way as Socrates, for none of his words exist in primary sources either.

The rhetorical tradition has readily accepted those secondary accounts of Socrates' influence, teaching, and beliefs, yet the same cannot be said about any female counterpart. Why not? What would happen if I considered female-authored words and ideas comparable to his? What if I read Aspasia through the palimpsest of her thoughts, knowing that her words and actions have been inscribed and reinscribed by those of men? We could come to know Aspasia the same way we know about Socrates—from secondary sources. The surviving fragments and references to Aspasia's intellect in the work of male authors compelled me to piece together those fragments to see what and who appeared, what was present, what was missing. Historiography, reading it crookedly and telling it slant, could help me shape—re-member—a female rhetorical presence.

FEMINIST RESEARCH AND SITUATING FEMALE RHETORICAL FIGURES

In concert with historiography, feminist research has also worked to resist the Western paternal narrative of rhetoric—a narrative Corbett described as "one of the most patriarchal of all the academic disciplines"—by recovering and recuperating women's contributions in the broad history of culture making. In 1990, Corbett could only hope for the recovery of names of women rhetors (377). Since then, we have recovered such names. In 1989, Karlyn Kohrs Campbell published *Man Cannot Speak for Her: A Critical Study of Early Feminist Rhetoric*, which catalogs successful rhetorical women, such as Sojourner Truth, Elizabeth Cady Stanton, and Lucretia Coffin Mott, who spoke from the often-controversial traditions of temperance, suffrage, and abolition work. In their 1990 *Rhetorical Tradition*, Bizzell and Herzberg include the rhetorical discourse of a number of women, starting in the Renaissance: Christine de Pisan, Laura Cereta, Martha Fell, Sarah Grimké, Hélène Cixous, and Julia Kristeva. In *Reclaiming Rhetorica*, editor Andrea A. Lunsford offers us a collection of women's rhetorical endeavors that includes essays ranging from Jan Swearingen on Diotima and Jenny Redfern on Christine de Pisan to Jamie Barlowe on Mary Wollstonecraft and Suzanne Clark on Julia Kristeva. These three collections offer a number of recovered women, as well as methodologies for recovering even more. Many other feminist scholars have employed a variety of methodologies for writing women into the history of rhetoric; the works of JoAnn Campbell, Vicki Tolar Collins, Drema Lipscomb, Shirley Wilson Logan, Yvonne Day Merrill, Joyce Irene Middleton, Catherine Peaden, Krista Ratcliffe, Jacqueline Jones Royster, and Molly Meijer Wertheimer immediately come to mind.

And although many feminist scholars have been working toward an inclusive rhetorical tradition, the results have not led automatically to unanimously happy or harmonious results within feminist communities. For instance, in "Coming to Terms with Recent Attempts to Write Women into the History of Rhetoric," Barbara Biesecker refers to the kinds of projects I have just mentioned as the "mere inclusion of women's texts in the rhetorical canon" (142). Drawing her representative generalizations from the much-celebrated work of Karlyn Campbell, Biesecker warns that a collection of cameo appearances by extraordinary women resolidifies rather than undoes the ideology of the received history of rhetoric (144). Biesecker's charges of "female tokenism" and "affirmative action" in current feminist scholarship (a point concurrent with Ballif's aforementioned argument) provoked an immediate and strong response from Campbell, entitled "Biesecker Cannot Speak for Her Either," in which Campbell countercharges that one scholar's "female tokenism" is another scholar's "incipient analysis of women's rhetoric" (154).

Regarding female tokenism, Campbell writes, "it was men who, over the years, excluded women from their rightful rhetorical place. Consider, then, the motive that could lead one to attack, *not the men*, but a woman who is trying to alter the rhetorical landscape" (154). According to Campbell, Biesecker is urging the "abandonment of individual women and the rhetoric they created," and Campbell herself is "adding to the store of knowledge about women's rhetoric" (158). Feminist historiographers need information about all the theoretical sites of exploration and contention, those ranging from separatism to contextualization and regendering. By regendering the rhetorical tradition, *Rhetoric Retold* expands our understanding of the relationship between males and females in rhetorical histories, as well as of the various Western rhetorical traditions themselves.

Even though feminist historiography points to a different set of subjects (in this case, women) for historical inquiry, such studies will not be merely compensatory or additive histories of women rhetoricians. Remapping rhetoric and regendering the tradition will demand much more of us. Given what we know about the writing of any intellectual history, given what we know about the limits of any one methodology, particularly an inchoate one, we cannot simply measure out the distance between women, chart their places on the rhetorical map, and travel. Instead, any remapping must locate female rhetorical accomplishments within and without the male-dominated and male-documented rhetorical tradition that it interrogates.

When Biesecker moves us beyond an argument of methodology or scholarship, she moves us even closer to those necessary demands. She asks us to push the envelope of our (feminist) research to do more than add women to the canon: "the *radical* contextualization of all rhetorical acts can enable us to forge a new storying of our tradition that circumvents the veiled cultural supremacy operative in mainstream histories of Rhetoric" ("Coming" 147). Such restorying (on whatever grounds—gender, class, or race, for example) can take place only within a reevaluation of rhetorical theories in general (Blair and Kahl).

Therefore, whatever theoretical, practical, or political challenges—whatever agreements, disagreements, or locations—feminist rhetoricians bring to the map of rhetoric, their contributions are moving us beyond the restoration of women to rhetorical history; they are revitalizing rhetorical theory by shaking the conceptual foundations of rhetorical study itself. In the broadest sense, then, feminist historiography is performative—it *does* something. Toward that end of bringing feminism to rhetoric and rhetoric to feminism, recent issues of both *Rhetoric Society Quarterly* and *Southern Communication Journal* have been devoted to feminist research (Jarratt, *Rhetoric*; Rushing). Yet despite all the established and ongoing feminist historiographic work, much work remains to be done; for each time we face the rhetorical woman, we still see *terra nova*, barely perceptible on our horizon.

It was only by incorporating various feminist methodologies that I was able to move my own work forward. My initial, graduate-school work on Aspasia (which ran for merely seven pages in my dissertation) now seems to me a purely descriptive, somewhat solitary account. Only when I was able to broaden my definition of rhetoric and its practice, only when I was able to give Aspasia the kind of acceptance I had always given Socrates, did I realize that I had discovered a pocket of rhetorical activity. Such small methodological steps, but what a rich payoff: I could write a fuller, relational account of Aspasia's place and participation in rhetorical history, as a woman, as a foreigner, and as an intellectual and political force. Feminist historiography insisted that I contextualize her, the better to see her and her significance.

Thus, feminist historiography is performative in that it embodies a promise of connecting women and history and rhetoric, a nexus that enables us to (insists that we) write contextualized rather than merely separatist rhetorical histories. Feminist historiography points toward what Tania Modleski describes as "the freer world it is in the process of inaugurating" (48). It points to a simultaneously committed and utopian rhetorical world, in which women's participation is not always upstaged, dubbed over, or completely ignored by men.

GENDER STUDIES AS A CATEGORY FOR ANALYSIS

The last of the critiques I want to discuss, however briefly, is gender studies. Despite the feminist intellectual work of the past five years, the rhetorical map still most familiar to us, regardless of its contours, is one exclusive of women. Because those rhetorical maps are always inscribed by the relation of language and power, such maps have replicated the power politics of gender, with men in the highest social elevation and rank. It is no coincidence, now, that feminist scholarship has pressed us toward examining the social construction of gender and gendered power, a move that is "the single most important advance in feminist theory" (Flax 43). Susan Bordo tells us that "gender theorists . . . cleared a space, described a new territory, which radically altered the male-normative terms of discussion about reality and experience; they forced recognition of the difference gender makes" (137). And what a difference. Figuring gender denaturalizes the concept of sexual differences and investigates the cultural construction of men and women, thereby revitalizing our thinking about the appropriate or inappropriate roles and opportunities for sexed bodies. Thus, gender studies include both women and men, a shift in focus (from feminist studies) that holds potential for transforming rhetorical studies.

Gender is nothing more or less, according to Joan Wallach Scott, than "a social category imposed on a sexed body" (32). But that "more or less" directly relates to power. For two thousand years, humans have been conditioned to accept the opinions of "thinkers from Aristotle and Rousseau to Talcott Parsons and Erik Erikson . . . [who] have argued that women not only differ from men but are not as equipped mentally and physically to function in the spheres of society in which men *predominate*" (Epstein 2, emphasis added). Each of these men seems to have returned to the beliefs of Aristotle, who wrote that "between the sexes, the male is by nature superior and the female inferior, the male ruler and the female subject" (*Politics* 1.2.12), and "one quality or action is nobler than another if it is that of a naturally finer being: thus a man's will be nobler than a woman's" (*Rhetoric* 1.9.15). For Aristotle, then, the "natural" deficiencies of women rendered them naturally subordinate to those naturally finer beings, men, who were awarded the right and privilege of a public voice. The universally subordinate evaluation of women in relation to men has provided the tautology that women were closed out of the rhetorical tradition only because they were women. Nevertheless, once feminist historians began looking around, forward and backward for intellectual and rhetorical sisters, they discovered traces of rhetorical women (and gendered theories and practices) in the very places women were thought to be forbidden or nonexistent.

Putting gender studies on the rhetorical map problemizes the power politics of rhetoric itself in several provocative and related ways. First of all, gender studies is more about power, performance, and societal expectations than about male and female biology; therefore, gender studies successfully unsettles "the manner in which decidedly male experiences have been made to stand in for the history of Rhetoric" (Biesecker, "Coming" 141). Second, gender studies obstructs the master narrative mapped earlier in this chapter, that "preservative, continuous history of rhetoric from ancient Greece to contemporary America" (Blair, "Refiguring" 181). Hence, the rhetorical power of the oppressed and marginalized (the Sophists or Aspasia, for example) has yet to be in the mainstream (or what Mary O'Brien calls the "*male*-stream") of rhetoric, yet, paradoxically, the influence of the oppressed and marginalized is no longer gendered as a space reserved to enhance the center. They are coming into their own rhetorically. Finally, gender studies complicates "the notion of classical rhetoric as a preferred archetype from which all departures are greater or lesser" (Ehninger, "On Systems" 140).

Because the archetypal rhetor of antiquity was male, gender studies automatically moves us away from the belief in the exclusive validity of classical rhetoric and its male practitioners. Classical technique no longer delimits rhetoric, and masculine performance no longer delimits rhetoric either—particularly now that various rhetorical performances and performers are being considered in their own right. Although "the standards according to which any particular speech is assessed [have traditionally been] constructed on the basis of male attributes, capacities, and modes of activity" (Biesecker, "Towards" 88), we have broadened our conception of rhetorical activity and performance to be more inclusive and therefore more accurate.

Clearly, gender studies provides a different lens by which to survey rhetoric. Gone is the dualist lens of male-female biology; instead, we have a lens that regards the construct of gender as a social product, an institution of power relations learned through and perpetuated by culture. Gender studies remains closely allied with feminist research; nevertheless, the two lenses continue to supply different views and different methodologies. Thus, scholars surveying the same rhetorical territory are seeing different shapes and contours and are discovering different absences. In their surveys, historiographers, for instance, are locating pockets of uncharted rhetorical activity; feminists have discovered unappreciated female orators, such as Aspasia; and gender theorists are calibrating the rhetorical activity located along the fault line of gender. Naturally, such conflicting and complementary visions serve to arouse and enrich the various analyses of both marginalized and centralized rhetorics and rhetors.[5]

Gender theory is an exceptionally useful analytical category for writing women into the history of rhetoric. Feminist studies helped me locate Aspasia, an upper-class courtesan who successfully and perhaps wisely translated her sexual access to Pericles into access to his intellectual and political circle as well. But by contextualizing Aspasia within the gendered limits and expectations of her time, I am now able to explain her political, social, and intellectual influence—and her rhetorical accomplishments—in terms other than erotic. Aspasia's intellectual participation in Athenian culture was unprecedented; it is difficult to emphasize how extraordinary the foreign-born Aspasia would have been in fifth-century BCE Athenian society.

But if we think of gender as a cultural role, as a social rank, or as "a primary way of signifying relations of power" (Laqueur 12), then we can more easily trace Aspasia's movement across gendered boundaries of appropriate roles for both non-Athenian, citizen-class women and men during her historical moment. The story of Aspasia's gendering is about more than her being sexed female; it is also about her being a foreigner, being educated, and being unacculturated as an Athenian. Considered as such, Aspasia appears as an intellectually forceful woman—not merely as a successful courtesan. And this learned woman seems to have profited by her excursion into the male domains of politics and intellect. In chapter 2, I explore her profiteering: she opened an academy for young women of good families that soon became a popular salon—not a brothel—for the most influential men of the day (Socrates, Plato, Anaxagoras, Sophocles, Phidias, and Pericles); she established a reputation as a rhetorician, as a philosopher, and as a member of the Athenian intelligentsia; she was memorialized by a number of those same men; and she left firmly and fully realized contributions to the history and theory of rhetoric, which we are just beginning to appreciate. However, for those very same reasons (being female, being a foreigner), her contributions were later directed through a powerful, gendered lens to both refract and reflect Socrates and Pericles, rather than herself.

How could she have been a powerful force in Periclean Athens, an influence on Plato and Socrates? How could she have been a teacher, much less a rhetorician? After all, by the principle of *entelechy* (the vital force urging one toward fulfilling one's actual essence), she would have naturally followed her predetermined life course as a traditional wife and mother, her progress toward fulfillment distinctly marked off and limited to a degree of perfection less than that for a man. Denied the telos of perfect maleness, Athenian citizen-class women, such as Aspasia, were denied a passport into the male intellectual battlegrounds of politics, philosophy, and rhetoric. But somehow Aspasia had approached the border—and trespassed into the masculine territory of classical rhetoric.

Both historiographic and feminist research pointed me toward using gender studies to explore the societal gendering (power) inherent in the expectations, strictures, and possibilities for humans of different sex, as well as the ways in which we think about the social order and hierarchy. I have profited from what gender studies can reveal about power. But no single analytical category (historiography, feminism, or gender studies, for instance), no single route into rhetorical territory, can address all our divisions or questions as we rewrite rhetorical histories.

Gender studies, in particular, cannot be used alone, for "gender never exhibits itself in pure form but in the context of lives that are shaped by a multiplicity of influences, which cannot be neatly sorted out" (Bordo 147). After all, whatever we think we know about the sexed body is inevitably culturally produced anyway: anatomical sketches and biological explanations of the body throughout the ages have continually reflected and "proved" each society's beliefs about the body. In fact, during the time of Aspasia's excursions into rhetorical territory, her female body would have been considered that of an undeveloped male, for the Athenians believed Aristotle when he said that "the female body was a less hot, less perfect, and hence less potent version of the canonical body" (Laqueur 34–35). In *The Children of Athena*, Nicole Loraux tells us that "there is not, and never has been, a real female Athenian. The political process does not recognize a 'citizeness,' the language has no word for a woman from Athens" (10). Aspasia, then, spent her life with Athenians and with "women," a category that included any person who did not meet the prestigious requirements of Athenian citizenship; such a person was automatically feminized, gendered "nonmale."

Whatever the reinterpretations of the body or whatever the model of gender(s), the point is that each model accounts for and prescribes the movement of females and males along and across the range of gendered performances.[6] If we understand the particular and contextually specific ways gender and society (or culture) interinanimate one another, we can more knowledgeably chart and account for those gendered limits and powers as we take a specific route along the borders of rhetorical history. But we must keep in mind that narratives of gender analysis (male/female, powerful/disempowered, black/white) can harbor the same grandiose and totalizing concepts as rhetoric's now-disputed paternal narrative, that grand narrative of masculinist display that many of us want to complicate, disrupt, interrupt—but finally enrich.

NEW MAPS, NEW DIRECTIONS

So what? So what if the traditional rhetorical map flattened the truth, leaving scarcely a ridge on the surface that could suggest all the disenfranchised rhetorics just off the main road? After all, "the rhetorical tradition is a fiction that has just about outlived its usefulness" anyway (T. Miller, "Reinventing" 26). So why revisit the history of rhetoric? Why challenge that dominant narrative? Why find new points of interest? Why bother to remap it? And why encourage any new mappings?

By acknowledging that rhetorical history is not neutral territory, the refiguring of Aspasia, or any other woman, for that matter, as a bona fide rhetorical figure transforms the rhetorical terrain. Until recently, we had not thought of looking for a woman in rhetoric. It had already been assumed, a priori, that no women participated in the rhetorical tradition. We had been willing to believe the tautology that no women have been involved in rhetorical history because not a single rhetorical treatise by a woman appears in lists of primary works (we resolutely ignore Lucia Olbrechts-Tyteca) and because, until most recently, not a single woman has appeared in the indices of the most comprehensive histories of Western rhetoric.

For too long, the arbiters of canonical acceptance have operated on the basis of $X + 1$. Whenever a woman has accomplished the same goals as her male counterpart (theorizing, public speaking, successful argument, persuasive letter writing, for example), the stakes immediately rise. She may have achieved X, but she needs X *plus* 1 to earn a place in rhetoric. Men who have conceptualized theories of rhetoric are rhetoricians. Aspasia conceptualized rhetorical theories, but since none of her texts are extant, she is not a rhetorician. But " 'sexual difference' appears to be interrupting the smooth transmission of the male dominated rhetorical tradition," Biesecker writes, "destabilizing the subject of rhetorical history that up to this point has been exclusively male" ("Towards" 87; "Coming" 142). So as more and more women are searched out and located on the rhetorical terrain, as their work becomes recognized and validated, the unfolding of their stories will continuously realign our concept of rhetorical histories.

Our disruption of that seamless narrative we have for too long been willing to accept as rhetorical history implicates both past and future scholarship. Our first obligation, then, as scholars is to look backwards at all the unquestioned rhetorical scholarship that has come before. Our willingness to interrogate, test, and unfold that scholarship will advance our rethinking, reseeing, and rewriting of rhetorical history, much of which will always be "rhetorical iterations, saturated with the impure representations, intrinsic interestedness, and general obstreperousness of *any* discourse" (Blair, "Contested" 417, emphasis added).

Our advances, however, will not always be welcome, for "in light of classical rhetoric's long and venerable history of preservation, any 'new' rhetoric [will be] suspect, or ... . rendered as a marker of decline, reduced to a flawed or inadequate version of the tradition" (410). Nevertheless, our profession must continue to historicize and theorize, remapping our notions of rhetorical *theoria* and praxis. In "Revisionary History," Berlin assures us that we should continue in our attempts to strike a balance among new ideas, new research, and traditional scholarship:

> No completely accurate and reliable historical account is attainable, yet this does not absolve us of the responsibility for attempting such accounts. . . . All accounts are partial, but all reveal something about history and about the movement of our thought in coming to terms with it. Just as we cannot know the future but must nonetheless make judgments about it and act on them, we cannot completely know the past, yet we must work to understand and judge it in order to understand and judge ourselves in our own moment. We are doomed to be partial, incomplete, mistaken, yet we cannot for all this abstain from acting. (59)

As more scholars work to write and rewrite rhetorical histories, even more women and men will become scenic (or perhaps mis-taken) routes on our intellectual landscape. Some of these new maps already provide us new pathways—new options—as we explore rhetorical territory. They not only demonstrate to us how infinitely varied rhetorical accomplishments can be, but they also remind us just how abstract—how fragile, ephemeral, and plastic—maps themselves are. With each new discovery, the map must be drawn and illustrated again.

If historical narratives are primarily motivated actions to *do* something, and if that something has to do with power, then perhaps we should find ways to connect our current rhetorical inquiries, histories, and mappings with our contemporary academic and social concerns. After all, the only way we can displace the old map of rhetoric, which Welch refers to as the "Heritage School" map of masculine performance, is to replace it with maps that *do* something else, that are recognized as being better suited to our present needs (*Contemporary* 9).

Rhetoric has taken root in many other disciplines (philosophy, classics, history, speech, communication, English, and composition), all of which tap rhetoric for theory, practice, and pedagogy. Hence, now is a propitious time to reconsider, define, profess, and learn from rhetoric, its traditions, and its histories (T. Poulakos, "Introduction" 2–3; T. Enos, "Brand" 11; T. Enos and Brown, *Defining* vii–xiii). By inviting our remapping activities into our institutions, we can—regardless of the discipline—introduce into our classrooms new curricula, new syllabi, new research and mentoring projects, new readings, and new writings. For instance, Thomas P. Miller suggests that we use our courses in classical rhetoric to provide "opportunities for research on the rhetorical practices of more diverse groups" other than the intellectual gatekeepers or owners of intellectual production ("Teaching" 72). He goes on to suggest that we use our courses to analyze "the discursive formations that establish positions of authorship, condition how people read, and locate the purposes of writing and reading within the social relations of time" (74). Welch suggests that we foreground the frequently unseen problems of classical rhetoric—history, hierarchy, and gender—in ways that students can recognize and identify as problems, not with themselves as female or minority students but with "the universalized reader—the white, male, middle class, bookish decoder whose values, ideologies, and desires underlie many of the assumptions of standard readings" ("Plato" 7). Bizzell would have both teachers and students remap and resist the paternal narrative by seeking out and teaching lost voices ("Opportunities"; "Praising"). Each time we encourage such remappings and reconceptualize basic assumptions about rhetoric, we are redrawing the boundaries of rhetoric to include new practitioners and new practices.

Even if (or because) we do not "form any one school of historical-rhetorical thought" (Vitanza, "Editor's" viii), we need to help one another and the new scholars with their own mappings, for remapping rhetorical territory is an important way we can locate ourselves or our students or our various rhetorical activities in the field we are studying. We also need to support the classroom activities that result from such remappings. Those of us living in English departments should realize that some thirty-five hundred college writing teachers are professionalizing themselves by learning the history, theory, and praxis— the maps—of rhetoric (T. Enos, "Brand" 7). And just a glance at a Convention on College Composition and Communication (CCCC) program, for instance, will reveal the various mappings available to us all: in addition to the traditional great male figures, the CCCC offers analyses of male and female figures; minority groups (ethnic, religious, social); professional, religious, and popular discourse practices (including twelve-step programs); solitary and collaborative activities, all of which are being figured onto rhetorical maps. Intrinsic to each of these remappings is the necessary historical inquiry that empowers political action, whether social, academic, or religious, for historical inquiry helps people situate problems in a broader context and discover the available means of persuading their communities to act from their shared historical experiences and needs. Indeed, all of these rhetorics must *do* something new if they are to fulfill our present needs: our needs as citizens, researchers, teachers, students, and colleagues in the diverse and multidisciplinary professions of rhetorics.

TWO

Classical Rhetoric Conceptualized, or Vocal Men and Muted Women

INTRODUCTION

The earliest literary examples of what would become rhetorical practices were two: first, the eloquence of male and female literary characters; then, the arguments of historical male writers and public men. Although male writers and literary characters most often articulated public rhetorical practices, a few female literary characters used language persuasively in the private sphere, and two groups of historical women, Sappho's coterie and the female Pythagoreans, spoke their way into the public domain. Given how very little of their work has survived, it is impossible to measure women's contributions to what would become rhetorical practice. But as I trace the much-disputed origins and eventual codification of rhetoric, identify women rhetors, and evaluate their contributions, I argue that those women who found access to education and rhetorical accomplishment were indeed supporting, complementing, and enhancing the contributions of their male counterparts to the development of male-dominated rhetorical art, an art in ascendance.

Early on, Sappho herself knew that her contributions to the intellectual movement would not be forgotten. Nor would the contributions of Aspasia of Miletus, who took a leadership role in constructing the sophistic movement and in influencing the course of its development—as well as the fork in its development that led to the codification of rhetoric. Rhetoric can be retold and regendered only if gender relations are deemed influential upon social and intellectual events and change. Therefore, this chapter is punctuated with investigations and explanations of the cultural dynamics of Greek and Roman society, specifically in terms of the powers and limits of gender(ed) roles on sexed bodies. Since any (socially recognized) thinking woman—Greek or Roman—would have been an exception, those women who entered the masculine, public sphere of rhetoric left their indelible and inimitable mark.

THE ASCENDANCE OF RHETORIC: PRACTICE BEFORE THEORY

"Dead, I / won't be forgotten," sang Sappho some twenty-five hundred years ago, her words recited by professional Greek singers and then transcribed and retranscribed by copyists (Sappho, *Poems*, Frag. 99). Sappho was right: she would not be forgotten. Despite the unreliability of those transcriptions, the fragmentary nature of her literary legacy, the continuous and troubling focus on her sexuality, the passage of time, and the willful attempts to silence the voices of women, Sappho is one of our most important literary foremothers. But women such as Sappho can be located within the rhetorical tradition—as rhetorical foremothers—only when the rhetorical tradition itself has been laid out in such a fashion as to reveal what seems to have been its precodified roots and spread out to include the measure of women's contributions and participation.

Walter Ong reminds us that the agonistic patterns we automatically accept as rhetorical argument and dialectic were inscribed by gender—the male gender:

> In . . . earlier cultures, contest and high-stress operations suggestive of contest marked a variety of phenomena at first seemingly unconnected: the dominance of rhetoric and dialectic or logic in the curricula, the use of a language other than the mother tongue acquired (with negligible exceptions) only by males and under stress situations, for all formally intellectual work, the totally male population of academia, the vigorous and often brutal disciplining of pupils, the dominantly agonistic teaching procedures, the constant recycling of all knowledge, even that acquired by reading, through agora of public oral disputation, the programmatically combative oral testing of knowledge, and much else. (*Fighting* 24–25)

This argument, however, obscures the fact that women, from the beginning of recorded time, have been excluded from participating in those practices that informed and codified the practice of rhetoric, practices that were, handily enough, labeled *rhetoric*. Thus the dominant ideology of most of the ancient world offered women no place in public discourse. The exclusion of women from politics and power was simply one side of that much greater disability—their lack of any right to be heard. At first, men silenced them and ventriloquized their characters in still-popular poems and plays. But a few women challenged the ideology of female silence and found their own voices, speaking for themselves in poetry, philosophy, religious ritual, and prophecy.

Although eloquence and rhetoric are not synonymous, their powers overlap. A speaker (or writer) who self-consciously manipulates the medium solely and purposefully to ensure that the message has the most favorable reception possible on the part of the particular audience being addressed enjoys the power of eloquence as well as rhetoric. If rhetoric is the art of using language in such a way as to produce a desired impression upon the hearer (or reader), then the practice of rhetoric existed many hundreds of years before any rhetorical theory was codified, before rhetoric became a discipline. And the literature of ancient Greece provides us an entrance into the earliest forms of rhetorical practice.

Homer

Homer's *Iliad* and *Odyssey* are perhaps the earliest examples (900–700 BCE) of purposeful and persuasive language use, eloquent orations calculated to achieve a desired effect. On the basis of his "inspired" rather than his "studied" eloquent power, however, some ancients, as well as some contemporary scholars, oppose using Homer as a rhetorical model. Thomas Cole describes such early practice as "arhetorical" (42), yet Richard Leo Enos explains that those "prerhetorical" oral and written systems of composition (of epic and lyric poetry) evolved in inextricable unity to establish rhetoric and to secure its popular reception and perpetuation (*Greek* x).[1] The power of eloquence, a rhetorical consciousness so to speak, is evident and recognized in the earliest Greek writings. Achilles, for example, has been purposefully prepared for a life as "a rhetor of speech and a doer of deeds" (*Iliad* 9.443)—the earliest extant mention of "rhetor" in Homer's works.

However, women were excluded from dominant social forms, which included the public practice of what would become rhetoric, as well as from the production of literary works like Homer's. Nonetheless, Homer's fictional women, as well as the fictional men, are knowledgeable, acknowledged, and eloquent rhetors who participate in the also-fictional public domain: both Andromache and Helen pronounce their personal response to the Trojan War. And the sulking Alexander/Paris explains that Helen uses especially reasoned discourse to urge him to return to war: "It was not so much because of anger and indignation at the Trojans that I remained sitting in my chamber, but I desired to give myself up to grief. And just now my wife, persuading me with soft words, urged me to war" (6.336–38). Defining her reasoned discourse as a good example of "protreptic" discourse, Enos delights in this fictional female character who is "to illustrate a capacity for rationality in time of stress" (R. Enos, *Greek* 8).[2]

Sappho

The power of purposeful language, of pretheoretical rhetorical practice, was evidenced in other early Greek writings as well, namely in the works of Sappho (properly Psappho) of Lesbos (fl. c. 600 BCE), the only woman in all antiquity whose literary productions placed her on the same level as the greatest male poets, in other words, with Homer. According to Jane McIntosh Snyder, "the earliest woman writer in Western literature whose work has—at least in part—survived the passage of time and the willful attempts to silence the voices of women, Sappho is also the most famous" (1).

Plato invokes Sappho as the tenth Muse; Aristotle honors her as a wise woman; and Strabo calls her the marvel among women—all because they were unaccustomed to supreme lyric talent in a woman. By calling Sappho a Muse, however, Judith P. Hallett writes, these later ancients "ranked her an inspired and immortal figure to whom poetic self-expression and success came naturally" ("Sappho" 448), which suggests that she "had not earned literary stature through toil and competition, as did the men of her field" (447).

Whether Muse or competitive genius, as a productive poet, Sappho is extraordinary by any standard. She wrote nine books of lyric poems, nearly two hundred of which remain in fragments, only one poem surviving in its entirety. Most of her fragments survived only in the quotations made by ancient authors; that is, until the late nineteenth century. At that time, excavations from Hellenistic cemeteries brought to light nearly two hundred tattered poetic fragments that had endured on shreds of papyrus rolls and vellum codices. Written at dates ranging from the second to the sixth or seventh centuries AD, these terribly mutilated but authentic transcriptions of Sappho are remarkable for the integrity of their tradition.[3]

The scholarly reconstruction of those fragments put an end to the millennia of fictions about Sappho, most of which focused obsessively on her sexuality— and the freedom it signified. Whether a poet of such stature was also a figure of female homoerotic desire was the critical question for scholars, some of whom staunchly defended Sappho's heterosexuality, some of whom denied her any sexuality whatsoever, while others coined a pair of Sapphos, the poet and the sexual being by the same name. Even as late as 1963, David M. Robinson would deny that Sappho had any impurities (or sexuality whatsoever), for "an imagination with such a marvellous range as this is never given to the child of sodden vice" (45); "Sappho, then, was a pure and good woman, busily and successfully engaged in the work of her chosen profession" (238).

But once scholars distinguished clearly between autobiography and literature—between the narrator and the flesh-and-blood author of the work, between literary words and actual deeds—and once they achieved consensus on the particular fragments, specifically whether a missing letter should be a delta or a theta, it became clear that most of Sappho's love lyrics were addressed to persons of the female gender and that the speaking subject of the poems was, indeed, a lover of women. Unlike any other poet of the era, Sappho created a narrator, as well as literary texts, that accorded women their full humanity:

> [Her voice was]
> far sweeter than any flute . . .
> [her hair,]
> more golden than gold . . .
> [and her skin,]
> far whiter than an egg. . . .   (*Poems*, Frag. 23)

Yet fabulation surrounds even the most serious scholarly commentaries about this poetic genius. All writings—including the recovered fragments—postdate her life by at least three hundred years, so we know very little about this seventh-century poet except for a few brief, and perhaps irrelevant, biographical details regarding her place of birth, her aristocratic family, and her all-female coterie. Only a few of the many and often-conflicting statements made about her by ancient authors can be checked by her own writings. But it would seem possible that she was born between 630 and 610 BCE, that her parents were Skamandronymos and Kleis of Mytilene on Lesbos, and that she had three brothers, Erigyios, Charaxos, and Larichos, whose government service on the council in Mytilene suggests that the family was aristocratic. She may have been married to Kerkylas of Andros, who is never mentioned in any of the extant fragments of her poetry, and she may have had a daughter, who—named after her own mother (Kleis)—appears to be mentioned in the fragments:

> I have a beautiful daughter, golden
> like a flower, my beloved Cleis,
> for her, in her place, I would not accept
> the whole of Lydia. . . .   (*Poems*, Frag. 75)

The only contemporary reference to her is in a fragment of poetry written by her male compatriot Alcaeus: "O weaver of violets, holy, sweet-smiling Sappho," an acknowledgment of her beautiful verse weaving and her own mention of her own name in the "Hymn to Aphrodite."

Sappho wrote in Greek (about two hundred years after the works of Homer were first recorded) during a time of political unrest throughout Greece, in general, and on Lesbos, specifically. For all the Greek city-states, the movement from aristocratic to democratic rule was a turbulent transition that required citizens to develop a fresh political consciousness. Lesbos, in particular, was not immune to these troubles: though in power, its aristocracy was a class in crisis; furthermore, from about 610 BCE Lesbos was involved in a war with Athenian colonists at Sigeum, near Troy, on the coast of Asia Minor. There is poetic evidence of Sappho's awareness of this political turmoil—and, like other aristocrats, may have been involved to the point of having taken refuge in (or been exiled to) faraway Sicily, for one of her fragments speaks of the difficulty of getting luxuries (a headband) while in exile:

> . . . My mother . . .
>
> in her youth it was great
> adornment if someone had her hair
> wrapped round with a purple [braid,]
>
> it really was.
> But for the one with hair
> more golden than a pinetorch

. . . fitted with garlands
of blooming flowers.
Recently a hairband of many hues

from Sardis . . .
. . . cities . . .

But for you, Kleis, I have no colorful
hairband—where will it come from?—
by the Mytilenean . . .
*

*

. . . many-hued . . .

these keepsakes of exile . . .
Kleanax's sons . . .
These have wasted away terribly. . . .   (*Sappho's*, Frag. 46)

Other than the mention by Alcaeus, Sappho's intellectual training and achievements were not connected with, recorded by, or attributed to a male contemporary—not to a father, brother, or husband. Therefore, we do not have to rely solely on a man's representation of a woman's discourse and of her world. Of course, poetry is neither history nor (auto)biography. But since tradition has long accorded Homer's verse a measure of historiographic significance, we can, for once, turn to a woman's view. We have Sappho's poetic view of Sappho's world, a world of women, of female beauty, of divine and natural loveliness, of marriage rituals, and of day-to-day pleasures. But because she confided in neither diaries nor biographers, scholars cannot describe with certainty the material circumstances of Sappho's poetic practices—except that those circumstances allowed her to enter the masculine sphere of honoring and inspiring members of one's own sex with poetry.

Like Homer's and Alcaeus's, Sappho's society was for the most part sexually segregated. Wellborn women had little contact with males either before or after marriage, not even with their husbands, who were often selected for them by their fathers. Except for their participation in religious pageantry, women were subordinated to the *oikos*, while men remained in the polis. But Sappho, the original poet of female desire, came to writing within the feminized *oikos* and outside the patriarchal and militaristic culture inhabited by Homer and Alcaeus. And her "coming to writing" (Cixous and Clément 69) allowed her to assume her extraordinary literary gift, demonstrating female language use and consciousness in ways evidenced neither by her predecessor Homer nor by her contemporary Alcaeus.[4] Indeed, Homer ventriloquizes the aforementioned legendary female characters, and Alcaeus puts emotional lines in the mouths of a single, love-struck female: "Me, a woman pitiable, me, who am spared no misery . . . / destiny of shame . . . For upon me comes grievous injury" (Frag. A10[B], qtd. in Page).

Excluded from social, political, or economic activity, women were meant only for marriage, for *ekdosis*, an ancient Greek word that also means "loan." This semantic connection betrays its function and character: a Greek marriage was a transaction whereby a woman's father lent her out to the head of another *oikos*, perhaps meeting her husband for the first time at their marriage, so that she might perform for the latter the functions of wife and mother (Arthur 68). After marriage, a woman remained excluded from the worldly pursuits, often meeting with her husband only long enough to guarantee her pregnancy and thereby her husband's *oikos*.

Thus, the island of Lesbos seems to have provided extraordinary social and intellectual opportunity for Greek women. Even though sixth-century BCE Lesbos was given over to political agitation and burgeoning commerce, it still maintained provisions for unmarried women to be educated. The first Greek women to be educated systematically alongside men may have been the Spartans, their compulsory education purposefully subordinate to the good of the state—and of men. Lesbian women, on the other hand, could find a measure of cultural education within Sappho's circle of women, women who voluntarily lived separately from men. Legend supports the implications of Sappho's poems that, despite any Lesbian domestic turmoil, young women from all parts of Ionia were educated by way of an all-female fellowship, a *thiasos*. Riane Eisler would describe such an education as celebrating female life-giving and life-sustaining sources (115). And H. I. Marrou says that theirs was an education "dedicated to the goddesses of culture—a form that was also to be adopted by the schools of philosophy from the time of Pythagoras onwards" (34).

But to imbue Sappho with respectability—to insist that Sappho's circle was dedicated only to achieving the highest nobility of spirit or that Sappho was a paragon of virtue or that Sappho was a headmistress or priestess—is "absurd" (Snyder 12). "There is simply no evidence for [these] notion[s] in either the fragments themselves or in the ancient biographical materials" (12). All we know for sure is that, whatever forms their education took, these young women received it among the company of other young and single women. Although we lack concrete information about women's education and about their ability to read and write, we must suppose that they were largely excluded from educational practices—that is, except on Lesbos, for the "illustrious case of Sappho . . . should be regarded as exceptional though not unique, her family having been a privileged one" (Harris 48).

Groups of women living together and educating one another was an uncommon but understandable occurrence; after all, it was perfectly acceptable for like-minded men of this same period to live apart from women. For example, the kinship and fealty of Alcaeus's band of noble friends (his *hetaireiai*) was constantly displayed in their common military actions and in their peacetime activities: they celebrated common cults, and they bunked, sang, dined, and drank together as often as they could, giving little or no thought to the emotional or sexual needs of their wives or brides-to-be.[5] While it was perfectly acceptable for these men to be intellectual, military, and sexual mentors to the younger males in their group, it remained controversial for Sappho to celebrate and express the female sexuality of her *hetaerae*, young girls preparing for adulthood—not for harlotry.

Like their male counterparts, the girls studied music and dancing, as well as physical fitness and development—all arts that support the study of poetry, the only literature of the day. But "Sappho's group . . . drew inwards, keeping its members back in quietude and touching the community only in ritual moments; its public gestures were restricted to the dance, and its songs were made to emphasize the esoteric quality of its closed experience" (Burnett 209). Werner Jaeger tells us that

> [t]he very existence of Sappho's circle assumes the educational conception of poetry which was accepted by the Greeks of her time; but the novelty and greatness of it is that through it women were admitted to a man's world, and conquered that part of it to which they had a rightful claim. For it was a real conquest: it meant that women now took their part in serving the Muses and that this service blended with the process of forming their character. (1: 133)

Released from a male-dominated society, Sappho exercised her verbal prowess, using her poetry to celebrate women's education, women's alliances, and, especially, women's public use of persuasive language:

> "I simply wish to die."
> Weeping she left me
> and said this too:
> "We've suffered terribly
> Sappho I leave you against my will."
> I answered, go happily
> and remember me,
> you know how we cared for you,
> if not, let me remind you
> . . . the lovely times we shared.
>
> Many crowns of violets,
> roses and crocuses
> . . . together you set before me
> and many scented wreaths
> made from blossoms
> around your soft throat . . .
> . . . with pure, sweet oil
> . . . you anointed me,
> and on a soft, gentle bed . . .
> you quenched your desire . . .
> . . . no holy site . . .
> we left uncovered,
> no grove . . . dance
> . . . sound.   (*Sappho's*, Frag. 14)

At the center of an all-female fellowship, Sappho used her poetic language to explore and expand the limits of male-dominated forms of poetry—without diluting any of its potency: "Pain penetrates / Me drop / by drop" (*New*, Frag. 61).

The speaking subject of Sappho's poems was a woman, a woman claiming the right to talk, the right to use her own voice. And that woman's voice, that speaking subject, is what is at stake in these poems—not the objects of the poems, not sexuality, not lesbianism, not even female friendship. In the manner of a prototypical rhetor, then, Sappho's concern was how the "woman's voice" could best be heard and understood by an audience:

> Thank you, my dear
>
> You came, and you did
> well to come: I needed
> you. You have made
>
> love blaze up in
> my breast—bless you!
> Bless you as often
>
> as the hours have been endless to me
> while you were gone   (*New*, Frag. 46)

Sappho was afforded some opportunity to write, and she demonstrated woman's ability to equal or surpass the male poets of her day. The ideas of the old Greek aristocracy had been expressed in the Homeric epics, through the doughty deeds of divinely descended and godlike characters. Hesiod had wrought into poetry the practical wisdom and experience of the peasant's life and morality.[6] And Tyrtaeus's elegies had eternalized the severe code of the Spartan state, exhorting his fellow citizens to win glory in defense of their country. But the new ideal of a polis, an aristocratic democracy, seems, at first glance, to have no comparable expression in contemporary poetry, that is, not until individuality rather than community became an acceptable poetic theme.

When the Ionian poets (Archilochus, Semonides, Mimnermus of Colophon—misogynists all) narrowed their focus within the city walls, to the world of the individual, they discovered a new theme that made clear the deepest reasons for the political revolution: the individual's will to live and concomitant right to enjoy life, politics, society, and sex. Seventh-century Ionian poetry, then, concentrates on individual hedonism but is addressed to individuals within a political community.

However, the Aeolian lyric poets Sappho and Alcaeus address a more particular audience, for they express the individual's inner life itself.[7] Composing within the space between the epic and tragedy, Alcaeus and Sappho wrote lyrics addressed not to a public audience (not to an entire city) but to a few close friends. Alcaeus often addressed appropriate poetry to his circle of drinking companions, restless men, who were bound together for life. While Sappho, on the other hand, sang to a leisurely, transitional group of females, her *hetaerae*. In a tone of meditative irony, she sang wedding or love songs, the speaking voice of her poems often extending beyond her immediate audience, to mothers, daughters, and future husbands:

> We drink your health
>
> Lucky bridegroom!
> Now the wedding you
> asked for is over
>
> and your wife is the girl you asked for;
> she's a bride who is
>
> charming to look at,
> with eyes as soft as
> honey, and a face
>
> that Love has lighted
> with his won beauty.
> Aphrodite has surely
>
> outdone herself in doing honor to you!   (*New*, Frag. 30)

Sappho takes the newly established joy-of-life lyric one step further, celebrating personal emotion and self-expression—and women. She moves the lyric from an expression of masculine heroism, political dominance, and male individuality to the ardor and nobility of the feminine soul, thereby contributing to literary rhetoric (poetics) and disrupting the continuum of male-dominated poetics. In her articulation of womanly concerns, of sensual desire, and of her own experience, she closes her eyes as she writes, sometimes addressing only herself: "Beauty endures only for as long as it can be seen; / goodness, beautiful today, will remain so tomorrow" (*Poems*, Frag. 119).

Of all the Greek lyricists, Sappho, in both reputation and actual achievement, holds by far the highest place. In the technique of her art—metrical skill, the music of verse—she is at least the equal of any poet who has lived since her day. Fragments of her poetry reveal her expertise in and resistance to all the traditional, male-approved forms and subjects: epithalamia (bridal-chamber songs), epiphany (prayer or invocation), and *priamel* (epigrammic catalog). Her poems celebrate the desires, rituals, and stages in a woman's life, as well as affirm female beauty and the pleasures residing in day-to-day living. In a Kristevan sense, then, Sappho's writings reflect a woman's sense of both cyclical and linear time.[8] Sappho's female subjects are mostly defined by and limited to their physical *being* and states of emotion.[9] They are not immortalized, as were the subjects of male poetry, for glory achieved by *doing*—that is, except in Fragment 4:

> Some say an army of horsemen, others
> say foot-soldiers, still others, a fleet,
> is the fairest thing on the dark earth:
> I say it is whatever one loves.
>
> Everyone can understand this—
> consider that Helen, far surpassing
> the beauty of mortals, leaving behind
> the best man of all,
>
> sailed away to Troy. She had no
> memory of her child or dear parents,
> since she was led astray
> [by Kypris] . . .
>
> *
>
> . . . lightly
> . . . reminding me now of Anaktoria
> being gone,
>
> I would rather see her lovely step
> and the radiant sparkle of her face
> than all the war-chariots in Lydia
> and soldiers battling in shining bronze.   (*Poems*, Frag. 4)

Although purely conventional in its outward shape, Fragment 4 is uniquely Sapphic in its treatment—and rhetorical purpose. Sappho frames the narrator's desire for Anaktoria with the rhetorical device of the catalog, a traditional *priamel* listing the "fairest" objects of the male gaze: epic-scale naval expeditions, displays of military might, and the supreme exemplum of loveliness, Helen of Troy.[10] But Sappho molds the catalog, or *priamel*, to suit her own purposes: the speaking voice of the poem lists and then rejects each of those sights, including Helen, keeping the audience in suspense. The narrator's overwhelming preference is for the "radiant, sparkl[ing] . . . face" of Anaktoria, the "fairest" object being "whatever one loves"—a concluding statement that ties the list of items together. This shift in perspective transforms what Laura Mulvey calls the "male gaze" into a female gaze, for Sappho's narrator gazes at Anaktoria, who signifies, in this case, female desire.[11]

· Furthermore, in the same fragment she gives her version of the Homeric Helen a feminist twist: no longer the passive object of a man's desire, the beautiful Helen is the active, choice-making *subject*—with her own desire for her own "fairest thing." The choice of Helen, as well as of the narrator, is based on the power of that "fairest thing," the object of their love. And since whatever is fairest is what one loves, Fragment 4 is actually about the power of love, a woman's love. From the time of the earliest Greeks, it was decreed that, since desire operates through the eyes, women were forbidden to look directly on their male objects or in their eyes. But Sappho subverts this decree as well; her women desire with their eyes in a female equivalent of a male gaze:

He is more than a hero

He is a god in my eyes—
the man who is allowed
to sit beside you—he

who listens intimately
to the sweet murmur of
your voice, the enticing

laughter that makes my own
heart beat fast. If I meet
you suddenly, I can't

speak—my tongue is broken;
a thin flame runs under
my skin; seeing nothing,

hearing only my own ears
drumming, I drip with sweat;
trembling shakes my body

and I turn paler than
dry grass. At such times
death isn't far from me.   (*New*, Frag. 39)

The shift in perspective from the traditional to the personal makes Sappho's poetry and her use of language both remarkable and memorable: she uses Homer to heroize her own world and to set up a female perspective on male activity that illustrates the exclusion of women from male arenas. Homer's Helen cursed herself for abandoning her husband and coming to Troy; Sappho's Helen is held up as proof that it is right to desire one thing, "the fairest," above all others and to follow it. Sappho's desire for beautiful Anaktoria compares with Helen's desire for Paris. And the female voice of a poem identifies completely with a male, a hero and god, no less, who sits beside the object of her gaze and desire. A student of her own school, Sappho worships the beauty of the present while embracing the beauty inherited from the past. Thus the most powerful seventh-century Ionian woman of words takes her rightful place in the pretheoretical rhetorical tradition.

The Pythagoreans

Literary greats such as Homer and Sappho made many contributions to what would become the art of rhetoric; their attention to form, delivery, appropriateness, and audience nourished a pretheoretical rhetorical consciousness. But the nascent study of philosophy also fed the development of rhetoric, despite the fact that philosophers concentrated on establishing the *truth* and eschewed the rhetoricians' willingness to settle for belief and probability. Like the literary contribution, most philosophical input into rhetoric would come from males who wanted to explain (to themselves and to their students) the universe: humans, physics, chemistry, astronomy, biology, psychology. But women participated in philosophy on a "fairly constant basis throughout Greek antiquity"—and thus in the formation of rhetorical tradition (Wider 22).

The followers of sixth-century Pythagoras of Croton composed a religious fellowship, a *thiasos* (order), dedicated to wisdom and to the goddesses of culture—an educational system resonating with philosophical study. Pythagoras was credited with having six hundred close disciples (*koinobioi*), who shared in the communist life of the Pythagorean society and were provided the possibility for intellectual achievement and understanding.

In his *Life of Pythagoras*, Phorphyry (AD 233–c. 310), following Dicaearchus, describes Pythagoras as so extraordinarily impressive in looks, voice, and bearing that

> the rulers bade him give some advice to the young men on questions relating to youth. This was after he had swayed the council of elders with many fine words. Afterwards he spoke to the assembled school-children; then to the women who were gathered together to hear him. After these speeches his fame increased rapidly, and he made many disciples from the city itself, not only men but also women. One of the women is especially famous, Theano by name; and he made many converts among the neighbouring region of the native inhabitants, including rulers and princes. No one knows exactly what he said to those assembled because the Pythagoreans have an exceptionally strict rule of silence. (qtd. in Gorman 94–95)

Although no contemporary accounts of the Pythagoreans exist (perhaps because of the renowned silence of his followers), subsequent reports and the Pythagorean writings indicate that their academic goals became the template of Greek education that was to inform Plato's Academy, Aristotle's Lyceum, and Epicurus's school.[12]

Unlike the ancient school of the *hetaerae* type, with master and students on the same level (e.g., Sappho's school), the Pythagorean school took holistic charge of the entire student, requiring students, whether young or old, male or female, to adopt a way of life dedicated to moderation, social order, and cosmic harmony. With Pythagoras, the motive for philosophy became the "search for a way of life whereby a right relationship might be established between the philosopher and the universe" (W. Guthrie 1: 148). And those admitted to his circle were pledged to uphold and practice Pythagoras's teaching in their daily lives, for he was as much a religious and political teacher as a philosopher.

Although Pythagoras's school was distinguished by the genius and vast learning of its headmaster, it was immortalized because it received both female and male pupils. Two centuries before Plato, Pythagoras laid down the principle of equal opportunity for the sexes, a principle he practiced as well as preached. Recognizing the natural differences in function between the sexes, he gave his women pupils considerable training in philosophy and literature, but he also had them instructed in the maternal and domestic arts. In contrast to the ancient Greek attitude that women should be spoken of as little as possible, the Pythagoreans extolled their women as "just." For example, while men require legal security in the form of witnesses or a pledge when they lend anything to others (if they lend at all), according to Pythagorean tradition, women are "just": women are willing to share what is their own with others, and this with perfect ease and harmony. In fact, one reason that Pythagorean men (unlike other Greek men) were exhorted to remain faithful and attentive to their Pythagorean wives was that the women were of such high quality, perhaps the highest "feminine" type that Greece ever produced.

The mainstay of Pythagorean philosophy was *harmonia*, the body of inflexible cosmic rules that informed sculpture, architecture, poetry, music, rhetoric, religion, morality, and human life. Pythagoras's program of moral reform aimed to eliminate discontent among the citizens and to produce, instead, a state of *homonoia*, or union of hearts and minds. Diogenes Laertius condenses *harmonia* thus: "Virtue is harmony, and so are health and all good and God himself; this is why they say that all things are constructed according to the laws of harmony. The love of friends is just concord and equality" (2.8.33). Pythagorean men could practice their philosophy openly and publicly within Greek culture, but it was the Pythagorean women who helped spread this philosophy of thought and who adapted it from the cosmos to the microcosm: from the state to the home.

The extant female-authored Pythagorean writings clearly mark the intersection of influential Pythagorean women with domestic, personal *harmonia*. These fragments, whole letters, and complete essays concern themselves with "practical ethics," with the ways women should and can preserve "personal and familial relationships" (Ward 57, 59). Seventeenth-century scholar Gilles Ménage mentions the contributions of twenty-eight Pythagorean women (47–50). Ménage draws on Laertius's *Life of Pythagoras* (AD 400) to write that Pythagoras's Themistoclea, a Delphic priestess-philosopher, was the source of Pythagoras's aesthetic principles (Laertius 2.8.7, 2.8.21). No further details can be found about her.

Perhaps Pythagoras's wife, Theano, is most deserving of attention because she, more than any other of the women, explains the Pythagorean philosophy and the practical application of *harmonia* to the home and everyday life. Of the sixteen extant letters by both women and men, ten are by women; and of these, eight are attributed to Theano, who used letter writing as a form of moral education for other women (Ward 59–60).[13] According to Theano, women, being naturally temperate, bear the responsibility for using moderation (Theano's "Golden Rule") and for respecting the natural laws of hierarchy (e.g., male over female) within family and marriage, which were thought to be the microcosm of the state. To that end, every Pythagorean demonstrated an obligation to preserve, promote, and protect the concord of domestic and public social relations.

Laertius mentions Theano's writing, as well as her influence. Like Pythagoras, she supported the harmony and purity of the family, particularly the parent-child relationship but also the husband-wife relationship.[14] It was generally held that sexual intercourse made one impure, so that whoever wished to enter the temple had to wait a day or so after intercourse, taking time to become purified. However, when Theano was asked "how many days it was before a woman becomes pure after intercourse, she replied, 'With her own husband at once, with another man never' " (Laertius 2.8.43). The "just" thing was "just," whether performed at home or in public. After all, the primary meaning of *harmonia* is not musical but is, instead, a "fitting together," made possible by a craftsmanship that results in a unified object, or a "perfect fit." Consequently, Pythagorean women understood and accepted their measure of domestic power and acted on their responsibility for creating the conditions under which harmony, order, law, and justice could exist in the state and in the home.

One of the few extant writings, albeit a fragment, is from the late Pythagorean Phintys of Sparta. *On the Moderation of Women* continues the argument that, although the social responsibilities of men and women are different, men and women remain equal and that the normative principle of *harmonia* provides for satisfaction within the context of those specific social responsibilities, both public and private. According to Phintys, women were equal to men in terms of courage, justice, and reflection; but men used these virtues for waging war and governing, while women managed the private sphere of home and family. Phintys argues persuasively, as a woman and for women, meeting any opposition to women philosophers head-on:

> Now, perhaps many think it is not fitting for a woman to philosophize, just as it is not fitting for her to ride horses or speak in public. But I think that some things are peculiar to a man, some to a woman, some are common to both, some belong more to a man than a woman, some more to a woman than a man. . . . But I say that courage and justice and wisdom are common to both. Excellences of the body are appropriate for both a man and a woman, likewise those of the soul. And just as it is beneficial for the body of each to be healthy, so too, is it beneficial for the soul to be healthy. The excellences of the body are health, strength, keenness of perception and beauty. (qtd. in Waithe 27)

Thus, according to Phintys, any differences between men and women should not prevent women from taking their rightful place in the development, maintenance, and teaching of philosophy.

Another late Pythagorean work that focuses on the social and moral status of women in society is *On the Harmony of Women*, written, many scholars think, by Perictyone, mother of Plato. Much more utilitarian than Phintys's work and therefore perhaps more accessible to her lay readers, Perictyone writes of ways for women best to achieve harmony within their circumscribed worlds, not within an idealized world. Pragmatic and insightful, Perictyone's theories seem to prefigure rhetorical ones: she expounds rules that proceed from moral and legal judgments that society actually makes, yet she appeals to feelings, for she addresses a popular audience. She opens her exhortation with these words:

> A woman should be a harmony of thoughtfulness and temperance. Her soul should be zealous to acquire virtue so that she may be just, brave, prudent, frugal, and hating vainglory. Furnished with these virtues she will, when she becomes a wife, act worthily towards herself, her husband, her children and her family. Frequently also such a woman will act beautifully towards cities if she happens to rule over cities and nations, as we see is sometimes the case in a kingdom. (qtd. in K. Guthrie 239)

If Perictyone the Pythagorean is indeed Plato's mother, she may well have influenced his *Symposium*, in which he extols the virtue and wisdom and philosophy of another female Pythagorean, Diotima. Using a combination of wisdom and good speech, a rhetorical consciousness as it were, both Perictyone and Phintys produce a desired effect upon their readers—in a time when most women were excluded from intellectual pursuits and well before a theory of rhetoric had yet been developed.

THE GREEK RHETORICAL TRADITION

"Rhetoric did not originate at a single moment in history. Rather, it was an evolving, developing consciousness about the relationship between thought and expression" (R. Enos, *Greek* ix). Most well known to us, however, is the use of rhetoric in the establishment of a democracy in Syracuse. Rhetoric began as a practical art, a vital part of civic life in this new democracy fraught with a mass of litigation on property claims. Formerly exiled claimants who had no documents of ownership had to rely on inferential reasoning to plead their own cases. Without any idea of how to state and arrange the complicated details, they needed professional advice—hence Corax's custom-designed art of rhetoric, an art his pupil Tisias transmitted to Greece.

Corax's art of rhetoric was immeasurably influential, for it would serve as the foundation for the rhetorical theories of Plato, Aristotle, Cicero, Quintilian, Gorgias, Isocrates, and Pericles. In the burgeoning democracy of Athens, men only argued for civic and political *areté*.[15] Such public oratory fed the spirit of Panhellenism, a doctrine sorely needed to unify the Greek city-states. Women could testify, but only men argued. Receptive to the art, Athens became the center for the flourishing study and practice of rhetoric; therefore, men came to Athens to prepare for a career in politics.

Sicilian ambassador to Athens in 427 BCE, Gorgias settled in Athens and opened a school of rhetoric, not a school in the institutional sense but rather a circle of collective tutoring. Gorgias's philosophy of education was dedicated to producing a capable statesman and to forming his personality, his *areté*. *Areté* denoted to Gorgias an intellectual power and oratorical ability. And his student Pericles was *areté* personified, an ideal citizen-orator. Not a philosopher, a thinker, or a seeker of truth, Gorgias was a teacher. But he became known for more than his teaching. Recognized as one of the first to appreciate and articulate the persuasive power of emotional appeal, of pathos, he laid the groundwork for centuries of debate concerning the efficacy of the individual artistic proofs (logos, pathos, ethos). Also because he believed that the probable deserves more respect than the true, he perfected the ability to promote probabilities, part of the power that is found in logos. Gorgias is best known, however, for his ability to merge rhetoric with poetics, for his distinctive, ornate prose style. Gorgias belonged to the Sophist school in that he was indeed a teacher of superior grade who distinguished himself by providing a liberal education that would supplement the customary instruction in reading, writing, gymnastics, and music.

Despite his prodigious success, Gorgias was not to be the most influential of the teachers in the Sophist schools; that distinction would go to Isocrates. Along with Aristotle, Isocrates is often hailed as one of the most influential of the Greek rhetoricians. Isocrates, whose school had offered a greater breadth of education than that of the Sophists, had himself received the best education Athens provided: he had studied with Tisias, Gorgias, and Socrates and ultimately identified himself as a Sophist, a term that in his early years had no negative connotation.

Although Isocrates began his career as a *logographos*, a hired writer of courtroom speeches, his real vocation was teaching. About 392 BCE, he founded his famous school near the Lyceum, its goal being the formation of an intellectual elite by way of a grave and upright education. He drew hundreds of paying pupils from the Panhellenic world and, in the process, amassed a considerable fortune. Although he often referred to himself as a philosopher, he was in fact a Sophist, albeit of a different stripe than Gorgias. If Gorgias's education was based ultimately on the idea of probability, that of Isocrates relied on the virtues of speech itself, of logos.

Isocrates's real eminence lay in his giving an artistic finish to the literary branch of rhetoric—accurate diction, logical transitions, smooth sounds and rhythm, periodic sentences, holistic aim—setting a standard in form and rhythm for prose style. He was regarded by the Greeks as representing the school of smooth prose style—he refined Gorgias's artificial style into an artistic prose—and as making oratory a literary form. And he was the "first major 'orator' who did not deliver his speeches orally. They were carefully edited, polished, and published in written . . . form. By his action speech was converted into literature, another influence toward the *letteraturizzazione* [secondary form] of rhetoric" (Kennedy, *Classical* 35). In this way, he helped raise oratory to the level of a literary art and preserve that influence of the spoken word on literature that—helped by the custom of reading aloud—was to remain one of the dominant features of Greek literature.

Isocrates's prose style was his legacy to the literature of modern Europe, and his confidence in the power of words was the wellspring of what would become humanist scholarship. He undertook to saturate his art with a content of real values, for his eloquence had a distinct civic and patriotic purpose, and his students were to be citizen-orators. As such, his sophistry, his educational system with its sound moral influence and its rhetorical base, was a system of general culture.

The Sophists, then, were supplying a social and political need, but they were also creating new ones. Their humanist philosophy propounded individual responsibility, as well as political and social action. The fruit of their philosophy was activated conscience and rhetorical maturity. The gods were no longer responsible for earthly actions; *individuals* were responsible for their own actions and were collectively responsible for the actions of the state. In addition to the conducive climate of their historical moment, the Sophists owed much to individual patronage and, above all, to the patronage of one man: Pericles—a fact that has not perhaps been recognized as fully as it should in accounts of the Sophists' movement. Offering democracy to the masses, Pericles (fl. 442 BCE), the most powerful and influential of Athenians, appreciated fine intellect and command of language, so he surrounded himself with the greatest thinkers of his age: with Sophists, philosophers, scientists, and rhetoricians.

Fifth-Century BCE Athens

In the burgeoning democracy of Periclean Athens, men were consciously forming human character in accordance with the new cultural ideals of military strength and justice (*diké*) tempered by the traditional concepts of *areté*. Only aristocratic male citizens, equal in their *homonoia* (being of one mind), argued for civic and political *areté*, the essential principle of government by the elite—a democratic oligarchy. Yet Plato's Socrates called for *areté* according to social role, be it male or female, free or slave (*Republic* 1.353.b); and later, Aristotle would write that both the rulers and the ruled, males and females alike, "must possess virtue" and that "all must partake of [moral virtues] . . . in such measure as is proper to each in relation to his own function" (*Politics* 1.5.5, 7.5.7). Thus was manifested the complex tension between the elitist *areté* and the more democratic *homonoia*.

In *The Origins of Greek Thought*, Jean-Pierre Vernant tells us that "Greek political life aimed to become the subject of public debate, in the broad daylight of the agora, between citizens who were defined as equals and for whom the state was the common undertaking" (11). Such public oratory fed the spirit of Panhellenism, a doctrine sorely needed to unify the Greek city-states, just as it satiated the male appetite for public display. As a system, the polis implied "the extraordinary preeminence of speech over all other instruments of power, [speech becoming] the political tool par excellence, the key to authority in the state, the means of commanding and dominating others" (49). In what would be an inestimable contribution to a democratic oratory possessed by aristocratic characteristics, former logographer (speech writer) Isocrates practiced rhetoric as a literary form, one imbued with civic, patriotic, and moral purpose. Confident in the power of words, he practiced and taught a morally influenced and rhetorically based system of general culture that propounded individual responsibility, as well as political and social action. No longer were men deferring to their sovereign or the gods, who could reinforce *nomos* (beliefs, customs, laws, provisional codes enforced by universal opinion) with *physis* (nature, ultimate reality). "With this denial of the absolute status of law and moral things, the stage [was] set for a controversy between the two . . . [and for drawing] different practical conclusions from it" (W. Gutherie 3: 60). Individuals would be responsible for their own actions and collectively responsible for the actions of the democratic state, the polis.

The Athenian polis was founded upon the exclusion of foreigners and slaves (Vidal-Naquet 145). Although females born of Athenian-citizen parents were citizen-class and subjects within the polis, they were not actual citizens in any sense. Nor could foreign-born women or men hope for citizenship, regardless of their political influence on, civic contributions to, or intellectual ties with those in power. Therefore, noncitizens, such as Protagoras, Gorgias, Prodicus, Thrasymachus, Anaxagoras, and Aspasia, functioned within the polis, yet outside its restraints.

Aspasia of Miletus

In the fifth century BCE, Miletus was a far-eastern Greek subject-ally, a cultivated city (in what is now Turkey) renowned for its literacy and philosophies of moral thought and nature.[16] A non-Athenian, citizen-class Greek, Aspasia arrived in Athens brilliantly educated by means that have never been fully explained.[17] Whether she was educated within a literate Milesian family or within a school for *hetaerae* (upper-class courtesans), she was exceptionally fortunate, for "there is no evidence at all that in the classical period girls attended schools, and it is entirely consistent with what we know about the seclusion of women in Athens that Athenian girls did not do so (some other cities may have been less benighted in this respect)" (Harris 96).[18] Married at an early age, Athenian women neither attended schools nor participated in the polis. H. D. F. Kitto places Athenian women in Oriental seclusion, a practice he considers sensible yet worth mentioning: "In this pre-eminently masculine society women moved in so restricted a sphere that we may reasonably regard them as a 'depressed area' " (222).

Yet the system of the polis, which implied both civic consciousness and the "extraordinary preeminence of speech over all other instruments of power" (Vernant, *Origins* 49), tripped the mechanism that powered the active diffusion and acquisition of literacy among Greek males (proper citizens). And we must assume that at least a few Athenian or Athenian-colony women of the citizen-class, even those defined by good families and cultural constraints, became literate—and became conscious of civic rights and responsibilities (S. Cole 222–23; Harris 103, 107).[19] Aspasia of Miletus was one of those women.

As a free woman brought up in the transitional society of Asia Minor, Aspasia was freed from the rigidity of traditional marriage and from the identity that arose from that fixed role. And upon emigrating from Miletus, Aspasia emerged in Athens linked with Pericles, the aristocratic democrat who placed Athenian democratic power "in the hands not of a minority but of the whole people," with everyone equal before the law (Thucydides 2.37.1). Thus, this non-Athenian, or "stranger-woman," was subject to Athenian law but did not have citizen rights. Nor was she accountable to the severe strictures applied to an aristocratic Athenian woman, whose activity, movement, education, marriage, and rights as a citizen and property holder were extremely circumscribed by male relatives. Aspasia could ignore—even rupture—the traditional enclosure of the female body. She could subvert Pericles's advice for ideal womanhood: "Your greatest glory is not to be inferior to what God has made you" (Thucydides 5.46.2). She could—and she did.

That Aspasia is mentioned by her male contemporaries is remarkable, for rare is the mention of any intellectual woman. Surviving fragments and references in the works of male authors provide tantalizing indications that the intellectual efforts of Aspasia were, at least occasionally, committed to writing—and to architecture. Aspasia is memorialized in a fresco over the portal of the University of Athens, in the company of Phidias, Pericles (on whom she leans), Sophocles, Antisthenes, Anaxagoras, Alcibiades, and Socrates.

When other women were systematically relegated to the domestic sphere, Aspasia seems to have been the only woman in classical Greece to have distinguished herself in the public domain. Her reputation as both rhetorician and philosopher was memorialized by Plato (427–348 BCE), Xenophon (c. 431–c. 352 BCE), Cicero (106–43 BCE), Plutarch (AD 46–c. 120), and Athenaeus (fl. AD 200)—as was, of course, her enduring romantic attachment to Pericles. For those authors, Aspasia clearly represented the intelligentsia of Periclean Athens, and the story of her intellectual contributions to rhetoric may suggest the existence of an unrecognized subculture within that community.

The best-known source of information about Aspasia is Plutarch's *Lives of the Noble Grecians and Romans* (AD 100), an account written several hundred years after her death. Nevertheless, all earlier mentions of Aspasia confirm this

inquiry about the woman, what art or charming facility she had that enabled her to captivate, as she did, the greatest statesmen, and to give the philosophers occasions to speak so much about her, and that, too, not to her disparagement. That she was a Milesian by birth, the daughter of Axiochus, is a thing acknowledged. And they say it was in emulation of Thargelia, a courtesan of the old Ionian times, that she made her addresses to men of great power. Thargelia was a great beauty, extremely charming, and at the same time sagacious; she had numerous suitors among the Greeks. . . . Aspasia, some say, was courted and caressed by

Pericles upon account of her knowledge and skill in politics. Socrates himself would sometimes go to visit her, and some of his acquaintances with him; and those who frequented her company would carry their wives with them to listen to her. Her occupation was anything but creditable, her house being a home for young courtesans. . . . [I]n Plato's *Menexenus*, though we do not take the introduction as quite serious, still thus much seems to be historical, that she had the repute of being resorted to by many of the Athenians for instruction in the art of speaking. Pericles's inclination for her seems, however, to have rather proceeded from the passion of love. He had a wife that was near of kin to him, who had been married first to Hipponicus, by whom she had Callias, surnamed the Rich; and also she brought Pericles, while she lived with him, two sons, Xanthippus and Paralus. Afterwards, when they did not well agree, nor like to live together, he parted with her, with her own consent, to another man, and himself took Aspasia, and loved her with wonderful affection; every day, both as he went out and as he came in from the market-place, he saluted and kissed her. (200–1)

By every historical account, Aspasia ventured out into the common land, distinguishing herself by her rhetorical accomplishments, her sexual attachment to Pericles, and her public participation in political affairs. Her alleged connection with the courtesan life is only important so far as it explains her intellectual prowess and social attainments—and the surprise of an Athenian citizenry unaccustomed to (or perhaps jealous or suspicious of) a public woman:[20]

No one would have thought the less of Pericles for making love to young boys . . . but they *were* shocked by his treating [Aspasia] like a human being—by the fact that he *lived* with her instead of relegating her to the *gynaikeion* [women's quarters], and included his friends' wives when he issued invitations to dinner. It was all too amazing to be proper; and Aspasia was so brilliant she could not possibly be respectable. (Delcourt 77)

Gendered boundaries. Aspasia's appearance among the educated, accomplished, and powerful was unprecedented at a time when the construction of gender ensured that women would be praised only for such attributes as their inherent modesty, their inborn reluctance to join males (even kinsmen) for society or dining, and their absolute incapacity to participate as educated beings within the polis; at a time when a woman's only political contribution was serving as a nameless channel for the transmission of citizenship from her father to her son (Keuls 90); and at a time when Pericles pronounced that "the greatest glory of a woman is to be least talked about by men, whether they are praising . . . or criticizing" (Thucydides 5.46.2).[21] It is difficult to overemphasize how extraordinary the foreign-born Aspasia—a public woman, philosopher, political influence, and rhetorician—would have been in fifth-century BCE Athenian society (Pomeroy 19; Just 144).[22]

But when we think of gender as a cultural role or a social rank, we can more easily trace Aspasia's movement across gendered boundaries of appropriate roles for women and men in fifth-century BCE Athens. She seems to have profited by her excursion into the male domain of politics and intellect, even at the expense of her respectability, reputation, and authority. Named among the rather short "list of Athenian citizen[-class] women" known to us from literature (Schaps 323), the assertively intelligent Aspasia has been interpreted as self-indulgent, licentious, immoral. Historical records have successfully effaced the voice of the ideal Greek woman, rendering silent her enclosed body. And those same historical records have defaced any subversion of that ideal woman, rendering her unconfined body invalid.

Thus, even though her contributions to rhetoric are firmly situated and fully realized within the rhetorical tradition, those contributions have been directed through a powerful gendered lens to both refract toward and reflect Socrates and Pericles. Ironically, then, Aspasia's accomplishments and influence have been enumerated by men and most often attributed to men—or installed in the apocryphal, the safest place for wise (and therefore fictitious) women. As for Aspasia's popular salon, it is often accredited to Pericles instead of to his female companion.

Aspasia, Pericles, and the funeral oration. Pericles, perhaps the most socially responsible, powerful, and influential of Athenians, was surrounded by "a brain trust" that included Sophists, "experts in political manipulation who were flocking to Athens from other Greek poleis," as well as Aspasia, "the power behind the throne" (Ober 89–90).[23] Plato's Socrates calls Pericles "the most perfect orator in existence," attributing Pericles's eloquence to the successful combination of his natural talents with the high-mindedness and art of speaking he learned from Anaxagoras (*Phaedrus* 269.e–270.a, in *Euthyphro*). Cicero later concurred that Anaxagoras was "a man distinguished for his knowledge of the highest sciences; and consequently Pericles was eminent in learning, wisdom and eloquence, and for forty years was supreme at Athens both in politics and at the same time in the conduct of war" (*De oratore* 3.34.138–39).

Yet several years later, Philostratus (fl. AD 250) wrote in his *Epistle* 73 that "Aspasia of Miletus is said to have sharpened the tongue of Pericles in imitation of Gorgias," with "the digressions and transitions of Gorgias' speeches [becoming] the fashion" (qtd. in Sprague 41–42). Philostratus echoes Plato, the earliest writer to mention Aspasia. In the *Menexenus*, Plato's Socrates reveals Aspasia to be the author of Pericles's funeral oration (*epitaphios*), an assertion I explore below. Aspasia becomes even more implicated in Pericles's education if we consider the "familiar knowledge at Athens that Aspasia had sat at the feet of Anaxagoras in natural philosophy" (Courtney 491). The rhetorician most closely associated with Pericles would no doubt have served as his logographer, as logography (the written composition of speech) was commonly the province of rhetoricians. Hence, Aspasia surely must have influenced Pericles in the composition of those speeches that both established him as a persuasive speaker and informed him as the most respected citizen-orator of the age.

Although Plutarch credits Aspasia with contributing greatly to intellectual life, specifically to philosophy, politics, and rhetoric, many scholars have since discredited her. Plutarch draws on a now-incomplete work of Aeschines (389–14 BCE) to describe Aspasia, but neither his nor Aspasia's case has been strengthened by the fragments of Aeschines's work that survived. Those fragments present a controversial statement on gender equality: "the goodness of a woman is the same as that of a man," an assertion Aeschines illustrates with the political abilities of Aspasia (qtd. in Taylor 278).[24] Both Xenophon and Cicero (and, later, medieval abbess Héloïse, perhaps best known for her attachment to Peter Abelard), however, tap that same complete text, giving credence to the text—as well as to the existence of a historical Aspasia.[25]

According to several ancient sources, all of whom knitted together secondary sources to shape a reliable Socrates, Socrates deeply respected Aspasia's thinking and admired her rhetorical prowess, disregarding, it seems, her status as a woman and a *hetaera*. In Xenophon's *Memorabilia*, for instance, Socrates explains to Critobulus the "art of catching friends" and of using an "intermediary":

> I can quote Aspasia. . . . She once told me that good matchmakers are successful only when the good reports they carry to and fro are true; false reports she would not recommend for the victims of deceptions hate one another and the matchmaker too. I am convinced that this is sound, so I think it is not open to me to say anything in your praise that I cannot say truthfully. (2.36)

In Xenophon's *Oeconomicus*, Socrates ascribes to Aspasia the marital advice he gives to Critobulus: "There's nothing like investigation, I will introduce Aspasia to you, and she will explain the whole matter [of good wives] to you with more knowledge than I possess" (3.15, in *Memorabilia*). Plutarch writes, "Socrates sometimes came to see her [Aspasia] with his disciples, and his intimate friends brought their wives to her to hear her discourse . . . as a teacher of rhetoric" (*Lives* 200); Athenaeus calls Aspasia "clever . . . Socrates' teacher in rhetoric" (5.29) and goes on to account for the extent of Aspasia's influence over Socrates:

> [I]n the verses which are extant under her name and which are quoted by Herodicus . . . [she says]: "Socrates, I have not failed to notice that thy heart is smitten with desire for [Alcibiades]. . . . But hearken, if thou wouldst prosper in thy suit. Disregard not my message, and it will be much better for thee. For so soon as I heard, my body was suffused with the glow of joy, and tears not unwelcome fell from my eyelids. Restrain thyself, filling thy soul with the conquering Muse; and with her aid thou shalt win him; pour her into the ears of his desire. For she is the true beginning of love in both; through her thou shalt master him, by offering to his ears gifts for the unveiling of his soul."
> So, then, the noble Socrates goes a-hunting, employing the woman of Miletus as his preceptor in love, instead of being hunted himself, as Plato has said, [Socrates] being caught [as he was] in Alcibiades' net. (5.219)

Furthermore, in the *Menexenus*, Plato's Socrates agrees that, were the council chamber to elect him to make the recitation over the dead (the *epitaphios*), he "should be able to make the speech . . . for she [Aspasia] who is my instructor is by no means weak in the art of rhetoric; on the contrary, she has turned out many fine orators, and amongst them one who surpassed all other Greeks, Pericles" (*Menexenus* 235.e, in *Timaeus*). But it was Pericles—not Aspasia—who delivered that funeral oration.

The *Menexenus* contains Plato's version of Socrates's version of Aspasia's version of Pericles's funeral oration, further recognition of Socrates's version of Aspasia's reputation as rhetorician, as philosopher, and as influential colleague in the sophistic movement, a movement devoted to the analysis and creation of rhetoric—and of truth. Moreover, the funeral oration itself held political, philosophical, and rhetorical significance: by its delivery alone, the funeral oration played out "rhetoric's important role in shaping community" (Mackin 251). After all, the funeral oration served as an "*institution*—an institution of speech in which the symbolic constantly encroached upon the functional, since in each oration the codified praise of the dead spilled over into generalized praise of Athens" (Loraux, *Invention* 2). Besides conflating praise of the Athenians with praise of Athens, this institutionalized and specialized epideictic was useful for developing "consubstantiality" (*homonoia*) and for creating a "similar rhetorical experience" for everyone present, be they citizens, foreigners, or women related to the dead. As Thucydides writes: "Everyone who wishes to, both citizens and foreigners, can join in the procession, and the women who are related to the dead are there to make their laments at the tomb" (2.34). The shared experience of this rhetorical ritual linked everyone present even as it connected them "with other audiences in the past" (Mackin 251). As "one of the authorized mouthpieces of classical Athens," the funeral oration translated into "Greek patriotism" or "Athenian eloquence" "adapted to the needs of a given historical situation" (Loraux, *Invention* 5). As such, the issues of translation and adaptation easily connect the *epitaphios* with sophistic philosophy.

"For the Sophists, human perception and discourse were the only measure of truths, all of which are contingent" (Jarratt, *Rereading* 64); therefore, they focused on "the ability to create accounts of communal possibilities through persuasive speech" (98). In every *epitaphios*, "the personality of the orator has to yield to the impersonality of the genre . . . as an institution and as a literary form" (Loraux, *Invention* 11). Aspasia's sophistic training, political capacity, and powerful influence on Pericles's persuasive oratory easily translated into Socrates's pronouncement to Menexenus that Aspasia had composed the famous funeral oration delivered by Pericles:

I was listening only yesterday to Aspasia going through a funeral speech for [the Athenians]. . . . [S]he rehearsed to me the speech in the form it should take, extemporizing in part, while other parts of it she had previously prepared, . . . at the time when she was composing the funeral oration which Pericles delivered. (Plato, *Menexenus* 236.b, in *Timaeus*)

That Aspasia may well have composed Pericles's speech makes sense: after all, being honored by the opportunity to deliver the *epitaphios*, he would have prepared well, seeking and following the advice of his colleagues, including Aspasia, on points of style and substance. That she wrote it becomes more convincing when we consider the assurance that "the political orator must have the ascendant over the logographer" and that the Sophist would preserve the "essential features of the civic representations" (Loraux, *Invention* 11, 107). Given Aspasia's proximity to Pericles, as well as her intellectual training, she no doubt contributed to Pericles's work.

Before demonstrating her expertise at composing moving, patriotic epideictic oratory, Aspasia reminds Socrates of the efficacy of rhetoric. In the *Menexenus*, Plato's Aspasia explains that "it is by means of speech finely spoken that deeds nobly done gain for their doers from the hearers the meed of memory and renown" (236.e)—an accurate description of contingent truth. Jarratt explains the sophistic rhetorical technique and its social-constructionist underpinning with her definition of *nomos* as a "self-conscious arrangement of discourse to create politically and socially significant knowledge . . . thus it is always a social construct with ethical dimensions" (*Rereading* 60).

Hence, the author of the *epitaphios*—whether viewed as Aspasia or Pericles—makes clear the power of oratory to influence the public's belief that its history was other than it was: "a Sophist and a rhetor would have used the official oration in order to write a fictitious logos; within the corpus, then, the 'false' follows hard upon the 'true' " (Loraux, *Invention* 9). Accordingly, the most aggressive exploits of Attic imperialism are represented as bringing "freedom [to] all the dwellers of this continent" (*Menexenus* 240.e, in *Timaeus*), as "fighting in defence of the liberties of the Boeotians" (242.b), as "fighting for the freedom of Leontini" (243.a), as "setting free . . . friends" (243.c), and as "saving their walls from ruin" (244.c). In offering this version of Pericles's funeral oration, an exaggerated encomium abounding with historical misstatements and anachronisms, Plato makes explicit his own feelings about the use of rhetoric—just as Thucydides uses his own version of the *epitaphios* to make explicit his belief in the necessary subjection of individual citizenship to the polis: "A man who takes no interest in politics is a man . . . who has no business here at all" (2.40).

Thinly disguised in the *Menexenus* is Plato's cynicism. In his opinion, the development of oratory had negative consequences for Athens, the most glaring defect being its indifference to truth. A rhetorician such as Aspasia was, indeed, interested more in believability than in truth, more interested in constructing than in delivering truth, more interested in *nomos* than in *physis*, interests leading to Thucydides's claims that such "prose chroniclers . . . are less interested in telling the truth than in catching the attention of their public" (1.21). In the opening dialogue of the *Menexenus*, Plato's Socrates disparages the orators in much the same way he does in the *Symposium*, saying that "in speeches long beforehand . . . they praise in such splendid fashion, that . . . they bewitch our souls. . . . [E]very time I listen fascinated [by their praise] I am exalted and imagine myself to have become all at once taller and nobler and more handsome . . . owing to the persuasive eloquence of the speaker" (*Menexenus* 235.b, in *Timaeus*). Thus Plato recoils from the touch of rhetoric.

Aspasia's influence. Aspasia was an active member of the most famous intellectual circle in Athens, her influence extending to Plato and his concept of rhetoric as well. Like Aspasia, Plato taught that belief and truth are not necessarily the same, a sentiment he makes evident in his *Gorgias* when Gorgias admits that rhetoric produces mere "belief without knowledge" (*Gorgias* 454.e, in *Symposium*). Plato also agrees with Aspasia that rhetoric, which is the daughter of truth-disclosing philosophy, does not always carry on the family tradition; rhetoric can be used to obscure the truth, to control and deceive believers into belief. In the *Gorgias*, his Socrates says, "[R]hetoric seems not to be an artistic pursuit at all, but that of a shrewd, courageous spirit which is naturally clever at dealing with men; and I call the chief part of it flattery" (463.b). And in the *Phaedrus*, Plato writes that "in the courts, they say, nobody cares for the truth about these matters [things which are just or good], but for that which is convincing; and that is probability" (*Phaedrus* 272.d–e, in *Euthyphro*).

Like Aspasia, Plato approved of a rhetoric of persuasion; he too sees the political potential of public rhetoric. But his rhetoric is foremost a search for the truth; only truth—not fictive effect over accuracy—should constitute persuasive rhetoric. His perfect orator of the *Phaedrus* "must know the truth about all the particular things of which he speaks and writes . . . [and] must understand the nature of the soul" (277.c), for the ideal rhetorician speaks "in a manner pleasing to the gods" (273.e). What Plato could have learned, then, from Aspasia was the potentially harmful uses of rhetoric as a branch of philosophy—as well as the as-yet-uncalibrated potential of rhetoric to create belief.

In addition to influencing Socrates and Plato, Aspasia also influenced Xenophon and his wife, specifically in the art of inductive argument. In *De inventione*, Cicero uses Aspasia's lesson on induction as the centerpiece for his argumentation chapter. Like others before him, Cicero too acknowledges Aspasia's influence on Socrates, as well as the existence of the Aeschines text:

In a dialogue by Aeschines Socraticus[,] Socrates reveals that Aspasia reasoned thus with Xenophon's wife and with Xenophon himself: "Please tell me, madam, if your neighbour had a better gold ornament than you have, would you prefer that one or your own?" "That one," she replied. "Now, if she had dresses and other feminine finery more expensive than you have, would you prefer yours or hers?" "Hers, of course," she replied. "Well, now, if she had a better husband than you have, would you prefer your husband or hers?" At this the woman blushed. But Aspasia then began to speak to Xenophon. "I wish you would tell me, Xenophon," she said, "if your neighbour had a better horse than yours, would you prefer your horse or his?" "His," was the answer. "And if he had a better farm than you have, which farm would you prefer to have?" "The better farm, naturally," he said. "Now if he had a better wife than you have, would you prefer yours or his?" And at this Xenophon, too, himself was silent. Then Aspasia: "Since both of you have failed to tell me the only thing I wished to hear, I myself will tell you what you both are thinking. That is you, madam, wish to have the best husband, and you, Xenophon, desire above all things to have the finest wife. Therefore, unless you can contrive that there be no better man or finer woman on earth you will certainly always be in dire want of what you consider best, namely, that you be the husband of the very best of wives, and that she be wedded to the very best of men." To this instance, because assent has been given to undisputed statements, the result is that the point which would appear doubtful if asked by itself is through analogy conceded as certain, and this is due to the method employed in putting the question. Socrates used this conversation method a good deal, because he wished to present no arguments himself, but preferred to get a result from the material which the interlocutor had given him—a result which the interlocutor was bound to approve as following necessarily from what he had already granted. (1.31.51–53)

Few women participated in the intellectual life of ancient Greece. Aspasia has emerged as an exceptional hero in a new rhetorical narrative.

Diotima of Mantinea

In addition to Aspasia, Diotima of Mantinea is a striking exception to the exclusion of women from intellectual life. Known to us only through her appearance as a central character in Plato's *Symposium*, Diotima informed the thinking of those Greek philosophers and rhetoricians who listened to her discourse on eros, love, and the pursuit of possession. Roughly translated, "Diotima of Mantinea" means "the Zeus-worshipper from Prophetville" (Halperin, "Why" 121), but her name can also be given the more positive spin of "god honoring," perhaps a better translation considering the substance of Diotima's discourse: procreation, both intellectual and physical. Except for Zeus, whose daughter sprang from his brow, all men are inferior to all women in their ability to bear children. Thus, Diotima of Mantinea honors Zeus as she speaks to the issue of male love, (homo)sexuality, and the concomitant desires for intellectual and physical possession that reproduce one's soul in another. The great energy of nature, eros translates to "love," one of the highest cultural ideals, but it is also associated closely with "desire," with an irrational, irresistible, inevitable madness (Ervin 75). A nexus of love, desire, and immortality, a "soul can only reach immortality in a metaphysical sense by its prolific operation . . . by leaving a name and a reputation to survive it" (Grote 17–18).

Controversy surrounds this philosopher-priestess whenever the question of her historicity is raised—raised by the fact that "the introduction of purely fictitious named personages into a discourse seems to be a literary device unknown to Plato" (Taylor 224). Plato's own Socrates, no less, seeks out Diotima as "an instructor," asking her to "tell [him] the cause of these effects . . . that have relation to love matters" (Plato, *Symposium* 207.d).

Diotima's significance lies both in the crux of her argument and in her female representation of a worthy and competent teacher for Socrates, Plato's own master (207.c). Diotima's presence resonates with the passions, the body, the family and the private realm, as well as with the processes of life and birth (Saxonhouse, "Eros" 6). Yet her feminine presence enhances—rather than detracts from—the powerful homoeroticism of Plato's *Symposium*. The backdrop for the dialogue is Plato's own well-established reputation as a homosexual, a mystic, a moralist, but foregrounded is the dialogue on love that sublimates the base and barren physicality of Plato's sexual identity and instead transcends to a philosophy of perfect love and intellectual intercourse that reproduces the form of immutable beauty:

> And now I shall . . . proceed with the discourse upon Love which I heard one day from a Mantinean woman named Diotima; in this subject she was skilled. . . . [I] will give my description that form of question and answer which the stranger woman used for hers that day. For I spoke to her . . . , saying Love was a great god, and was of beautiful things; and she refuted me with [those] very arguments. (Socrates, in Plato, *Symposium* 201.d)[26]

In the *Symposium*, Plato stretches the scientific study of passionate erotic love over the frame of inductive logical method. And he places that inductive argument in the mouth of Diotima, who leads Socrates toward conclusions much different from the sensual-spiritual dichotomy he reached in the *Phaedrus*. In the *Phaedrus*, Plato's Socrates accepts erotic passion as a degrading madness and a physical urgency that disturbs stable contemplation, as well as any understanding of the good and the beautiful. To illustrate his argument, Socrates describes the soul as a charioteer, pulled by two strong horses, each tugging in a different direction: one toward the physical, the other toward the spiritual. The charioteer's goal is to keep those horses moving ahead, balanced at the same pace and in the same direction.

In the *Symposium*, however, Diotima offers a theory and practice of erotic love that unfolds naturally into an understanding and procreation of the beautiful—just like philosophy. Speaking through Socrates, who invokes her tutelage, her friendship, and the presence of her absence, Diotima explains that love cannot be happy if it lacks goodness or beauty: "Such, my good Socrates, is the nature of this spirit. That you should have formed your other notion of

Love is no surprising accident" (Plato, *Symposium* 204.c). She goes on to tell Socrates that he is "wrong . . . in supposing that love is *of* the beautiful"; rather, love is "engendering and begetting *upon* the beautiful. . . . Love is of *immortality*" (Plato, *Symposium* 206.e, 207.a, emphasis added). Just like philosophy.

Therefore, a lover of the beautiful will scale a ladder of love that starts with love for beautiful individuals, moves to the creation of beautiful ideas, and then culminates in love for the reproduction and expression of those ideas. Those merely physical lovers, "who are teeming in body," will "betake them rather to women, and are amorous on this wise: by getting children they acquire an immortality, a memorial and a state of bliss, which in their imagining they 'for all succeeding time procure' " (Plato, *Symposium* 208.e). Heterosexual eros, then, is bodily, particularly in contrast with the homoerotic love that concerns itself with the soul, with conceiving the beautiful in the soul:

> [T]here are persons . . . who in their souls still more than in their bodies conceive those things [prudence and virtue] which are proper for soul to conceive and bring forth. . . . So when a man's soul is so far divine that it is made pregnant with these from his youth, and on attaining manhood immediately desires to bring forth and beget, he too, I imagine, goes about seeking the beautiful object whereon he may do his begetting, since he will never beget upon the ugly. . . . [A]nd if he chances also on a soul that is fair and noble and well-endowed, he gladly cherishes the two combined in one; and straightway in addressing such a person he is resourceful in discoursing of virtue and of what should be the good man's character and what his pursuits; and so he takes in hand the other's education. . . . [B]y contact with the fair one and by consorting with him he bears and brings forth his long-felt conception. . . . Equally too with him he shares the nurturing of what is begotten, so that men in this condition enjoy a far fuller community with each other than that which comes with children, and a far surer friendship, since the children of their union are fairer and more deathless . . . [and] leave behind to procure them a glory immortally renewed in the memory of men.
> (Plato, *Symposium* 208.e–209.d)

Diotima emphasizes the superior value of intellect and links the erotic appetite with beauty; eros motivates her lover's ascension towards contemplation, towards seeing intellect as sexual. Thus, rather than seeking love for the fulfillment of biological reproduction, eros leads us toward the Idea of the Beautiful, the true immortality that comes only through an intellectual legacy, through reproduction of beauty's values and ideas.

For Diotima, then, the generative power of eros (or the philosophy of love) is an ongoing pursuit, a striving, rather than any kind of completion or final attainment: "For wisdom has to do with the fairest things, and Love is a love directed to what is fair; so that Love must needs be a friend of wisdom" (Plato, *Symposium* 204.b). Diotima's philosophical lover must recognize that the transient beauty attached to his beloved's fair body is cognate to the eternal and changeless beauty attached to certain ways of life and laws that are pure of flesh or other mortal rubbish. And only if he places a higher value on intercourse with beautiful souls and ideas over intercourse with beautiful bodies will he qualify for the love of the gods and for the possibility of immortality. Thus, in Plato's rendition of Socrates's retelling of Diotima's lesson, the power of erotic love is likened to divine ecstasy that reaches out to beauty itself, an ultimate principle of all things. And knowledge itself is feminized to indicate all that "prevents the soul from appropriating truth, from penetrating directly to where it lies hidden" (Sissela 51).

Not surprisingly, Diotima's speech resonates with Platonic love, his theory of forms, and a justification of homoeroticism. But her belief in the regeneration of the soul through the procreation of the beautiful strongly deviates from Plato's belief in reincarnation. In the *Phaedrus*, he writes at length about the transmigration of immortal souls, the finest of which are "perfect and fully winged," mounted upward and governing the whole world.[7]

Though constructed by Plato and spoken by Socrates, Diotima does not follow their beliefs regarding the transmigration of souls. Instead, she espouses the reproduction of one's soul in others—the engendering of value in the beloved is the best begetting possible. Such begetting is an opportunity available only to lovers of the beautiful, who reproduce themselves by giving birth to the values by which those molded by them live and die. Hence, a person becomes immortal by reconstituting in the beloved the complex qualities that have come to constitute that person's soul. And Diotima's soul is not eternal—if the lover fails to generate an offspring of his soul, the soul ceases to exist when the body dies, and the lover fails to achieve immortality.

Yet despite these theoretical inconsistencies among Plato and his personages, Diotima and Socrates, their theories converge on the philosophy of rhetoric. Like Diotima's theory of eros, rhetoric should be devoted to beauty and goodness found in knowledge and ideas. In the *Gorgias*, Plato's Socrates tells us that rhetoric can be "noble—the endeavour, that is, to make the citizens' souls as good as possible, and the persistent effort to say what is best, whether it prove more or less pleasant to one's hearers," for "rhetoric is to be used for this one purpose always, of pointing to what is just" (*Gorgias* 503.b, 527.c, in *Symposium*). And in the *Phaedrus*, he tells us the true rhetorician must "be able to speak and to do everything, so far as possible, in a manner pleasing to the gods" (273.e, in *Euthyphro*). For Plato, then, the intense and passionate attachment to one's beloved is akin to the attachment to abstractions, such as social reform, poetry, philosophy, and rhetoric. And Plato explains this attachment in terms of another drive, the hunger to create, a hunger "we all seek to appease in every activity propelled by beauty" (Vlastos 27–28).

In the *Symposium*, Plato warns us against loving just one beautiful body or beautiful bodies in general. His *scala amoris* requires that lovers follow Diotima's advice and set a higher value on the beauty of souls than on that of the body, so that however little the grace that may bloom in any likely soul it shall suffice him for loving and caring, and for bringing forth and soliciting such converse as will tend to the betterment of the young. . . . Beginning from obvious beauties he must for the sake of that highest beauty be ever climbing aloft, as on the rungs of a ladder . . . ; so that in the end he comes to know the very essence of beauty . . . pure and unalloyed; not infected with the flesh and colour of humanity. (210.b, 211.c, e)

Thus we are to love the "image" of beauty in persons only so far as it reminds us of the universal beauty and goodness signified in systems of social reform, rhetorical practice, or science and philosophy—those systems that please the gods.

In Diotima's claim that the ultimate impulse behind erotic desire is the natural mortal longing for immortality, she seems to prefigure Aristotle's thinking, that the urge to reproduce is natural to all living things:

Of the things which are, some are eternal and divine . . . ; Soul is better than body, and a thing which has Soul in it is better than one which has not, in virtue of that Soul. . . . These are the causes on account of which generation of animals takes place, because since the nature of a class of this sort is unable to be eternal, that which comes into being is eternal in the manner that is open to it. Now it is impossible for it to be so *numerically*, since the "being" of things is to be found in the particular, and if it really were so, then it would be eternal; it is, however, open to it to be so *specifically*. (*Generation* 2.4.731.b.25–35)

Whether Diotima was historical or literary, a priestess or a Pythagorean philosopher, seems not as important as her having been a female influence on both Socrates and Plato. She impressed them not only with her metaphysics but with her argument, her substance and practice informing Platonic rhetorical theory. And like Aspasia, she too is referred to as Socrates's teacher (*Symposium* 207.c). Yet because of their gender, both women have long inhabited the margins of rhetorical study.

Aspasia and Diotima Challenge the Greek Rhetorical Tradition

Aspasia colonized the patriarchal territory, but her colony was quickly appropriated by males. Although she herself escaped being enclosed, although she publicly articulated her intelligence and her heterosexual love, she did not escape those who defined her. Her influence has been enclosed within the gendered rhetorical terrain—and neutralized. "And the trouble is that the map of an enclosed space describes only the territory inside the enclosure. Without knowing the surrounding geography, how are we to evaluate this woman's estate?" (Jehlen 80). Few of us have ever heard of Aspasia of Miletus, teacher of rhetoric, or of Diotima, priestess-philosopher. But if we locate each of their colonies within the "larger context" and "examine the borders along which [each woman] defined herself" (81)—the writings of the men she influenced,

Plato, Socrates, and (for Aspasia) Pericles—we can better map out how Aspasia and Diotima were perceived by those men and, perhaps, how she might have perceived her estate within the surrounding geography.

GENDER(ED) DYNAMICS IN GREEK SOCIETY: HISTORICAL AND LITERARY

Although Aspasia was a powerful force in Periclean Athens and Diotima an influential philosopher, although both women seem to have informed the thinking of Plato and Socrates, few Greek thinkers accepted women as their mental equals. Aristotle makes no provision for the intellectual woman, except for his nod to Sappho: "Everyone honours the wise. . . . [T]he Mytilenaeans [honour] Sappho, though she was a woman" (*Rhetoric* 2.23.1389.b). Otherwise, Aristotle denied any philosophical or rhetorical contributions by women. He quotes Sophocles when he writes " 'Silence gives grace to woman'—though that is not the case likewise with a man" (*Politics* 1.5.9). Reasoning from Aristotle's basic premise, Aspasia could not have become a teacher, much less a rhetorician. Certainly, Diotima could not have become a philosopher. By the principle of entelechy, each woman would have naturally followed her predetermined life course, her progress distinctly marked off and limited to a degree of perfection less than that for a man.

For the most part, Aristotle's accounts of women, buttressed by the defective scientific understanding of reproduction and biological processes, belie women's participation in the making of culture, leaving their daughters without access to any knowledge of a female tradition, continuity, or intellectual underpinning.[28] For Aristotle, men and women differed only in outward form—but the inequality was permanent:

> It will surely be for the sake of generation that "the male" and "the female" are present in the individuals which are male and female. . . . [T]he Form is *better* and more divine in its nature than the Matter. [I]t is *better* . . . that the superior one should be separate from the inferior one. That is why wherever possible and so far as possible the male is separate from the female, since it is something *better* and more divine in that it is the principle of movement for generated things, while the female serves as their matter. The male, however, comes together with the female and mingles with it for the business of generation, because this is something that concerns both of them. (*Generation* 2.4.732.a.1–10)

Other than "mingling," then, male and female should stay separate, if for no other reason than that woman's boundaries are porous and mutable, her power to govern them inadequate, her control of them unreliable. Woman's excess moisture, so evident in her menstruation and breasts, was reason enough to render her body inefficient in comparison to man's. Yet when used propitiously, women's bodies produced sons of the Greek polis.

The founding myth and essence of Athenian citizenship was *autochthony*, the belief that each Greek citizen emerged from the soil of the city and would return to the soil upon his death. As a guiding myth of the polis, autochthony summarily excluded the reality of women's bodies: not only was Athenian citizenship predicated upon the exclusion of women, but the belief in autochthony erased women from any kind of participation or production within the polis, the sphere of men. These contradictions of myth and reality—whether citizens emerge from the soil or from their mothers' bodies—are neatly put to rest by Plato's Socrates, who claims to be speaking the words of Aspasia:

> Now our land, which is also our mother, furnishes to the full this proof of her having brought forth men; for, of all the lands that then existed, she was the first and the only one to produce human nourishment, namely the grain of wheat and barley, whereby the race of mankind is most richly and well nourished, inasmuch as she herself was the true mother of this creature. And proofs such as this one ought to accept more readily on behalf of a country than on behalf of a woman; for it is not the country that imitates the woman in the matter of conception and birth, but the woman the country. . . .
> Such being the manner of their birth and of their education, the ancestors of these men framed for themselves and lived under a civic polity which it is right for us briefly to describe. For a polity is a thing which nurtures men, good men when it is noble, bad men when it is base. It is necessary, then, to demonstrate that the polity wherein our forefathers were nurtured was a noble one, such as caused goodness not only in them but also in their descendants of the present age, amongst whom we number these men who are fallen. For it is the same polity which existed then and exists now, under which polity we are living now and have been living ever since that age with hardly a break. (*Menexenus* 237.e–238.c, in *Timaeus*)

Citizens (male, of course) born of the soil need not acknowledge human mothers—a convenience for Aristotle, who could not seem to see beyond the contemporary and seemingly permanent inferior status of Greek women. In the *Politics*, Aristotle writes that "between the sexes, the male is by nature superior and the female inferior, the male ruler and the female subject" (1.2.12); in the *Rhetoric*, he writes that "one quality or action is nobler than another if it is that of a naturally finer being: thus a man's will be nobler than a woman's" (1.9.15).

And those naturally finer beings—men—were awarded a public voice, which enabled them to participate as speakers, thinkers, and writers in the polis, in the "good" of public life. A public voice was the right and privilege of those who were declared to possess reason and goodness to its fullest extent. Men only. Naturally then, women and slaves—inferior beings in every way— were condemned to silence as their appointed sphere and condition. And most women spoke no alternative, except as literary characters.

Drama remains a problematic resource regarding the lives of historical women and men; after all, the plays may simply represent what male poets (and, on stage, male actors) imagined about the mythic past and about women or used them to imagine. Even so, as a cultural product and an ideological formation of Greek thought, drama serves as a site for comparative investigation. For instance, in his treatise on domestic management, the historical Xenophon writes, "Since both the indoor and the outdoor tasks demand labour and attention, God from the first adapted the woman's nature, I think, to the indoor and man's to the outdoor tasks and cares" (*Oeconomicus* 7.22, in *Memorabilia*). "Thus, to the woman it is more honourable to stay indoors than to abide in the fields, but to the man it is unseemly rather to stay indoors than to attend to the work outside" (7.30). Xenophon's doctrine is reflected in such contemporary literary works as Aristophanes's *Lysistrata*, which opens with a description of the ordinary conditions of historical Athenian women:

> Wisdom from women? . . .
> All we can do is sit, primped and painted,
> made up and dressed up,
> ravishing in saffron wrappers,
> . . . exquisite negligees, those chic,
> expensive little slippers from the East.   (11)

And in the horrific scenarios that follow Medea's desertion by Jason, Euripides's Medea speaks no safe way out of her domestic confinement/entrapment:

> My husband, whom it did importune most
> To have a thorough knowledge of, he proves
> The worst of men. But sure among all those
> Who have with breath and reason been endued,
> We women are a most unhappy race.
> . . . .
> A man goes forth, his choler to appease,
> · And to some friend or comrade can reveal
> What he endures; but we to him alone
> For succour must look up. They still contend
> That we, at home remaining, lead a life
> Exempt from danger, while they launch the spear:
> False are these judgments; rather I would thrice,
> Armed with a target, in th' embattled field
> Maintain my stand, than suffer once the throes
> Of childbirth.   (Euripides, *Medea* 2: 76–77)[29]

When Phaedra finds herself in a marriage that leaves her directionless except for her attraction to her stepson and for her ultimate destruction, Euripides writes her loneliness, boredom, and frustrations into a script that also captures her keen perceptions of societal expectations:

> Well-knowing what is good,
> We practice not. Some do amiss through sloth,
> Others to virtue's rigid laws prefer
> Their pleasures; for with various pleasures life

Classical Rhetoric Conceptualized

Is furnished; conversation lengthened out
Beyond dire bounds; ease, that bewitching pest.
. . . .
May my virtues be conspicuous;
But when I act amiss, I would avoid
Too many witnesses. That on such deed,
And e'en the inclination to transgress
Disgrace attends, I knew, and was aware
That if from honour's paths a woman swerve
She to the world is odious.   (*Hippolytus*, in *Complete* 2: 128–29)

Speaking from another of his plays, Euripides's Iphigenia understands the grief and confusion of both Medea and Phaedra: "[W]e / Are women and have hearts by nature formed / To love each other, of our mutual trusts" (*Iphigenia in Tauris*, in *Complete* 1: 362).[30] Thus, a good woman does not exceed the boundary of her *oikos*, a sentiment echoed by Plutarch, who says the tortoise on which Aphrodite rests her foot symbolizes a woman's life, closed upon itself in its own domestic space. Women remained at home, then, while their fathers, husbands, sons, and brothers performed in the public sphere of action, justice, and men. The history of classical rhetoric is thus the history of great men speaking out—Aristotle, Plato, Gorgias, Pericles, Socrates. But the voices of classical women have been silenced—that is, except for Sappho, Aspasia, and Diotima.

Plato records women's voices, Aspasia's in particular, in his work. Unlike Aristotle, Plato believed that differences in bodies do not indicate differences in nature; for as Plato makes clear in the *Symposium*, the soul has a separate and distinct identity from the body. Plato's Timaeus recounts the creation myth, in which the creator mixed the soul of the universe with matter to make souls in equal numbers to the stars, one soul assigned to one star, and "he showed them the nature of the Universe, and declared unto them the laws of destiny" (*Timaeus* 41.e).[31] The souls are then

sown each into his own proper organ of time . . . [and since] human nature is two-fold, the superior sex is that which hereafter should be designated "man." . . . [H]e that has lived his appointed time well shall return again to his abode in his native star, and shall gain a life that is blessed and congenial; but whoso has failed therein shall be changed into woman's nature at the second birth; and if, in that shape, he still refraineth not from wickedness he shall be changed every time, according to the nature of his wickedness, into some bestial form after the similitude of his own nature. (42.a–b)

Plato, then, manages somehow to assimilate his belief in the separate existence of souls and bodies with the belief that women are made from secondary men. For him, those beliefs were consistent with the "reality" of women being the private property of their men. Only in the "ideal" state, a state of communal property and social obligation, could men and women live with any measure of equality.

In *The Republic* (book 5), the *locus classicus* of his feminism, Plato describes the roles and potentials of women and men in the ideal state. Although he does not promise that women are equal to men; he envisions a state with complete equality of opportunity for guardians of both sexes: women would participate fully in the military; men in the communal child rearing. In the ideal state, women would be released from the bondage of private life, of being private wives, and would receive the same education and training as men, including the opportunity to exercise nude (5.456.c). Ideally, then, women would be capable of performing the full range of activities and functions that men performed:

> If it appears that the male and female sex have distinct qualifications for any arts or pursuits, we shall affirm that they ought to be assigned respectively to each. But if it appears that they differ only in just this respect that the female bears and the male begets, we shall say that no proof has yet been produced that the woman differs from the man for our purposes, but we shall continue to think that our guardians and their wives ought to follow the same pursuits. (5.454.e)

Unfortunately, however, women's performance would still be less than that of men, despite the equality of opportunity. "The natural capacities are distributed alike among both creatures, and women naturally share in all pursuits and men in all—yet for all the woman is weaker than the man" (5.455.e). Thus, Plato tells us, in everything practiced by mankind, the masculine sex surpasses the female "on all points" (5.455.d). Not even in his fantasy could Plato envision gender equality, for although he believed in the equality of nature and opportunity, women remained always inferior in capacity.

Despite its limitations, Plato's *Republic* projects a clear vision of equal rights and unabridged social possibilities, a vision that allows us to accept accounts of Plato's admitting women into his Academy. Lasthenia of Mantinea and Axiothea of Philesia are both assumed to have entered the Academy, although not without restrictions. According to a fragment by Dicaearchus, Axiothea was compelled to disguise her sex, to dress like a man before joining Plato's lectures (Waithe, *History* 205). Drawing on that same fragment, Frederick Adam Wright tells us that

> in the inner circle of the Academy, the first University College of which we know, men and women met on equal terms, and shared responsibilities and privileges. The names of two such women (neither of them . . . Athenians) are recorded for us by Dicaearchus . . . Lasthenia of Mantinea and Axiothea of Phil[esia]. (177–78)

The teacher-Plato who would allow women to penetrate his intellectual sphere would be the same writer-Plato to mention female teachers, Aspasia and Diotima, in his work. So although Plato explores the gendered tensions between domestic and public life and opportunities, although his writings help reconstruct the intellectual, social, and political achievements of some women, he cannot explain those tensions away entirely.

Even Athenian class structure exacerbated the power differentials among the females themselves, differentials manifested in the divisions of women's labor. While Athenian matrons supervised the slaves in their household and child-care duties, remaining inside except to attend religious festivities, some citizen-class women worked in the fields with their husbands or plied retail trades. The Peloponnesian War crisis forced some Athenian wives, particularly the slave-less women, to take employment as wet nurses, midwives, day laborers, grape pickers, market vendors, errand runners, shoppers, and public mourners.

The ideal woman was expected to remain inside, but real women worked hard inside and outside the home. Running a household was a time-consuming business, and even proper matrons would have found it difficult to leave their homes. Lysistrata's friend, the fictional Kleonike, is buried beneath her domestic responsibilities:

> You know a woman's way is hard—
> . . . fuss over hubby,
> wake the maid up,
> put the baby down, bathe him,
> feed him."
> (Aristophanes, *Lysistrata* 9)

The Athenian wife was responsible for conscientious and prosperous house-keeping, including the protection of all property: pantry stores and wine cellars, female relatives and female slaves. Any unwelcomed intrusion upon the sanctified domestic domain, whether from within or without, violated the husband's honor. Just as all foodstuffs were ordered and accounted for, all reproduction of slaves and free matrons was supervised as well, the latter being an important matter of inheritance—it all being a matter of prosperity. Thus parts of the house were locked, including the women's quarters, or *gynaikeion*. Seclusion, then, served as the handmaiden of protection, and the proper Athenian woman was thought to need both. Women's legal seclusion signaled cultural efforts to keep women in the possession of men:

> A woman, like a piece of property, was always under legal control of some man; and if he should die in her lifetime, she and whatever was attached to her passed to the next male relative in the same elaborate order of succession used for any other property. If the woman was heiress to an estate, the estate went to the appropriate male relative whose wife she necessarily became; she had no more choice in the matter than . . . a vase. (Garner 84)

Despite so vulnerable a position, however, the elite Athenian woman was not entirely unprotected under the law; her single greatest security was her dowry, which stayed with her throughout her life. And her seclusion was not isolation.

Ideally, Athenian women might have been relegated to the private sphere, but in reality (as well as in literature), women made purposeful, socially sanctioned forays into the public sphere. Few Athenian families were wealthy enough to dispense with the typical economic and social activities of women that necessitated going out of the house: going to the fountain to wash clothes or fetch water; going to the marketplace to work or shop; visiting female neighbors or relatives; and participating in religious rituals, festivals, and funerals.

In fact, imaginative literature creates autonomous and powerful women more often than do historical accounts of so-called actual women, providing a rich dissonance in representational perspective. The strong, self-propelled women in *Lysistrata*, for instance, band together, ally and enemy alike, to bring their husbands to terms. Their husbands do not find consolation in the arms of *hetaerae*, nor are they content with the society of their own sex once their wives withdraw their favors. Clytemnestra avenges the murder of her daughter by killing her husband; Electra encourages her brother Orestes to kill their mother and her lover. In Attic tragedy, women come and go from their houses at will, publicly shamed only when they are wailing. Antigone is asked to go indoors— but only because she is creating an undignified disturbance.

Although the power politics of gender in ancient Greece manifested itself in gendered restrictions or opportunities of speech, movement, and bodies, the cultural construction of biological difference in medicine and art spoke a story of fundamental sameness, a sameness of the sexes distinguished through systematic hierarchy. According to the ancients (and into the eighteenth century), the teleology of perfect humanness culminated in adult males; women's bodies, then, were those of undeveloped males. After all, neither their penises (vaginas) nor testicles (ovaries and fallopian tubes) had developed and descended— both medical writings and illustrations alike display a remarkable consistency in depicting the female body as an undeveloped male, different only in breasts and menses. Artwork, too, reinforced this hierarchical range: bodies characterized by male chests, hips, arms, and legs are womanized by the obvious addition of feminine hairstyles and breasts. The difference between male and female bodies at the time was one of degree rather than of kind.

Examining ancient life through the lens of gender studies provides new ways of thinking about women and the legal, medical, literary, historical, and artistic representations of them in the ancient world, for *gender* is the set of social and cultural differences that societies construct (and constantly represent to themselves) to distinguish maleness and femaleness in almost every sphere of life, from warfare to morals (Beard 34). Mary Beard's emphasis on gender analysis moves beyond *what women did or did not do* into the realm of *representation*. For she rightly insists that male-authored "ancient literature is not evidence *for* women's lives in antiquity; it is a series of *representations* of women, by men; and we cannot hope to understand what it is saying, unless we reflect on who is speaking, to whom, in what context and why" (33). She goes on to write that

this recent stress on representation rather than social reality has gone hand in hand with a stress on gender as a focus of study, rather than *women*. . . . To study gender is to study a lot more than "women"; it is to study a set of oppositions and differences that underscore almost every aspect of ancient (and modern) life. (34–35)

In historical accounts, upper-class Athenian women are represented by their absence, clearly gendered in their seclusion and exclusion. In art, their representation as intellectual beings is also faint: vase paintings show female figures in domestic scenes holding or reading book rolls and carrying writing tablets (c. 450 BCE). Despite the lack of historical evidence that girls received any kind of regular academic instruction, these sketches allow us to imagine that some women could read and write (S. Cole 223–26), that some young girls may have shared in their brothers' lessons, and that whatever their educational opportunities, women (such as Sappho, Aspasia, and Diotima) made their intellectual marks.

Greek imaginative literature represents many women as vigorous participants in public life, perhaps modeling female characters on particular historical women whose lives have gone unwritten. Despite the dramatic irony in Greek imaginative literature, we can still believe that those actual Athenian males were impressed (if not cowed) by the actions of Medea, Lysistrata, Clytemnestra, and Electra and that they would demonstrate their respect and admiration for the poet Sappho, the immigrant Aspasia, and the philosopher-priestess Diotima. Greek culture produced the acceptable idea of a few intellectually accomplished, exceptionally influential women, each of whom approached the gendered border—and trespassed into masculine territory.

THE ROMAN RHETORICAL TRADITION

In the centuries between Aristotle and Cicero, rhetoric traveled between Athens and Rome, carried along in the general wave of Hellenism, or Athenian imperialism, that flowed westward. "The introduction of rhetoric in Rome was not so much the consequence of direct contact by Romans traveling to Athens but rather a prolonged process of exposure to schools of rhetoric from the Greek colonies in Sicily and southern Italy" (R. Enos, *Roman* 1). Athenian rhetoric offered much to the burgeoning Roman republic: not only could individual speakers advance themselves and enhance their political aspirations but they could also "direct civic affairs by securing action through persuasion" (3). But the increasingly urbane Roman republic, dotted with its southern Greek colonies, offered rich opportunities to the immigrant Greek rhetors and pedagogues. Thus, Athenian rhetorical colonies quickly took root and flourished.

Romans wanted to duplicate the Greek link of rhetoric to *vita activa*, of individual expression and the democracy. But early Roman oratory, or "show" rhetoric, with its Asiatic style, was nearly eclipsed by more austere Greek rhetorical practices in philosophy, science, and, of course, politics. Not until such writers as Theophrastus and Hermagoras staked out a small area of legitimacy and the beginnings of a theory for a more restrained Roman rhetoric would oratory be transformed into a thriving public practice and discipline, adapted to Roman needs, and formally codified and schematized in various Roman works.

None of these early Roman treatises have survived except for the desultory *Rhetorica ad Alexandrum*, written by Anaximenes of Lampsacus (the pseudo-Aristotle). However, if the work of Theophrastus still existed, we could trace back to him the reorganization of Aristotle's virtues of the three levels of style that Cicero would later expound; the four "virtues" of good prose style (correctness, clarity, ornamentation, and propriety); and the division between schemes and tropes made popular by the pseudo-Cicero in the *Rhetorica ad Caius Herennium* (Kennedy, *Classical* 80–89). Hermagoras, one of the most influential Greek teachers in the Roman republic, is the "earliest source we know for the full treatment of the five parts of technical rhetoric and a major authority for its identification with civic functions"; in addition, Hermagoras "laid down the basic lines of the important theory of *stasis*, or the basic issue of a case," which remains at the heart of rhetorical invention (88). Hermagoras's rhetoric would shape the Latin treatises that initiated a Roman rhetorical tradition: Cicero's *De inventione* (87 BCE), his youthful and incomplete account of rhetorical divisions, parts of an oration, types of speeches, and stasis; and the pseudo-Cicero's *Rhetorica ad Caius Herennium* (*On the Theory of Public Speaking*), the earliest extant rhetoric to concern itself with the kinds and orders of style, as well as to taxonomize the stylistic figures. Given this developing framework for arguing both sides of an issue, for the ordering of material, and for meeting political, legal, and educational exigencies of Roman life, Greek rhetoric was informed by Roman needs and joined with Roman rhetoric.

The sophistication and widespread success of Greek political and intellectual culture held promise for the young Roman republic. Education in Rome was in most respects a close copy of that of Greece: the teachers of rhetoric in the Roman republic were Greek, as were the early texts. Following in the Greek tradition, the Romans learned Greek rhetoric, grammar, and logic in school and then used rhetoric as a means of persuasion in the law courts and political arenas. But the Romans taught and practiced a more practical rhetoric than the philosophical rhetoric of the Greeks. Hence, Greek philosophers gradually withdrew from teaching rhetoric, and the subject of Greek philosophy fell by the wayside. In its stead, young men, particularly young aristocrats with military acumen, concentrated on the art of speaking, on oratory, as part of their training for public careers—and they learned first in Greek and then in Latin.

Cicero

Perhaps the most famous orator of the Roman republic, Cicero (106–43 BCE) reconciled the concept of the ideal orator with that of the eloquent philosopher, no doubt building on his own thorough training in Greek rhetoric and playing upon the allurement of Greek culture.[32] As young men, Cicero and his brothers had been educated by the illustrious Roman orator Crassus (with whom they lived) and had spoken many times with another great orator, Antonius.[33] From his early training, Cicero came to believe that the province of oratory, the education of the rhetorician, must include knowledge of all things, for "no man has ever succeeded in achieving splendour and excellence in oratory, I will not say merely without training in speaking, but without taking all knowledge for his province as well" (*De oratore* 2.1.4–5). Thus, Cicero's educational agenda expanded the Greek rhetorical realm of philosophy and science to a Roman rhetorical empire:

> For, while nearly all the other arts can look after themselves, the art of speaking well, that is to say, of speaking with knowledge, skill and elegance, has no delimited territory, within whose borders it is enclosed and confined. All things whatsoever, that can fall under the discussion of human beings, must be aptly dealt with by him who professes to have this power, or he must abandon the name of eloquent. (2.1.5)

From motives that were genuinely patriotic (as well as genuinely self-promoting) Cicero placed rhetoric and himself at the service of the republic, revitalizing the practice and theory of a utilitarian rhetoric that incorporated both the sobriety of Greek philosophy and the elitism of its practitioners.[34] Technical skill was the mainstay of his *eloquentia*, and mastery of all accessible Greek and Roman culture were necessary components; yet Cicero's orator also embodied a philosophical life, a belief he defends in *Nature of the Gods* (c. 45 BCE).[35]

Perhaps because Cicero's faculty of rhetoric is heavy with philosophical and real responsibilities, it attracts great admiration, for "the wise control of the complete orator is that which chiefly upholds not only his own dignity, but the safety of countless individuals and of the entire State" (*Nature* 1.8.34, in *Brutus, On*). In the *Brutus* [c. 44 BCE], Cicero records the early development of Roman rhetoric, often making himself the final objective, as though his rhetoric were the synthesis to which previous rhetoricians had progressively opened the way. For example, Isocrates's citizen-orator would become Cicero's rhetorical ideal as well, for "if the mind is the glory of man, then eloquence is the means whereby the mind diffuses its radiance, and thus those ancients were right when they declared that he who excelled in it was the choicest flower of the people, 'the souls of Persuasion' " (*Brutus* 15).

Regardless of the influential momentum of Greek rhetoric, only Cicero's devotion to the Latin language (for both teaching and speaking), combined with his political and cultural influence, could ensure a Roman rhetoric. His *De inventione*, a *techné* similar to *Rhetorica ad Caius Herennium* (84 BCE) in its fusion of Aristotelian and Hermagorean models, was meant to assist men with the discovery of ideas and subject matter suitable for their forensic contests.[36] But much more sophisticated and written at a later age was Cicero's triumphant response to Aristotle's assertion that rhetoric had no subject matter: *De oratore*, which "remains unequaled for the greatness of its theoretical and expository execution" (Barilli 32).[37] Privileging both rhetoric and himself, Cicero artfully argues for a broad, liberal education that allies rhetoric and philosophy as a means of preparing an orator best to argue a case, to know which side to take, and to have insight into human psychology. The citizen-orator ought to be ready to do anything for his country, but not everything was permissible—nothing that went against justice or morality or the law.

Quintilian

The association of rhetoric and public life, so rehearsed in Cicero's works, would be echoed by Quintilian, the Roman rhetorician and teacher whose name is most frequently coupled with Cicero's. Quintilian's *Institutio oratoria* (*Education of an Orator*, AD 92–94), considered the most systematic and detailed compendium of rhetoric and the multiple roles it played throughout a Roman's life, would come to be his official magnum opus. In this massive enterprise, Quintilian seems to have painstakingly and tirelessly collected materials and endeavored to reconcile and include every point of view, retrospectively.

Because his aim was to educate the whole man for peacetime, as well as for war, Quintilian argued that political questions provide only a part of rhetoric's material, "for political questions are material for eloquence but not the only material" (2.21.2). After all, the political situation in Rome had evolved from the burgeoning republic to the more stable Empire.[38] In some ways, Quintilian's scope was far broader than Cicero's: he wanted to educate the whole man rather than the public orator. But in other ways, his view was more narrow, for he spoke from the schoolroom not from the *Forum Romanum*. Cicero had achieved fame in a long career as a political and forensic orator, but Quintilian would make his reputation as an intellectual and teacher.[39]

Commissioned first as the state professor of rhetoric, Quintilian was eventually appointed by Emperor Domitian to tutor the royal nephews, and he undertook to establish a comprehensive educational system that would produce citizen-orators for the Roman world. His treatise on education, *Institutio oratoria*, comprises a manual of rhetoric, a reader's guide to the best authors, and a handbook on the moral duties of the orator. By studying and imitating the best of authors, Quintilian's students would learn all the parts of a speech, the appropriate appeals, and the best examples; in addition, they would develop an appreciation for the elements of style (including the figures and tropes) and for persuasive ability. Quintilian cannot stress enough the value of analyzing and imitating distinguished prose and poetry, but he makes certain his readers believe that the roots and foundations of eloquence lie not in reading but in writing: "It is writing that provides the holy of holies where the wealth of oratory is stored, and whence it is produced to meet the demands of sudden emergencies" (10.3.3).

Under Quintilian, Roman rhetorical theory matures; it is no longer dependent on the Greek practices espoused by Cicero. Yet in the spirit of Cicero, of whom he speaks with unbounded eulogy, Quintilian continues to regard the broadly educated man as the fittest candidate for a course in rhetoric and for a role in public life, though with the end of the republic came the end of rhetoric as a political force in Roman society.[40] With rhetoric as the heart of his educational system, Quintilian expands the province of the ideal orator to include being of strong moral character as well, an idea Cicero only implied. Quintilian writes, "My aim then is the education of the perfect orator. The first essential for such a one is that he should be a good man, and consequently we demand of him not merely the possession of exceptional gifts of speech, but of all the excellences of character as well" (1.Pr.9).

By emphasizing moral purpose along with rhetorical skill, Quintilian distinguishes *Institutio oratoria* from all preceding rhetorics, just as he defines the study of rhetoric differently from those who came before him. After all, when rhetoric was no longer desired or empowered by politics, it came to inhabit education. In terms, then, of educating the Roman populace in ways that could resurrect Rome's former greatness, Quintilian treats oratory as the end to which the entire mental and moral development of the student is to be directed.[41] Children of both sexes must be educated to become the well-educated nurses, Roman matrons, and *pater familii*, who, in turn, would teach their own charges: "Above all see that the child's nurse speaks correctly. The idea, according to Chrysippus, would be that she should be a philosopher. . . . No doubt the most important point is that they should be of good character: but they should speak correctly as well" (1.1.4). And as for parents, Quintilian wants to see them as highly educated as possible, not restricting this expectation to fathers alone. To be sure, the Roman city was a men's club; nevertheless, a Roman woman was a *civis romana* who gave birth to a *civis romanus*. And Quintilian expected her, too, to take responsibility for the proper education of her children. To help her do so, he provided precedents:

> We are told that the eloquence of the Gracchi owed much to their mother
> Cornelia, whose letters even to-day testify to the cultivation of her style. Laelia,
> the daughter of Gaius Laelius, is said to have reproduced the elegance of her fa-
> ther's language in her own speech, while the oration delivered before the triumvirs
> by Hortensia, the daughter of Quintus Hortensius, is still read and not merely as a
> compliment to her sex. (1.1.6)

Plato had talked in *The Republic* about equal educational opportunities for women, but his talk had been theoretical. For Quintilian, rhetoric is "concerned with action; for in action it accomplishes that which it is its duty to do" (2.18.2). Quintilian argues for the practicality of equal education that enacts impressive results for all Roman citizens.

He dedicates his last book to the discipline of the whole man in his life beyond rhetorical studies: "my temerity is such that I shall essay to form my orator's character and to teach him his duties" (12.Intr.4). In this book, he accepts Marcus Cato's definition of the perfect orator: "a good man, skilled in speaking" (*vir bonus dicendi peritus*, 12.1.1). But above all, the orator must be a good man, devoting his attention to the complete formation of his moral character and acquiring a complete knowledge of all that is just and honorable.[42]

Quintilian's good man must study wise sayings and noble deeds: "for a long time . . . we should read none save the best authors" (10.1.20). He provides explicit instructions for whom and how to read throughout the whole *Institutio oratoria*. His orator would leave school devoted to the complete formation of his own moral character, as well as to the acquisition of a complete knowledge of all that is just and honorable. Above all things, Quintilian's orator must study morality, for he will not get noble thoughts from philosophy alone but from wise sayings and noble deeds, of which there is nowhere so rich a store as in the records of all the great Romans. The Greeks excel in moral precepts, the Romans in moral performances.[43]

Convinced that the purpose of education was to train citizens fully equipped in character, intellect, and all the high qualities of leadership, Quintilian provided an educational system for doing just that. His orator must learn from the past and think of posterity, equipping himself with a rich store of examples, both old and new, historical and fictitious; he must learn civil law and the custom and religion of his state; and he must practice temperance (what the Greeks called *sophrosyne*) at all times, at all levels of oratory, plain, middle, and grand. Quintilian closes his treatise with these sober words: "If the knowledge of these principles proves to be of small practical utility to the young student, it should at least produce what I value more, —the will to do well" (12.11.31). After all, he writes, "The rhetoric . . . which I am endeavouring to establish and the ideal of which I have in my mind's eye, that rhetoric which befits a good man and is in a word the only true rhetoric, will be a virtue" (2.20.4).

WOMAN'S PLACE IN ROMAN SOCIETY: HISTORICAL AND LITERARY

Could women become citizen-orators in the style of Cicero or by way of Quintilian's educational system? A particular point of Roman male pride seems to have been the deliberate exclusion of women from civil and public duties; and in the first centuries of its history, Roman law reflected rigid legal inequalities between males and females. Cicero reportedly contemplated with utter dismay a society which "included women in assemblies" and which allowed women "soldiery and magistracies and commands." "How great will be the misfortune of that city, in which women will assume the public duties of men" (Lactantius, *Epitomes* 33.[38.]1–5, ascribed to *De re publica* 4–5, qtd. in Hallett, *Fathers* 8).

No doubt, Cicero would have approved of the second-century AD Roman Empire, where a young man of the privileged classes grew up looking at the world from a position of unchallenged dominance. For such a young man, "women, slaves, and barbarians were unalterably different from him and inferior to him. The most obtrusive polarity of all, that between himself and women, was explained to him in terms of a hierarchy based upon nature itself. Biologically, the doctors said, males were those fetuses who had realized their full potential" (Brown 10). Women, by contrast, were failed males.

Over centuries, Roman law constructed and guaranteed the sexual distinction—and division—between males and females. The differential between the legal status of women and that of men was justified by the natural inferiority of women: their congenital weakness, limited intellectual faculties, and ignorance of law. But even while honoring these gendered distinctions, legal practices fluctuated over time.

The persistent popular ideal of female domesticity, *Domum servavit. Lanam fecit* ("She kept up her household. She made wool."), endured—despite the pragmatism permitting women to exercise leadership during the absence of men on military and governmental missions, despite enormous wealth and aristocratic indulgence, despite the fluctuations in the legal system throughout the republic and the Empire. In 195 BCE, for example, legislators debated the repeal of the 215 BCE sumptuary legislation (*Lex Oppia*) that imposed specific restrictions on women: "no woman should possess more than half an ounce of gold, or wear parti-coloured [purple-trimmed] clothing, or ride in a horse-drawn vehicle in a city or town, or within a mile therefrom, unless taking part in a public religious act" (Livy, *Rome* 141).

Lex Oppia was eventually repealed on terms of fairness to Roman matrons who had already, on many occasions, demonstrated their financial generosity during times of crisis. But the repeal was not without controversy regarding women's rightful place, particularly since so many women and men attended the debate on Capitoline Hill. Marcus Cato, the Censor, argued that women's unlawful extravagance could bring down the Roman Empire.[44] However, Tribune Lucius Valerius saw the constraint of women in a different light, arguing that the matrons had long ago set a precedent for supporting their country financially: "The matrons by unanimous consent contributed their gold to the nation. In the last war . . . it is common knowledge that, when money was scarce, the widows aided the treasury with their stores of money" (Livy, *Rome* 147). And he went on to elucidate the irrationality of a law that permitted men to display their wealth and status (to wear purple, for instance) but not women.[45] The repeal of *Lex Oppia* removed only one of many laws and practices that continued to subordinate Roman women.

In essence, Roman women were perpetually restrained by law. Although by mid fifth century BCE they were legally empowered to inherit, own, and bequeath property, any such transaction was to be done only under male *auctoritas*, or guardianship.[46] By the beginning of the second century AD, however, women who had borne three children gained the freedom to designate heirs and inherit, though she could not adopt sons or serve as a guardian. In addition to administering their property and inheritance, those same women could enter into legal transactions (entering contracts, constituting dowries, selling property, collecting debts). But because Roman women possessed no power over other people, because they were excluded from "virile" civil offices, their autonomy was illusory: "in both private and pubic law, citizenship and masculinity were one whenever an action exceeded the limits of a single person or patrimony and affected others. This was precisely the sphere of those *officia* that women were forbidden to hold: representation, guardianship, intercession, proxy, advocacy, prosecution" (Y. Thomas 136). Thus, even the most emancipated and self-assertive Roman woman lived in subjugation in comparison to the most retiring Roman male.

The Roman matron was (to use anthropological terminology) *structurally central* to her family: legally restricted to the narrow sphere of private interest, she invested her economic and educational advantages to her domestic life, expected to be nothing less than entirely devoted to the welfare and well-being of her family.[47] The hardy virtues of the Roman matron, or *domina*—combined with superior knowledge, refinement, and civilization—prevailed among the higher classes during the Empire. Wellborn Roman women were expected to play a crucial part in their children's education (as Quintilian attests [1.1.6]) and in their children's marriage arrangements as well, aligning their roles with the Code of Justinian (AD 207) under Septimius Severus: "the affairs of others cannot be entrusted to women unless, through the actions they are directed to bring, they are pursuing their own interest and profit" (qtd. in Y. Thomas 136). Like the Greek matron, then, the Roman woman was oppressively busy managing her household and family; yet, within the narrow sphere of her "own interest and profit," she pursued social, business, and political affairs.

Verginia

Nearly all upper-class women were sufficiently cultivated and educated to be able to run large households, and many were prepared to participate in the intellectual life of their male associates. Although little is known about precisely how young girls received their educations, we do know that some were tutored at home by their parents or by their brothers' teachers (thereby receiving instruction in Greek, Homer, Latin poetry and composition), while others, of all social classes, studied at the Forum. The story of Verginia indicates that it was not unusual for the daughter of a lowly plebeian centurion to attend elementary school in the Forum, where various schoolmasters' booths stood. According to accounts by Cicero, Livy, and Dionysius of Halicarnassus, Verginia was walking to her schoolmaster's booth when Appius Claudius, the chief of the decemvirs, became "captivated by her beauty and became still more frenzied . . . , already mastered by his passion" (Dionysius 11.28.1). Because

Verginia was already betrothed, because Appius himself had a lawfully wedded wife, and because he himself inscribed in the Twelve Tables the law preventing marriage between patricians and plebeians, Appius had no legal means of obtaining her. So he pronounced her to be the daughter of his own slave; therefore, his slave—not the daughter of Verginius. Or as Livy tells it,

> She was a grown girl, remarkably beautiful, and Appius, crazed with love, attempted to seduce her with money and promises. But finding that her modesty was proof against everything, he resolved on a course of cruel and tyrannical violence. He commissioned Marcus Claudius, his client, to claim the girl as his slave, and not to yield to those who demanded her liberation, thinking that the absen[c]e of the maiden's father afforded an opportunity for the wrong. . . . Verginia was entering the Forum—for there, in booths, were the elementary schools. (*Complete* 3.44.4–6)

But perhaps just as important as the evidence of her schooling is the evidence that Verginia could be owned by one of three men: her father, her future husband, or her alleged master. To liberate her from debauchery, her father, according to Cicero, "killed his maiden daughter with his own hand rather than surrender her to the lust of Appius Claudius, who then held the highest power in the state" (*De finibus* 2.20.66). In short, Verginius "killed his daughter to save her from shame . . . inspired by the splendour of moral greatness" (5.22.64).

Most descriptions of educated Roman females are limited to those of the upper-class, not young plebeians such as Verginia. Few mentions are made of the young, but in Pliny the Younger's letters (all of which were literary compositions intended for eventual publication), he writes about a thirteen-year-old who died just before she was to be married. Pliny (AD 62–113) was active in government as both a senator and an author, but it was, perhaps, his early association with Quintilian that formed his sensitivity to the education of young women:

> I am writing to you in great distress. . . . I never saw a girl so gay and loveable. . . .
> She had not yet reached the age of fourteen, and yet she combined the wisdom of age and dignity of womanhood with the sweetness and modesty of youth and innocence. . . . [S]he loved her nurses, her attendants and her teachers, each one for the service given her; she applied herself intelligently to her books and was moderate and restrained in her play. . . . You will forgive and even admire [her father] if you think of what he has lost—a daughter who resembled him in character no less than in face and expression, and was her father's living image in a wonderful way. (Pliny 5.16.1–9)

He also writes about his own (upper-class) wife, referring to her high intelligence and devotion to him, which together have "given her an interest in literature: she keeps copies of my works to read again and again and even learn by heart" (4.19.3).

Cornelia

Plutarch describes Cornelia, last wife of Pompey the Great, as a young lady· who had other "attractions besides those of youth and beauty." "[S]he was highly educated, played well upon the lute, and understood geometry, and had been accustomed to listen with profit to lectures on philosophy; all this, too, without in any degree becoming unamiable or pretentious, as sometimes young women do when they pursue such studies" (*Lives* 779). Tradition has it that Cornelia was like her father, Metellus Scipio, in her love of literature. But despite his high praise and detailed information, Plutarch provides no actual source for Cornelia's education, an exceptional one based on the Greek curriculum. Not even Roman men received instruction in music and geometry.

Furthermore, not all the educational accomplishments of Roman women were appreciated. In *Satire 6*, for example, Juvenal (fl. AD 100) berates the woman who tries to educate herself into the male sphere:

> She is . . . more intolerable when she affects to play the Critick at Table, applauds the Genius of Virgil, and excuses poor Dido dying for Love. She quotes the Poets and compares them; Virgil she weighs in one Scale, and Homer in the other. The Grammarians are Fools to her, the Rhetoricians are struck dumb, the whole Company is mute, not even a Lawyer, a common Crier, not one of her Female Gossips, can put in a Syllable where she is; she comes down with such a Torrent of Words, that you would swear so many Baso[o]ns or Bells were ringing. . . . Such a lady . . . pretends to more than ordinary Learning and Eloquence [and wants] to be distinguished as a Philosopher. . . .
>
> Let not the Wife of thy Bosom, that lies by thee, know any thing of the Art of Logick, how to come over you smartly with a short Enthymeme, or pretend to be perfect in History. I'll allow her to have some Taste of Books, but she should not understand too much; I hate a Woman that is always conning, and turning over her Grammar Rules like a Pedant, and placing her words exactly in Mood and Tense, who is for ever plaguing me with her old-fashioned verses that I know nothing of, and correcting her gossiping Companions for speaking a Word improperly, which a man would take no notice of; a Husband surely may be allowed to break Prisian's Head, without danger to his own. (170–71)

Juvenal's *Satire* is no doubt exaggerated. But we may be sure that some contemporary thinkers were, at best, amused and, at worst, threatened by the educated woman. Education was the first step for women who moved into the public sphere from the private one, the first step toward political and rhetorical consciousness.

ROMAN WOMEN IN THE MASCULINE SPHERE
OF POLITICS AND RHETORIC

Some upper-class educated Roman women took pause from domesticity to become politically influential figures in the late republic and early Empire. But even during their forays into the public sphere, they often foregrounded their motherhood and emphasized their domestic and familial power.

Cornelia

Perhaps the most famous of these influential matrons is Cornelia (c. 180–5 BCE), mother of Tiberius and Gaius Gracchus, a woman renowned for her eloquence and political prowess.[48] The accomplished, bilingual daughter of Scipio Africanus and widow of Tiberius Sempronius, she devoted herself entirely to the education of her twelve children, only three of whom survived. Her two sons became distinguished statesmen and orators, mainly owing to her judicious training.[49] She brought Greek philosophers, Blossius from Cumae and Diophanes from Mytilene, to educate the young men, and most surely herself. Plutarch writes that she brought her sons up "with such care, though they were without dispute in natural endowments and dispositions the first among Romans at their time, yet they seemed to owe their virtues even more to their education than to their birth" (*Lives* 994). At a time when nature was still considered to be the primary influence on development (and although her sons had an impeccable bloodline), Cornelia proved that a scrupulous education (along with, according to Plutarch, "frequent upbraiding" [998]) was at least equally effective in the development of the citizen-orator.

Her then-extant letters, models of composition, greatly impressed Cicero. In the *Brutus*, he writes: "We have read the letters of Cornelia, mother of the Gracchi; and we know from them that she nourished her sons not only at her breast but by her speech" (131). During the late republic, when the conservatives were exhausted from protecting their lands and wealth from the effects of the Gracchi's (revolutionary) social agendas, a letter alleged to be from Cornelia to her younger son, Gaius, was celebrated for its right thinking:

> I would venture to take a solemn oath that except for the men who killed Tiberius Gracchus no enemy has given me so much trouble and toil as you have done because of these matters. You should rather have borne the care that I should have the least possible anxiety in old age, that whatever you did you thought it sinful to do anything of major importance against my views, especially since so little of my life remains. . . . Will our family ever desist from madness? . . . Will we ever feel shame at throwing the state into turmoil and confusion? But if that really cannot be, seek the tribunate after I am dead. (Nepos 43)

Thus a letter of controversial provenance was thought to indicate that even their own model of a mother disapproved of the Gracchi's social agenda. But despite any contemporary controversy between mother and sons, Cicero's ideal *progymnasmata* and Quintilian's education of the orator could begin at home, with Mother.

However hyperbolic the descriptions of Cornelia's domestic control and filial success, she is not the only mother who receives credit for her sons' accomplishments—and for the greatness of Rome. In his *Institutio oratoria*, Quintilian had written about maternal influence in the way that Tacitus (fl. AD 100) recounts in his own retrospective account of positive maternal influence. In his *Dialogue on Oratory*, Tacitus's character Messalla reminds us that

> in the good old days, every man's son, born in wedlock, was brought up not in the chamber of some hireling nurse, but in his mother's lap, and at her knee. And that mother could have no higher praise than that she managed the house and gave herself to her children. . . . Religiously and with the utmost delicacy, she regulated not only the serious tasks of her youthful charges, but their recreations also and their games. It was in this spirit, we are told, that Cornelia, the mother of the Gracchi, directed their upbringing, Aurelia that of Caesar, Atia of Augustus: thus it was that these mothers trained their princely children. The object of this rigorous system was that the natural disposition of every child, while still sound at core and untainted, not warped as yet by any vicious tendencies, might at once lay hold with heart and soul on virtuous accomplishments, and whether its bent was towards the army, or the law, or the pursuit of eloquence, might make that its sole aim and its all-absorbing interest. (28)

The assumption that women of high birth were instrumental in affecting the course of Roman republican and imperial politics manifests itself frequently in ancient Roman sources authored by males. In the *Brutus*, as already mentioned, Cicero retells the story of the Gracchi being "guided by the loving solicitude of [their] mother Cornelia," who "nourished her sons not only at her breast but by her speech" (*Brutus* 99, 131). Tacitus tells us that Julia Procilla, the mother of Gnaeus Julius Agricola, was a "woman of rare virtue. From her fond bosom, [Agricola] passed in the pursuit of all liberal accomplishments. . . . [I]n early life he was inclined to drink more deeply of philosophy than is permitted to a Roman Senator, had not his mother's discretion imposed a check upon his enkindled and glowing imagination" (*Agricola*, in *Dialogue* 4).

Because the family was the basic political unit, a mother's structural centrality furnished her with a power base and with resources. Tradition has it that, when Cornelia was asked to display her jewels to a visiting matron, she presented Tiberius and Gaius, and said, "These are my jewels." Still, it is nearly impossible to distinguish the Roman mother's actual from her imagined influence in political matters—unless we look at her actual primary participation. Besides being influential mothers, a few Roman women themselves became involved in public affairs. They participated in politics as women in their own right, not as influential mothers, during times of rapid change.

Hortensia

Cornelia and Laelia are both mentioned as eloquent and erudite speakers (see Quintilian 1.1.6; Cicero, *Brutus* 131); however, the nature of Roman politics constrained their political influence to the vicarious activities of their sons, husbands, fathers. Only Hortensia, daughter of Cicero's oratorical rival Quintus

Hortensius, exists in the extant records of admirable rhetorical performance.[50] Unlike Aspasia who, within her circle of powerful, public men, established a reputation for herself in rhetoric and philosophy, Hortensia's foray into public speaking seems to have been a one-time effort. That her speech merited recording by her male compatriots suggests that hers was an "occasional" rather than professional performance, a public display of her talent on the strict understanding that it would not become a regular event. Hortensia "had interested herself in her father's profession to such a degree that, even though women were not allowed to plead at the bar in Rome, she was able to argue the cause of the wives of the proscribed on whom the triumvirs had imposed an excessively burdensome tax" (Best 203). No man dared argue this particular case.[51]

In 42 BCE, the triumvirs had published an edict requiring fourteen hundred of the richest women to submit a valuation of their property, with severe penalties for concealment or undervaluation. A portion of these means would then be applied to the war effort. Already distressed by the proscription (and absence) of their male relatives, the women were exasperated by such a tax. Unrepresented by any man, then, the women "resolved to beseech the women-folk of the triumvirs. With the sister of Octavian and the mother of Antony they did not fail, but they were repulsed from the doors of Fulvia, the wife of Antony, whose rudeness they could scarce endure" (Appian 4.4.32). As legend has it, they finally forced their way into the Forum, so they could speak directly to the tribunal of the triumvirs, "the people and the guards dividing to let them pass" (4.4.32). There, Hortensia represented all the women when she spoke.

> As befitted women of our rank addressing a petition to you, we had recourse to the ladies of your households; but having been treated as did not befit us, at the hands of Fulvia, we have been driven by her to the forum. You have already deprived us of our fathers, our sons, our husbands, and our brothers, whom you accused of having wronged you; if you take away our property also, you reduce us to a condition unbecoming our birth, our manners, our sex. If we have done you wrong, as you say our husbands have, proscribe us as you do them. But if we women have not voted any of you public enemies, have not torn down your houses, destroyed your army, or led another one against you; if we have not hindered you in obtaining offices and honours, —why do we share the penalty when we did not share the guilt?
>
> Why should we pay taxes when we have no part in the honours, the commands, the state-craft, for which you contend against each other with such harmful results? "Because this is a time of war," do you say? When have there not been wars, and when have taxes ever been imposed on women, who are exempted by their sex among all mankind? Our mothers did once rise superior to their sex and made contributions when you were in danger of losing the whole empire and the city itself through the conflict with the Carthaginians. But then they contributed voluntarily, not from their landed property, their fields, their dowries, or their houses, without which life is not possible to free women, but only from their own jewellery, and even these not according to fixed valuation, not under fear of in-

formers or accusers, not by force and violence, but what they themselves were will-ing to give. What alarm is there now for the empire or the country? Let war with the Gauls or the Parthians come, and we shall not be inferior to our mothers in zeal for the common safety; but for civil wars may we never contribute, nor ever assist you against each other! We did not contribute to Caesar or to Pompey. Nei-ther Marius nor Cinna imposed taxes upon us. Nor did Sulla, who held despotic power in the state, do so, whereas you say that you are re-establishing the com-monwealth. (Appian 4.4.32–33)

According to Quintus Valerius Maximus, Hortensia's speech was praised by Quintilian and recorded later by Appian (AD c. 200) because it was a good speech, "for the image of her father's Eloquence obtained, that the greatest part of the Imposition was remitted" (Valerius Maximus 8.3.3). He went on to say that "Q. Hortensius then revived in the Female Sex, and breath'd in the words of his Daughter: Whose force and vigour if his Posterity of the Male Sex would follow, so great an inheritance of *Hortensian* Eloquence would not be cut off by one action of a woman" (8.3.3).

Although somewhat akin to a rhetorical exercise, Hortensia's "good speech" merits full examination for several reasons. First of all, she effectively raises rhetorical questions, questions such as why innocent women are being pun-ished financially, why women should become involved in civil wars. And she argues her points with legal precedents (e.g., *Lex Oppia*). Second, her anti-war arguments echo those of the Greek literary women (Andromache and Lysistrata, for example) as well as prefigure those of more modern speeches, as does the timelessness of her taxation-without-representation trope. In addition, rather than arguing for women's participation in political affairs, an argument that would have been both impossible and fantastic given her context, she uses women's nonparticipation to argue that women's war efforts be voluntary. In-stead of arguing for women's equality under the law, women's inequality un-derpins her argument. The stepwise logic and cogency of Hortensia's argu-ment are perhaps the most compelling (and traditionally masculine) features of her speech.

The triumvirs may have been impressed by Hortensia's eloquent argument, but Appian tells us that "while Hortensia . . . spoke the triumvirs were angry that women should dare to hold a public meeting when the men were silent; that they should demand from magistrates the reasons for their acts, and them-selves not so much as furnish money while the men were serving in the army" (4.4.34). In the end, however, Hortensia's speech was successful, for the trium-virs reduced the number of women who were to submit and, at the same time, extended the decree to include all men of a certain income bracket.[52]

Hortensia is received into the male tradition of public oratory, of persua-sive rhetoric—but only temporarily and only on male terms. Because she was the daughter of a famous orator, the filiafocal society of the Romans could understand and condone Hortensia's dalliance with rhetoric, particularly since she used public oratory to represent the needs of many Roman women (not just her own) before an irregular magistracy imposing an irregular tax. And Fulvia's repulsion of the women had only enhanced goodwill toward Hortensia. Thus, Hortensia stands alone in her oratorical achievement, singular though it was.

Amasia Sentia and Gaia Afrania

Roman daughters, as a group, did not follow Hortensia's example of participating in the public domain to advance their own causes or the cause of women. Those few who did received no praise. Daughterly emulation and maternal devotion might be memorable and valued, but womanly assertiveness was not. Valerius Maximus mentions two other women in connection with oratory, neither with the admiration he reserved for Hortensia:

> Nor must we omit those Women, whom the condition of their Sex, and the Garments of Modesty could not hinder from appearing and speaking in publick Courts of Judicature.
>
> *Amasia Sentia*, being guilty, before a great concourse of people pleaded her own cause [77 BCE]. *[Lucius] Titus*, the Praetor then sitting in Court; and observing all the parts and elegancies of a true Defense, not onely diligently but stoutly was quitted in her first Action by the Sentences of all. And because that under the shape of a woman she carried a manly resolution, they call her *Androgyne*.[33]
>
> *[Gaia] Afrania*, the wife of *Licinius Buccio*, the Senator, being extremely affected with Law-suits, always pleaded for herself before the Praetor. Not that she wanted Advocates, but because she abounded in Impudence. So that for her perpetual vexing the Tribunal with her bawling, to which the Court was unaccustomed, she grew to be a noted Example of Female Calumnie. So that the name *Afrania* was given to all contentious Women. She dyed when *Caesar* was Consul with *Servilius*. For it is better to remember when such a Monster went out of the world, than when she came in. (8.3.1–3)

Sempronia

Other Roman authors mention women whose names are linked to politics, masculine activities—and inappropriate behaviors, in general. A well-known verse maker, Sempronia, mother of Fulvia, was charged with conspiracy to the state. Sallust writes that Sempronia

> had often committed many crimes of masculine daring. This woman was quite fortunate in her family and looks, and especially in her husband and children; she was well read in Greek and Latin literature, able to play the lyre and dance more adeptly than any respectable woman would have need to [except for] . . . overindulgent living. . . . [Y]ou would have a hard time determining which she squandered more of, her money or her reputation; her sexual desires were so ardent that she took the initiative with men far more frequently than they did with her. Prior to the conspiracy she had often broken her word, disavowed her debts, been involved in murder. . . . Yet she possessed intellectual strengths which are by no means

laughable: the skill of writing verses, cracking jokes, speaking either modestly or tenderly or saucily—in a word, she had much wit and charm. (qtd. in Pomeroy 155–56)

Fulvia

Fulvia's reputation as the independently wealthy and formidable wife of Clodius, Curio, and then Mark Antony was recorded by Appian, Plutarch, and Cicero, all of whom wrote about her unprecedented and undignified role as a military leader and spokeswoman during the wars that followed Caesar's death. (These same authors also propagated adverse sentiment about each of her husbands, so some of the criticism leveled toward her might have to do with her husbands', as well as her own, political maneuvering.) Fulvia may well have been a prototypical "corporate wife" (Babcock 1), who invested her family connections and capital in her husbands' careers, but her political influence and meddling might have had more to do with the Roman matron's concern for her family (for protection of her children's name and finances) than for politics per se: "the image of Fulvia preserved in the ancient sources . . . [was] manipulated into an antithesis of the ideal Roman matron whose primary obligation was submission in order to promote harmonious domestic life, not conflict" (Delia 206). Fulvia came to represent the worst of *domina*, a virago. About news of Fulvia's death, Appian writes, "It was said that she was dispirited by Antony's reproaches and fell sick. . . . The death of this turbulent woman, who had stirred up so disastrous a war on account of her jealousy of Cleopatra, seemed extremely fortunate to both of the parties who were rid of her" (4.5.59). Such was the eulogy for the public Roman woman whose public movements were not subordinated to those of her male relatives.

Octavia

Fulvia has come to be the foil to Octavia, whom Plutarch describes as "quite a wonder of a woman" with "beauty, honour, and prudence, . . . much beloved by the Athenians" (1121–22, 1136). Also entering the public political sphere, by way of her selfless marriages to Marcellus and to (Fulvia's widowed husband) Mark Antony, Octavia was mythicized as the feminine ideal, a woman whose marriages were deemed unsurpassable benefits to affairs of the state rather than to herself. Octavia not only served as peacemaker between her brother, Octavian Augustus, and Mark Antony, she was considered her brother's finest supporter, going so far as to weave all the garments her brother wore.

Political Women

Cornelia, Hortensia, Amasia Sentia, Gaia Afrania, Sempronia, Fulvia, Octavia—these are the women whose names are linked with politics. The nature of Roman politics was such that women might properly exercise political power—but only vicariously through the male members of their families.

> [L]imitations were imposed by traditional ideology on public conduct of proper Roman women; women who strayed beyond these bounds were branded as both degenerate and dangerous. Moreover, the post-Augustan sources were, without exception, males who appear to have been both fascinated and repelled by the androgynous female stereotype. In their characterizations of Fulvia they perpetuated a distortion so grotesque and overwhelming that few traces of the real person have survived. She became a moral exemplum of the worst possible behavior for a Roman matron, just as the portrait of Octavia was deliberately groomed to project the feminine ideals formulated by Roman men. (Delia 206–7)

Indeed, some Roman women entered the masculine sphere of politics, but only Hortensia is recognized as successfully entering the domain of persuasive public oratory, or rhetoric.

Because the Romans clung to the ideal of the *domina*, of the strong privatized woman, they often reacted with perplexity or disgust at the women who pursued intellectual or political aspirations. Unlike the very few Greek women who found acceptance and admiration in the public domain, no Roman woman seems to have succeeded in establishing herself as a public figure in her own right. In fact, Hortensia's speech works more to reproduce and affirm the oppression of her reality than it does to affect the public good for the benefit of women.

CONCLUSION

During antiquity, the women's sphere was defined by men, a definition accepted and maintained by men and women alike, regardless of rank. Gendered to the private world of domestic and social affairs, a world exclusive of rhetorical study and practice, classical women were, as a rule, secluded from education for the public sphere. The public power of men, made visible and audible in their rhetorical displays, was "everywhere, not because it embrace[d] everything, but because it [came] from everywhere. . . . [*Power*] is the name that one attributes to a complex strategical situation in a particular society" (Foucault 93). During antiquity, every social institution, every member of society worked (sometimes consciously, most often not) to support gendered spheres of activity: the masculinity of the public sphere and the femininity of the private sphere.

In cultures founded upon and framed by matrices of gendered spheres, masculine power is constantly exercised "in the interplay of nonegalitarian and mobile relations" (94). And, as Foucault goes on to tell us, "where there is power, there is resistance" (95). Any thinking woman, particularly a respectable Greek or Roman matron, was—by her thinking—resisting the feminine sphere; and she was an exception. Yet in every way, her exceptional behavior worked to confirm the rule of exclusive male dominance in the intellectual arena. So a Sappho, an Aspasia, a Diotima, a Hortensia, or a Fulvia might enter the public sphere, might leave her indelible and inimitable mark; nevertheless, her resistance comes not from outside the power politics of gender but rather from inside, for such feminine resistances can only be inscribed in masculine power.

The Greeks and Romans regarded most women as ciphers, whose worth varied according to the property and family connections accompanying them. Women were to be traded among men. And historians—from the first—have had little more to say about these women, who were always, particularly in their exceptions, defined by the private, feminine sphere. The women in my study who passed into the public sphere, even if only temporarily, found themselves vulnerable to assaults on their families, their honor, their sexuality, their "feminine" influence. These women endured the closest of inspections and critiques by males and females alike, usually being disarmed of their influence and respect in the process.

Therefore, as I retell rhetoric, I am also trying to regender it in such a way that women's ventures into rhetorical territory seem safe and sane enough to analyze without defusing. The social events and changes that precipitated their so-called resistance to the power matrix must be regendered as well, so that women's history can merge with rhetorical history and both histories can become just that: history. Since history has traditionally been concerned exclusively with the public and the political, women have been excluded, relegated to the less-serious, private, and anecdotal sphere of everyday life. Thus, history itself has been controlled by the power politics of gender, with men validating historical texts by writing and enacting them—that is, until feminist historiographers began recovering and reconsidering women and their works.

THREE

Medieval Rhetoric: Pagan Roots, Christian Flowering, or Veiled Voices in the Medieval Rhetorical Tradition

INTRODUCTION

In the *Phaedrus*, Plato objects to rhetoric on moral grounds. He wants truth not merely belief, and thus his argument is for a "true" rhetoric: a man should toil diligently not "for the sake of speaking and acting before men, but that he may be able to speak and to do everything, so far as possible, in a manner pleasing to the gods" (*Phaedrus* 273.e, in *Euthyphro*). Aristotle takes up Plato's challenge in his *Rhetoric* by demonstrating that a true theory of rhetoric, one pleasing to the gods, both energizes knowledge and brings truth to bear upon men: rhetoric's "function is not simply to succeed in persuading, but rather to discover the means of coming as near such success as the circumstances of each particular case allow" (1355.b.10). By correlating rhetoric with inquiry and public policy, as well as with giving effectiveness to truth ("men usually have a sufficient natural instinct for what is true, and usually do arrive at the truth" [1355.a.15]), Aristotle vindicates rhetoric. For Aristotle, the difference between the sophistic rhetoric that Plato (so rightly) disparages and the "true" rhetoric that he promotes is the difference between a devotion to personal appeal and personal triumph and a devotion to truth and morality.

The controversies surrounding rhetoric led to a struggle in preeminence between philosophy and rhetoric in terms of influence and respect. But as an intellectual system, rhetoric remained central in educational programs for some eight centuries, exported from Athenian Greece to Rome and from Rome throughout the Roman Empire. The impact of Greco-Roman rhetoric throughout the Empire led Juvenal to write in his *Satire* 15, "Now the whole world has a Greek and Italian Athens; / Gaul with her eloquence has instructed the pleaders of Britain; / Even far-off Thule [Iceland] is talking of hiring professors" (109–11).

Rhetorical studies traveled with the Romans, who colonized what would become the British Isles, but educational practices were not enough to keep rhetoric flourishing. Christianity served to validate and invigorate pagan rhetoric by adapting it to religious ends. Around AD 400, St. Augustine of Hippo wrote *De doctrina Christiana* (*On Christian Doctrine*), perhaps the most influential book of its time, for he demonstrated how to "take the gold out of Egypt" to fortify what would become the Christian rhetorical practices of teaching, preaching, and moving (2.40.60).[1]

The medieval rhetorical tradition, then, evolved within the dual influences of Greco-Roman and Christian belief systems and cultures. Rhetoric was also, of course, informed by the gendered dynamics of medieval English society that isolated nearly everyone from intellectual and rhetorical activities. Medieval culture was wholly and decidedly masculine; yet most men, just like all women, were condemned to class-bound silence. The written word was controlled by clergy, the men of the cloth and the Church, who controlled the flow of knowledge for all men and women.

Yet within that perimeter of masculine culture and privilege, a few medieval women managed to participate in and contribute to rhetorical theory and practice—although their contributions to culture making have rarely been directly connected with rhetoric. Perpetua, Dhouda, Hrotsvitha, Héloïse, Hildegard of Bingen, Mechthild, Hadewijch, Marguerite Porete, St. Bridget, St. Catherine, Julian of Norwich, Margery Kempe, and Florencia Pinar have all been subjects of contemporary critical inquiry, but my study focuses on two religious Englishwomen, Julian of Norwich and Margery Kempe, whose religious devotion and fervor constituted their feminine rhetorical power. Bolstered by their Christian faith, these women inscribe the rhetorical tradition in new ways: they break their silence, speak in the vernacular, as women, and reach women and men of all classes.

MEDIEVAL CULTURAL DYNAMICS, VIEWED BROADLY

Inextricably interlaced with society, the Church stimulated the Christian flowering of a medieval culture with pagan roots. The Bible served as the supertext of medieval textuality; therefore, the terms of law, science, and medicine all spoke broadly to a society of masculine privilege and religious power. Christianity and the Bible colored law, political thinking, science, liturgy, common speech, idiomatic expression, dramatic performance, and art—for the highborn and the lowborn alike. The Bible was regarded as the ur-text of history, wisdom, and doctrine, as well as the ur-guide to proper actions and procedures in all the domains of human endeavor and existence.[2]

Law

Any society's law codes illuminate the actions the society wishes to prevent and persons it wishes to protect; medieval English law, for the most part, protected aristocratic men and their estates. By law, only men governed the entire kingdom, from estates and trades to towns and homes. Englishwomen were deemed the economic and bodily property of men, who could trade them off as "peace weavers" to protect an estate, as securities to expand an estate, or as a means of increasing economic and political power. Englishwomen were determined unable to bear arms, let alone lead troops. However, given the constant property fights among nobility, battles that took their menfolk away and left them in charge, many noblewomen, in addition to knowing every feature of managing their fortified lands, were also skilled in the military arts and could defend or supervise the defense of their lands.[3]

Like the powerful abbesses who, in utter contradiction to secular law, exercised wide prerogatives in the fiefs that belonged to their convents, rich and noblewomen constituted a special status of women. These women lived in the space between the letter and the spirit of the law. For example, inheritance by women often suited the needs of the great landholding families, as their unremitting efforts to secure such rights for their female members attest. If a woman inherited a fief that carried with it a certain office, she was supposed to transfer the office to a man—women were to be represented legally by their closest male relative. But in some cases, she represented herself. Even though a rich woman could hold wealth and influence, she was not to transfer her wealth unless she were widowed or left single by a husband's departure (to war, for instance).[4]

Married women labored under the most severe legal handicaps because peasant economy and society gave their husbands, as heads of households, the fullest rights—a system that worked to the advantage of widows. A widow enjoyed extensive rights and participated more actively in the public community than she could as a dame. If she were working-class, she could run her husband's business or land, even taking his place in the guild, supervising workshops, taking on apprentices and journeymen, and participating in most social and religious celebrations. Given that a guild master's wife would have been working alongside him for years, she already knew the family's work well.[5] Men controlled the crafts and guilds, though, and few women ever enjoyed a status equal to their deceased husbands'.

English peasant women were not isolated from the public world either; they owned land, occasionally appeared in court, and worked in the marketplace. And the daily life of domestic society was always under the direction of women, noble and peasant alike. Still, women's access to public power was limited by both their gender and their position in the household. Common law and customary law barred married women from exercising the legal and landholding rights accorded men. Yet resourceful, active women of all classes found work in the public sphere as craftswomen, shopkeepers, moneylenders, religious activists, midwives, and medical advisors (Howell 37).

Whether rich or poor, a woman had no legal right to censure her husband for extramarital sexual alliances; nevertheless, the rich and powerful exercised the prerogative.[6] Even within Christian marriages based on monogamy and exogamy, men were free to have concubines, many of whom were their slaves, some of whom were relatives, all of whom were within easy reach, as it were. But women could have been accumulated in any household for reasons other than sex and reproduction: since women were skilled in cooking, cloth manufacture, gardening, and similar household duties, most servants in manor houses were women. Besides, they could count on a measure of protection there.

Regardless of their diminished legal status, women had one major advantage: they were the sole conduits of male wealth and power. A child's class status was bestowed by the father, but all male ties ran through the female body; therefore, any lapse in monogamy could obscure lines of male descent. A man might be uncertain that his wife's children were representatives of his own stock, or semen, but he always could count on his blood relationship with his sister's children, in the same way that he could be more certain of a blood tie with his daughter's children than with his son's children. But class status remained a central concern.[7]

Science

Like the law, scientific beliefs supported a culture of subordinate women. Virtually unchanged since antiquity, many medical beliefs harkened back to Aristotle's teleological belief that the female was an incomplete male, an idea corroborated by the Judeo-Christian belief that Eve was created from Adam's rib, rendering her a secondary being created for the sole purpose of helping or serving her superior.[8] Woman best served man by bearing children, her purpose reduced to procreation, to the material body, to a purpose less than that for man, who transfers the very essence of humanness—the soul.[9] What twentieth-century readers recognize as ideologically charged social constructions of gender were indisputable ancient and medieval truths.

With his structural models of the male and female reproductive organs, second-century AD naturalist Galen of Pergamum informed medieval thinkers that women were, in essence, imperfect, undeveloped men, who lacked one vital and superior characteristic: heat. "Now just as mankind is the most perfect of all animals, so within mankind the man is more perfect than the woman, and the reason for his perfection is his excess of heat, for heat is Nature's primary instrument" (2: 630).[10] Woman's imperfections provided text for male writers who expanded upon and explained the physical differences between females and males (and the concomitant intellectual gap).[11]

Churchmen, too, held strong beliefs about the sexes founded upon defective scientific understanding. Both St. Augustine of Hippo (AD 354–430) and St. Thomas Aquinas (AD 1225–74) based woman's physical imperfection on her biologically determined preference for sensation over reason:

in the physical sense, woman has been made for man [who has the power of reason and understanding]. . . . [I]n sex she is physically subject to him in the same way as our natural impulses need to be subjected to the reasoning power of the mind, in order that the actions to which they lead may be inspired by the principles of good conduct. (Augustine, *Confessions* 13.32)

Thomas Aquinas supports and extends Augustine's view of woman's weaker temperament when he writes that "whatever she holds to, she holds to it weakly" and thus is more likely than man to sin (1.98.2). Woman's imperfection, then, rests in her physical being; hers was a procreative body undisciplined by mind, an imperfection that justified her subjection to man.

Religion

Mary, mother of Jesus, was a prime site of medieval Christian worship.[12] Exalted above all other women and sanctified above all other saints, Mary was Holy Mother, Blessed Virgin, Mother of God. Some Christians considered her the Holy Spirit of the Holy Trinity, while others equated her with Wisdom or Sophia.[13] Mary's procreative power, her female body, was honored not only as the power through which God created the world but also as the vehicle of redemption. Despite her exalted place, Mary's role in medieval Christianity did little to advance women's place in the Church; Mary was superior in every way to all other women, both in body and spirit.[14]

Just as worship of Mary was adjusted according to contemporary medieval mores, so were religious writings, scripture, and canon law (re)aligned, according to mores, both Christian and misogynistic. Old Testament texts considered immoral or unethical were reinterpreted by ecclesiastical writers.[15] Augustine, for example, defended hermeneutics and exegesis on the grounds that these methods allowed Christians like himself to borrow—or appropriate—worthwhile nuggets from pagan cultures:

> [A]ll the teachings of the pagans [the classics] contain not only simulated and superstitious imaginings . . . , which each one of us leaving the society of pagans under the leadership of Christ ought to abominate and avoid, but also liberal disciplines more suited to the uses of truth, and some most useful precepts concerning morals. Even some truths concerning the worship of one God are discovered among them. These are, as it were, their gold and silver. . . . [And] [w]hen the Christian separates himself in spirit from their miserable society, he should take this treasure with him for the just use of teaching the gospel. (*On Christian* 75)

Augustine is one of many early Church Fathers who converted the pagan into a usable past for the Church, one that could guide Christians in shaping their present and future. Like St. Ambrose, Paul, and Tertullian, Augustine found identity and strength in the images of past history, using them to justify the terms of human (in)equality.

In theory, the original Christian vision allowed full citizenship to all orthodox and obedient believers—of both sexes: "There is neither Jew nor Greek, there is neither slave nor free, there is neither male nor female; for you are all one in Christ Jesus" (Gal. 3.28). "And in the last days it shall be, God declares, that I will pour out my Spirit upon all flesh, and your sons and your daughters shall prophesy" (Acts 2.17). Therefore, the calling to Christianity was not a calling for subservience, it was rather for spiritual and evangelical responsibility. Jesus himself had preached such equality: "Come unto me, all ye that labour and are heavy laden, and I will give you rest." "For whosoever shall do the will of my Father which is in heaven, the same is my brother, and sister, and mother" (Matt. 11.28, 12.50). And Jesus's deeds broke any taboos of gender discrimination; he healed, comforted, and protected men and women alike.[16]

Indeed, in theory, early Christianity spoke to a new humanity, one of inclusion rather than exclusion.[17] But in practice, Christianity was not nearly so magnanimous.[18] Only those Christians who believed in a spiritualizing, personalized religious community, only those who held to a vision of mutual service could hold fast to the intrinsic equality of Christian men and women. For those believers, each woman who surrendered to the Church ungendered herself and became a man, an equal. After all, she was leaving behind her traditional familial (and gendered) role as daughter, wife, mother.[19]

St. Paul was ambivalent about the issue of male-female equality, at least according to the translations of his letters. Although he occasionally repeated Jesus's emphasis on the equal value of women's souls, he more often stressed women's inferiority, in keeping with the social conditions of his own day. Like many Christians, he used the Old Testament story of Eve to rationalize women's secondary status, an integral part of Pauline doctrine. Paul preached that in the private and public spheres "the head of every man is Christ, the head of a woman is her husband" (1 Cor. 11.3). And as for woman's participation in the Christian Church, he writes:

> Let a woman learn in silence with all submissiveness. I permit no woman to teach or to have authority over men; she is to keep silent. For Adam was formed first, then Eve; and Adam was not deceived, but the woman was deceived and became a transgressor. Yet woman will be saved through bearing children, if she continues in faith and love and holiness, with modesty. (1 Tim. 2.11–15)

These Pauline passages became the basis for the Christian view of women. Thus, in the place of genuine equal rights and equal roles for women, mainstream Christianity preached an ethic of equality for all people insofar as they could be viewed as men and pseudomen, but that equality was to be evidenced only "in Christ," not in the real world.

Society

The immeasurable power of the medieval Church influenced every cultural feature and social practice during the Middle Ages, from family life to royal rule, and that power is the fundamental feature that distinguishes the Middle Ages from earlier and later periods of history. Although the Church initially espoused equality between men and women, no woman stood equal to men in the eyes of the Church Fathers (AD 300–400)—or in the eyes of patriarchal society.[20] Nevertheless, from the fourth to the twelfth century, women took a prominent part in monastic life and, from the thirteenth century onward, in the resurgence of institutional piety; they were, however, excluded from established philosophical Christian debate and from the councils of the Church (Bell, "Medieval" 145).

Like the Church Fathers, with their androcentric hermeneutics, secular writers too balanced pagan and Christian beliefs to keep woman in her place. The *Beowulf* and *Pearl* poets, Sir Thomas Malory, Geoffrey Chaucer, the hagiographers, and the literary and religious scholars all took the gold out of Egypt in their efforts to bring the Greco-Roman intellectual heritage into equilibrium with Christianity and with medieval culture. As the Middle Ages began to shape its culture, the emphasis on the Virgin, supreme among women, slowly evolved into a cult of the beloved, a tradition of courtly romance that idealized sensual love, as well as the lady.[21]

In terms of their daily lives, however, most medieval people concerned themselves not with perfect love but with food, warmth, shelter, and health, all constant problems for the poor:

> [D]isease was rampant. The cities and country towns were . . . destitute of any regular system of sanitation. . . . From time to time plague and pestilence swept through the country, and the terrible Black Death, which carried off a third of the population and in some places left not sufficient survivors to bury the dead, was only the worst of many outbreaks. Skin diseases were rife, owing to the lack of personal cleanliness, and every town had its leper hospitals outside its walls and its lepers wandering through its streets. . . . The death-rate amongst young children must have been appalling. . . . Of those that reached manhood many, owing to bad food and other causes, were diseased or crippled. The towns were full of these unfortunates, unable to work and compelled to beg their living. (Salzman 25–26)

To speak about medieval English society, with its constants of religion, agriculture, and misogyny, is to speak broadly and to oversimplify. The Middle Ages, just like antiquity, the Renaissance, or modern times, was a vast expanse—and range—of days, people, and experiences.

WOMAN'S ROLE IN MEDIEVAL LITERATURE

Because all literature was colored by the Church, characterizations of women were hyperbolic (Mary or Eve) in both their romanticization and their harshness. And the confluence of courtly love poetry and the cult of the Virgin gave the appearance of empowering women and elevating their status; but, on the contrary, both movements actually coincided with a decrease in the real political and religious power exercised by women. Thus, despite the various literary characterizations of women's power over men, women remained socially constructed as inferior to men in every way.

Surviving literature offers a range of women and women's roles, from the fierce Grendel's mother and the wily Judith to the submissive Griselda and the holy, learned anchorites. Yet many of these medieval women play secondary roles in the stage play of medieval literature, serving as supporting actresses, extras, props, even scenery. In no case was the female character envisioned as an autonomous woman—or even human—except when she inscribed herself into her own story, as Julian of Norwich and Margery Kempe demonstrate.

Imaginative Literature

Despite the bias towards the masculine that is exhibited in the extant corpus of medieval literature, the voice of a woman expressing longing for her lover and grief at being parted from him is heard in "The Banished Wife's Complaint." The banished wife herself is both the voice and the protagonist of the poem, giving credence to the belief that it was female authored:[22]

> In solitude I sing this lonely song
> About my fate; and truly can I say
> That of the ills encountered since my youth,
> Ills new and old, most grievous far is this—
> Sorrows of endless exile I endure!
> . . . .
> Wherefore is my great grief,
> That him, most fitting of all men for me,
> False-hearted I have found and treacherous;
> With loving smile devising deadly sin.
> . . . .
> Must I, wrongly condemned, for evermore
> Endure the hate of him I wholly love? (Cook and Tinker 64–65)[23]

Moreover, the poem is unrestrained in its passion and emotion, two sensations deemed feminine (and thus inferior) by the culture. The superior faculty of reason, always in control of those sensations, would be constituted in male-authored works and enacted by male characters.[24]

Another passionate female protagonist is "Judith."[25] Composed before the Norman invasion, "Judith" presents an intrepid woman, strong and active; however, her power is neutralized by the Anglo-Saxon male gaze of idealized femininity that sees her as an "elfin [fairy] beauty," a "blessed maid," a "bright maid," a "holy woman" (Cook and Tinker 121–32). Judith finely arrays her beautiful self to steal into the military camp of debased, drunken Holofernes, the Assyrian king who plans to conquer the Israeli city of Bethulia. Judith's plan is to seduce Holofernes, disarm him, and murder him—which she does.[26]

Early in the Middle Ages, Judith's feats could be compared to the holy work of Juliana or of Elena, two other legendary women of military sanctity and chastity.[27] Even though Judith was not a saint, much less a Christian, these Anglo-Saxon poets celebrated all three women as valiant saints: "When the Anglo-Saxons converted to Christianity, they inherited a spiritual heroic past contained within the lives of the various apostles, martyrs, and confessors. These lives were bolstered by missionaries, relics, church dedications, and, especially in the seventh century, through manuscripts of saints' lives sent from Rome" (Chance 31). Stories of fighting saints were used for instruction, as well as for entertainment, among religious (monks and nuns) and secular folks alike, for, in every story, the woman defended her religious belief as though it were a political state. Thus, these stories not only spread early Christian beliefs but fed the jingoism necessary for establishing the English nation.[28]

Judith is the quintessential female of medieval literature: she is one-dimensional, either a heroic "Christian" or a Jewish seductress. Despite serving as the "Savior's handmaid then / Gloried," "the holy woman the handmaid of God," Judith serves as no venerable model of womanhood for her medieval audience (Cook and Tinker 126, 129). Regardless of her loyalties, her methods are larger than life, akin to those of the conniving Morgan le Fay: seduction, murder, jubilation. But she is permitted her daring escapade only with masculine support, the masculine trait of reason: God grants her wisdom and safekeeping, and Bethulian soldiers await her victorious return before they attack and destroy the Assyrian camp. Thus, powerful though she may be, Judith enacts woman's metaphysical inferiority to man; she is passionate rather than reasonable, of matter rather than essence.

The popular medieval romance never pretended to give an accurate picture of life, let alone of the medieval woman. It was fantasy, with love as a main motive and chivalric persons as main characters. Growing out of the cult of the Virgin, the passionate romance fed the adulation of the elevated noble lady, making her sole inspirer of all that was good in her lover. The lady of romance had two sides: she was idealized, superior, and untouchable, or she was supercilious, disdainful, and sometimes cruel—in either case, she was aristocratic, one-dimensional, artificial.

Often, the knights of the Round Table expended their time either rescuing these noble ladies from dangers (captors, robbers, monsters, magicians) or enduring patiently whatever trials or humiliations the ladies imposed upon them. For example, in Chrétien de Troyes's "Knight of the Cart," one of the earliest extant Arthurian romances, Lancelot must choose to debase and disgrace himself by riding in a cart (the symbol of guilt and disenfranchisement) if he is to see his beloved Guinevere.[29] Female control is ever present in the medieval romance and exerts itself in the response of the chivalric males, whose actions reflect their fealty to a feminized ideal: "he of the cart is occupied with deep reflections, like one who has no strength or defence against love which holds him in its sway"; "the knight has only one heart, and this one is really no longer his, but has been entrusted to some one else" (Chrétien 279, 286).

In Thomas Malory's *Morte D'Arthur*, "the noble hystories of the sayd Kyng Arthur," the women are also exaggerated, romantic notions.[30] In one story, the treacherous Morgan le Fay disguises herself as a "passing fair lady" so as to sleep with her brother King Arthur (1.1.19); in another story, the same fay magically heals a knight's wounds before he escapes her (1.10.37). Dame Bisen enchants Lancelot to sleep with Dame Elaine, and like King Arthur, Lancelot fathers a son from this entanglement. When Guinevere discovers Lancelot's adventure, she tongue-lashes him, with a force akin to that of an angry female saint: "False traitor knight that thou art, look thou never abide in my court, and avoid my chamber, and no so hardy, thou false traitor knight that thou art, that ever thou come in my sight!" (1.11.8). Lancelot swoons in the face of her furious gale.

Other noble ladies habitually make life and death intercessions in behalf of knights, demanding that the heads of false knights be brought to them or requesting that errant knights' lives be saved (1.3.8, 9, 12). Malory's women are exaggerated in their power to deceive, to control, to heal. The knights are privileged to serve these courtly ladies, for their unabashed service might earn them intimacies. Despite any measure of virtue or charm these women characters might have, despite the measure of knightly worship, these women, and elegant adultery, remain fictions of male desire. These were popular stories, written in the vernacular, printed by and distributed among the reading public. And these stories promulgated the gendered perceptions of women as emotional, physical, nonintellectual beings.

The medieval genre of the fabliau provides perhaps the crudest and the most conspicuous secular view of woman. In striking contrast to legends and romances, the fabliau is bourgeois, bawdy, sarcastic, and sometimes sadistic, its plot often hinging on a brutal practical joke. Like the romance, the fabliau has superficially drawn women (deceitful, faithless, eroticized) and wildly improbable plots; still, the fabliau is essentially antiromantic, in terms of its sharply realized settings, flat characters, and standard plot. Lascivious, clever matrons, eager wooers (usually students), gullible old husbands, and trickster bawds are cut to single patterns, little varied. In every case, women are discovered in flagrante delicto; and in every case, they are safeguarded by their own wiliness and their husband's unbelievable credulity.

One of the earliest extant fabliaux, the anonymous "Dame Sirith" (c. 1200) tells of double deception engineered by a woman whose cunning is more exaggerated than any similar character of Chaucer's (the Wife of Bath or the old witch-woman of her own tale, for example). Widowed, old Dame Sirith is not a professional bawd. She is, however, reputed to be knowledgeable and involved in the sexuality of those younger than she.[31] In this brief (450 lines), broadly sketched tale, deception unwinds the minute young Dame Margeri's old husband leaves for the fair of St. Bolstof in Lincolneschire and clever Wilekin arrives to take his place. Young wives, just need an excuse. So Wilekin goes immediately to the resourceful Dame Sirith to devise a plan.[32] The rest of the fabliau confirms the beliefs that, whether witches or tricksters, old women are manipulative, withered crones who, like Chaucer's Pandarus, derive vicarious pleasure from getting "love done" and also that all young wives are whorish.

Chaucer, too, demonstrates his skill with the fabliau form in tales that invariably denigrate women, despite the various motivations of his storytellers. In "The Miller's Tale," Alisoun represents all young wives; she has a "lecherous eye" and is "winsome . . . as a jolly colt" (lines 3245, 3263). She readily hoodwinks her husband to take a lover and takes pleasure in humiliating her second lover; she is prime material for the fabliau. The women in "The Reeve's Tale" are nothing more or less than the Reeve's property, for when they are debauched by the smarty students, they are serving only as instruments of revenue or reprisal. That the plotline of "The Merchant's Tale" is also that of a fabliau—with a deceiving and quick-witted wife—comes as no surprise after the pronouncement of the merchant in the prologue of his tale: "We wedded men live in sorrow and care" (line 1228). The most popular genre during the Middle Ages, the fabliau offered twisted and distorted pictures of woman that kept her subjugated in society and culture. And fabliaux were just one contribution to "The Book of Wicked Women," a veritable anthology of antifemale sentiments that drew on both Christian and classical Latin traditions.[33]

Marian Literature

Not even the religious and popular literature of Mariolatry, so pervasive during the Middle Ages, could advance or enhance the place of women. Alone among humans, the mother of Jesus had been healed of original sin.[34] Therefore, Mary's nobility was far superior to any historical or fictional woman's: she escaped the human condition, in terms of conception, birth, and death. She was a human creature totally enclosed in sacred space.[35]

Marian devotion captivated medieval writers and audiences alike. Her life and deeds were popularized in the various medieval English dramas, as well as in hymns, poetry, and feast days; alongside the crucifixion, the Madonna and child was by far the most common single subject for artistic representation. The central theme in all such literature is the perfection of Mary's life, a perfection unattainable by even the least inferior of earthly virgins or devout wives, and the perpetual comparison with Mary with any other woman (particularly with the fallen Eve, first sinner and mother of murder) served only to intensify the debasement of women.

Civic drama, particularly the Corpus Christi cycle plays, was one of the most popular of public literatures as early as the fourteenth century. Named for their city of origin, the Chester, York, Towneley (also called Wakefield), N-Town (*nomen*) Banns, and "Ludus Coventriae" (or Coventry) cycles affirmed Christian beliefs, most particularly redemption, as they prescribed Christian values and behaviors.[36] In nature and origin, they were a form of public worship and informed Christian values and behavior. In a time when most people could neither read nor write, the stage action and dialogue of civic drama could educate them more effectively than the Latin liturgy.[37]

Given the strong devotional trend of Marian piety during the later Middle Ages (fourteenth through early sixteenth centuries in England), the life of Mary became one theme in these plays.[38] The plays beguiled audiences into seeing Mary as an essentially perfect, yet human, figure and gave rise to an increased interest in the human Jesus (an interest underpinning mysticism) and to the mother and son as coredemptors.

Various pageants comprise one part of the "Ludus Coventriae," compressing and making room for apocryphal and legendary stories of Mary's life: her parents' notification of her immaculate conception; her visit to the temple, where she displays her brilliance and ecclesiastical understanding (at the age of three); the complications of a necessary betrothal for one dedicated to virginity; the reluctance of an impotent Joseph to marry an already pregnant, fourteen-year-old woman, who, by all accounts, should be stoned publicly; the miraculous flowering of Joseph's rod; the nativity; the flight into Egypt; the slaughter of the innocents; the life, crucifixion, and resurrection of her son; her own death; and her assumption. The glorification of Mary, patron saint of childbirth, coredemptrix, perfect mother of Jesus, shines no favor on actual women, who remained subjected to their human imperfection.[39]

On the moral scale, based on chastity, virgins were the equivalent of queens on the social scale. Although both virgins and queens represented unattainable superiority, they nevertheless embodied the moral values that all medieval women were expected to pursue to the limits of their condition. Women, literary and historical alike, were to dedicate themselves either to the Church or to the family. Uncontaminated virgins were considered golden vessels, totally committed to a spiritual life. Widows who had dispensed with the flesh to embrace the spirit were silver vessels. And the fertile matrons who were fulfilling their bodily obligation to procreate were, according to medieval custom, wooden vessels. Therefore, virgins were three times as likely to be saved as wives.[40]

Inspirational Literature

Historical rather than fictional Marian imitators, the three aristocratic women for whom the *Ancrene Wisse* (or *Ancrene Riwle*) was written withdrew from secular life better to serve the Lord and nourish their souls. These were young anchorites, prisoners of grace, who, in the manner of Julian of Norwich, vowed themselves to a life of withdrawal in little cells attached to churches, shutting themselves off from the world, shutting themselves off from carnal sins to concentrate on the spiritual sins of envy, pride, and wrath. Written by a chaplain about 1230, the *Ancrene Wisse* offers spiritual and practical advice initially to these three young anchorites and then, as the manuscript circulated, to anchorites all over England. In theory, the Church approved of eremitism, but practically, anchorites were secluded from the watchful eyes of male churchmen. Therefore, instructional and inspirational literature was aimed directly at them, advising them to

> [T]hink often with sorry of thy sins,
> Think often of Hell's woes, of heaven's happiness;
> Think of thine own death, of God's death on the cross;
> the grim doom of Doomsday remember often,
> Think how false is the world, which has her rewards.
> Think what thou owe God for his benefits
>
> (*Ancrene Wisse* 18.14–19, in Bennett and Smithers)[41]

We know his audience is upper-class, well-educated women, taking seriously their virginal devotion to the Church, for he speaks to them tenderly, encouraging them to thrive in their solitude not only by contemplating upon the Virgin but by bonding and growing together spiritually like any other community:

> You are the anchoresses of England—as many together, twenty now or more; as God is good, may you increase. . . . [G]o forth and prosper in your own way, for each is together with the other in a manner of living, as though you were a community of London and of Oxford, of Shrewsbury, or of Chester—[a community] with one manner shared and without individual distinction. Individual willfulness is a low thing in religion, for it destroys unity and manner shared that ought to be in order—this know then that you be all as a community is your high reputation, which to God is pleasing. [Your reputation is] already widely known, so that your community begins to spread towards England's edge. (18.222–35, in Bennett and Smithers)

The practices and symbols of anchorite experience embed themselves so deeply that their culture is inseparable from it. Devoted to contemplation and virginity, they are (to be) perfectly steadfast in their faith. Modeled after the Holy Virgin, queen of grace and courtesy, the anchorites themselves serve as model prisoners of grace and courtesy.

But true virginity demanded more than an intact hymen; women were to work constantly toward purity of heart, to listen always to Jesus. Thus, in their steadfast faith, these anchorites are akin to Chaucer's then-admired fictional heroines, the Man of Law's Lady Constance, who faces danger and horror like a daughter of the Holy Church, and the Clerk's long-suffering, virtuous Griselda, who withstands immeasurable loss for her husband and king. Like the anchorites, Chaucer's wholly romanticized and fictionalized characters are edifying examples of womanhood, not as fierce, perhaps, as the female saints, whose vitae were so popular at the time, but every bit as steadfast in their faith and devotion.

Women, Literature, and Culture

Medieval literature offers a range of stories featuring woman, but never is she accorded the full range of human feelings or characteristics: she might be an attractive snare and source of temptation or she might be an Amazonian warrior, but as an emotional creature, she remains inherently weaker than and inferior to rational man. Even the Holy Virgin, untouchable in her perfection, is excluded from full humanness; she is encircled by sanctity. None of the female literary characters is a human being.

The subordinate roles of female literary characters paralleled the secondary status of historical women, whose place in the intellectual sphere is best understood in the context of their place in overall society. With few exceptions, women could not vote or participate fully in the masculinized power structures of the Church, the military, the economy, or the guilds. Under such conditions, it was obviously rare for a woman to be able to make her public presence felt. But some strong women prevailed, primarily women associated with the Church. Most prominent among puissant medieval women are the abbesses, who exercised analogous temporal, as well as spiritual, jurisdiction over great territories—always in their own right and in virtue of their office.[42] But besides administrators, religious women such as Julian of Norwich and Margery Kempe actuated influence as well, by directing the spiritual lives of others, either from their cells or by evangelizing among the masses.

THE MEDIEVAL RHETORICAL TRADITION: THE RHETORIC OF RELIGION

Cutting short a brilliant secular career as a rhetorician to take up the Christian ministry, St. Augustine soon formulated what became the definitive Christian apologia for the study of pagan rhetoric, *On Christian Doctrine*. His broad principles transcended pagan oratorical goals and offered valuable suggestions to the Christian writer and preacher, further evidence of his ability to appropriate "Egyptian gold." Like Augustine, St. Jerome (AD c. 345–420) balanced his rhetorical training with his Christianity and recounted Old Testament law to support the range of his life's work. Just as a Jew could marry a captive Gentile woman if he shaved her head and eyebrows and clipped her nails (Deut. 21.10–13), so too could a Christian refashion his classical education. Like Augustine, Jerome had to defend his use of secular learning: "What is so surprising . . . about my wish to treat secular wisdom, which I admire for the beauty of its content and the elegance of its style, like this captive maiden, that is, to make her an Israelite once she has been clipped and shorn of idolatry, error and lust?" (Letter 70.2; see also 66.8, 21.13). Thus, rhetoric, admired for the beauty of its content and the elegance of its style, was refashioned for Christian use.

Rhetoric in Context

The age-old symbiosis between rhetoric and social conditions continued during the Middle Ages, with the Church guiding both rhetorical and social practices—hence the fusion of rhetoric and religion. In the Greek and Roman democracies, with their free speech and right to representation, rhetoric was essential to a citizen's legal and political involvement, in terms of his (or his representative's) eloquence in the courts or assemblies. However, during the medieval period, rhetoric took a different form: many of the major rhetorical texts either disappeared or survived only in damaged form. Cicero's *Orator* and *Brutus* vanished altogether; *De oratore* was known only to a few scholars; and Quintilian's *Institutio oratoria* appeared only in a badly mutilated version (Vickers, *In Defense* 215). Had these works been known in their fullest version, they "would have preserved a much wider conception of rhetoric's social and political role."[43] Thus, rhetoric in the traditional sense of the word was systematically neglected both in practice and in scholarship.

Despite the limitations of their own rhetorical educations, both Augustine and Jerome found ways to "take the gold out of Egypt," to marry the Jew and the Gentile, and, thereby, to converge the beauty and power of traditional rhetoric with the word and work of the Church. *On Christian Doctrine* was the first truly medieval treatise about the communicative arts.[44] In it, Augustine insists that rhetoric must be available to advance the truth of the Church.[45] He purified classical rhetoric for ecclesiastical use and adapted Roman eloquence to the service of Christian preaching: "If those who hear are to be moved rather than taught, so that they may not be sluggish in putting what they know into practice and so that they may fully accept those things which they acknowledge to be true, there is need for greater powers of speaking" (4.4.6).[46] He does, however, insist that eloquence be linked with wisdom. Alluding to Cicero (*De inventione* 1.1.1), Augustine writes that "wisdom without eloquence is of small benefit to states; but eloquence without wisdom is often extremely injurious and profits no one" (4.5.7).

Jerome remained sensitive to the aesthetic appeals of classical literature and the Christians' continuing need for useful secular knowledge as well, going so far as to carry out his own learning and writing during his years as a renunciate and hermit.[47] Jerome's nearly completed translation of the Bible from Greek to Latin proved to be the most comprehensive intellectual and spiritual undertaking up to that time, one that called on his vast linguistic, ecclesiastical, classical, and rhetorical learning. Early Christians found ways for the art of rhetoric to serve the Church; they used rhetoric to defend their beliefs from infidels and pagans but also to advance their beliefs. Rhetoric was not to be sidelined. From the first, Christianity kept a special relationship with intertextuality, with articulation and interpretation. The Christian God was itself modeled on language: "In the beginning was the Word, and the Word was with God, and the Word was God" (John 1.1).

Christianity, about words, their interpretation, belief, and practice, colored all intellectual activity, including each of the several liberal arts.[48] But despite the work of individual Christian rhetors, the Church politic saw no need for God's word to be improved by rhetoric. During the Middle Ages, then, rhetoric was nearly deprived of its most important function, that of training for eloquence and for political display; therefore, rhetoric lost much of its individuality—but not all of it. Individual efforts prevailed.

Medieval Rhetoric

Medieval Rhetorical Arts

The plasticity of rhetoric allowed it to adapt its classical self to the particular needs and discourses of Church and society—"the past should serve the particular needs of the present" (Murphy, *Rhetoric* 87).[49] Limited by the availability of rhetorical texts, medieval rhetoricians relied on the Aristotelian tradition, especially the relation of dialectic to scholastic *disputatio*, and they expanded upon Aristotle's logical works to demonstrate the interconnection of rhetoric and logic. They also tapped the foundation of language study, grammar.[50]

Ars poetica. The widely used grammatical works of fourth-century Aelius Donatus and the poetical treatise by Horace not only emphasized syntax and expanded grammar into the stylistic matter of the tropes and figures but also laid down specific advice to writers on how to go about the composition of poetry.[51] Donatus's *Ars grammatica* discusses schemata and tropi, thus representing the "first recorded intrusion of *grammatica* into a field heretofore appropriated by *rhetorica*. . . . [T]his marks a partial breakdown of ancient attempts to keep the two disciplines separate" (Murphy, *Rhetoric* 32–33). And Horace's *Ars poetica* "represents an extension—a further step, a projection forward—of the basic grammatical process. His comments are not merely judgments about the merit of previously completed works (which is usually termed 'criticism'). They extend into the future. The *Ars* poetics thus becomes a prescriptive or preceptive document," a preceptive useful for rhetorical studies (32). Thus, medieval grammatical studies flowed freely into rhetorical ones. Following the tradition of Quintilian's *Institutio oratoria*, for instance, Geoffrey of Vinsauf's preceptive *Poetria nova* ("the new poetics," as opposed to Horace's) bridged the gap between rhetoric and ancient grammar by speaking to issues of description, figures and tropes, and oral delivery. He also touched on rhetorical matters of arrangement and exordium. The rhetorical art of versification was being refined and codified, until it came to be considered "not a branch of grammar, but alternately a kind of argumentation or persuasion . . . and a form of composition (and as such to be treated in terms of style, organization, and figures borrowed from rhetoric)" (McKeon 28).

Ars dictaminis. The art of letter writing (*ars dictaminis*) was also attracting attention, for until the Middle Ages oral and written delivery were considered inseparable arts, natural outcomes of a broad rhetorical training. By the fourth century, however, letters had become related to less-formal discourse. Given the high level of illiteracy, rulers often dictated their letters to scribes who then arranged for the letters to be read aloud in the persona of the composer, often with an informal tone, and always in a manner delineating the social status and learning of composer, audience, and subject at hand. Though sometimes informal, these early letters (of Cicero, Augustine, Jerome, Paul, monarchs, and princes, for instance) resonated with practical importance; many of them are the only extant records of theological, governmental, and legal transactions.

Centuries later, a Ciceronian ideal of *ars dictaminis* became the means for the ever-expanding Roman Church to establish, maintain, and control its outposts, its institutionalized bureaucracy.[52] Such letter writing served to forward official Church positions and requests; it was the not argument-advancing *ars dictaminis* that legal studies would eventually promote.[53] The primary concern in successful letter writing was the salutation to the intended recipient, for astute audience awareness would guide the tone of the entire letter, with consequences for the letter writer and the writer's language. These early letters concentrated not only on purposeful arrangement but also on aesthetically pleasing poetic style, on *cursus*, the epistolary style made famous by the correspondence between Héloïse and Abelard.

Ars praedicandi. The groundwork so carefully laid and defended by Augustine and Jerome would eventually allow for a broad application of rhetoric to preaching (*ars praedicandi*). The pattern of using words to effect change was as old as creation itself. God had used words to create all of Heaven and earth, light and darkness, plants and animals, and humankind.[54]

If words can effect one's personal or public ends, where does language derive its power? The Sophists, Plato, Aristotle, and all the other early rhetorical theorists sought to discover the best means of persuasion for all arguments through elegance and skill in speaking. Christian doctrine, however, held that the power of persuasion came from God alone: either the speaker would serve as the mouthpiece for God's message, or the speaker would speak truth sparked with divine grace that would effect persuasion (Augustine, *On Christian* 4.27.59). Logic and eloquence meant nothing and were little used in the comparatively unshaped, less formal, almost conversational and homely style of speaking used by the early Church.

But Augustine and Jerome insist that "*all learning* useful to the propagation of the faith [should be brought] into the Christian arena" (Mountford 36). If missionaries and preachers were truly capable and worthy of spreading God's word, then, surely, they could learn by Christian example and practice (through their worship service); they would need no secular course in (pagan) rhetorical rules and theories.[55] For Augustine, the goal of public Christian discourse is a kind of natural clarity rather than artistry or elegance, and he borrows from Cicero three goals, as well as three levels of style, for the successful Christian speaker: to teach by means of the subdued style, to delight by means of the moderate style, and to move to action by means of the grand style.[56]

In spite of the clear injunction by Jesus concerning Christian duty—"Go ye into all the world, and preach the gospel to every creature" (Mark 16.15)— there had been no major attempt during the first 1200 years of the Christian era to embrace a special body of rhetorical precepts to aid preachers, except, of course, for *On Christian Doctrine.* "Despite the collapse of education during the barbarian invasions of Europe, despite the frequent avowals that study is necessary to the preacher, despite the consistent acceptance of preaching responsibility in council after council, no second Augustine appeared to propose a rhetoric of preaching" (Murphy, *Rhetoric* 297). Sermonizing and homiletics remained major features of the Church, but for those dozen centuries, the Church had been almost exclusively concerned with *what*—not *how*—to preach.

But by AD 1220, a theory of preaching that attended to both content and form began to emerge, *forma praedicandi*, a "fully developed theory of 'thematic' preaching" that made due allowance between the terrestrial and celestial city (Murphy, *Rhetoric* 275).[57] Writers became increasingly interested in discussing the form—as distinct from the subject matter—of preaching.[58] This shift in emphasis, establishing the genre in the shape it was to retain for centuries to come, was probably the result of academic sermons of the intellectual milieu of the schools of the period. Though exact origins of this genre have never been fully investigated, *ars praedicandi* was certainly the product of medieval humanism.

The work of Robert of Basevorn exemplifies this new theory of preaching and plays a major role in the rejuvenation of classical rhetoric.[59] Defining preaching as "the persuasion of many, within a moderate length of time, to meritorious conduct" (120), his *Forma praedicandi* (AD 1322) introduces a rhetorical "standard" for preaching that moves it beyond the familiar, personal homily, which had always been resolutely unorganized and unstylish. The sermon, by contrast, would tap the classical concepts of ethos, pathos, and logos and be structured on the standard rhetorical principles of division and proof.[60]

The dominant features of Robert's thematic sermon are *divisio* and *amplificatio*; a stated passage is divided and then commented upon. Medieval preachers needed both knowledge and skill to provide verbal concordances for the statements of the theme, but their success was always predicated on divine help and the goodwill of their audiences.[61] Robert shared with Augustine the belief that the persuasive power of Christian discourse came from God alone; the preacher served only as a vessel. Nevertheless, that vessel could be well prepared, intellectually, spiritually, and morally. Because preparing preachers is Robert's goal, he opens a new field for rhetoric to inhabit.[62] His *Forma praedicandi* breathes new life into classical rhetoric, transforming its deliberative function into exhortative, edifying oratory. By making highly selective use of the classical principles—of ethos, of knowledge, of the intricacies and resources of language and delivery, of audience awareness, of arrangement, and of style—fourteenth-century rhetoricians were able to apply the ideas of ancient rhetoric to the needs of the present, thereby preventing classical rhetoric from falling into disuse and oblivion.

Insofar as rhetoric deals with a basic and essential social ability—the power to speak or to write—it has been closely related to education since antiquity. The classical educational program outlasted the culture that gave it birth, transmitting the practices directly into the Middle Ages, practices that continued to exclude women. Advanced learning was necessary for neither marriage nor the convent, the traditional expectations for women. And since the world of the university was beyond the reach of all women, those who insisted on seeking an education could best be served by joining an intellectual convent. In the better convent schools, women learned the trivium, the Holy Scripture, the Fathers, and music. Because of Church-supported educational opportunities, nearly all the medieval women in rhetoric were convent educated; all of them were religious women.

VEILED VOICES: WOMEN IN THE MEDIEVAL RHETORICAL TRADITION

The Church Fathers pronounced pagan rhetoric to be ineffectual so far as Christian persuasion went, for successful evangelism depended on the grace of God. In Acts 20.32, Paul tells his hearers that God's grace is the gift that enables them to comprehend the word of God transmitted through a human speaker: "And now I commend you to God and to the word of his grace, which is able to build you up and to give you the inheritance among all those who are sanctified." In other words, the message itself has divine power.

St. Augustine and Robert of Basevorn, too, espoused the importance of the message itself rather than a purposeful arrangement or delivery. The individuality of each hearer informs the received message, for each hearer must balance the things she or he hears against what Augustine calls "interior truth," which is already resident in the person who hears the words of another; the message is more important than the medium.[63] This personal rhetoric of hearing enabled the medieval women to participate in the rhetorical tradition.

Excluded from classical university education and hence from rhetorical training, inexperienced in public life and the expectations of an audience, most educated women took nontraditional (i.e., feminine) rhetorical routes. Given the low rate of literacy among women and their exclusion from the public space (the universities, for instance) in which males gained and demonstrated their mastery of ancient learning, entry into a convent or another kind of religious community could mean release into literacy, across the sacred bridge of the Scriptures:

> For medieval women as well as men, literary productivity goes hand in hand with the opportunity for education, at least a modicum of scholarly idleness, access to materials needed for her work, some financial independence, patronage in social, religious, or financial form, and (sometimes in lieu of all the above) religious or political zeal. With women writers, an added prerequisite often entails the freedom from repeated pregnancies and childbearing. (K. Wilson, *Medieval* ix)

Such women as Julian of Norwich and Margery Kempe turned to the only intellectual world within woman's reach: the world of eternal—and internal— truth. Christian piety in women was commendable. Piety was the only high road to wisdom, feminine religious wisdom, that is: "Say to Wisdom, 'You are my sister,' and call insight your intimate friend" (Prov. 7.4). Wisdom and piety came to fruition in their visions, meditations, mystical experiences, and autobiographical sketches—stories composed for their children, the religious sisters and brothers, their fellow citizens, and themselves.

Women's visionary or mystical writings were an acceptable avenue of literacy and communication in a medieval world that otherwise discouraged women's academic literacy. Although unorthodox mystics, such as Margery Kempe, might be viewed with skepticism, orthodox mystics, such as anchorite Julian of Norwich, "were respected and highly acclaimed; their gifts of prophecy and clairvoyance were generously acknowledged; and the church made abundant use of the visions" (K. Wilson, *Medieval* xvii). Female mystics might be regarded as vessels of divine inspiration, but in no case would they have been considered vessels of literary erudition or academic acuity. The scriptural injunction that God "hath chosen foolish things of the world to confound the wise; and God hath chosen the weak things of the world to confound the things which are mighty" (1 Cor. 1.27), however, helped explain the power of female mystical inspiration that informed and sanctioned their "teaching, pleasing, and moving." Theirs was a rhetoric of unity and inclusion, of theology: as women, they spoke and wrote a female presence into the Trinity; they spoke and wrote the common people into their religious beliefs and their discussions.

Julian of Norwich and Her Rhetoric of Theology

Known only through *Revelations of Divine Love Showed to a Devout Ankress by Name Julian of Norwich,* Julian of Norwich (1343–1415) has emerged as an outstanding theological writer of the Church, a spectacular exception to the general rule that medieval Englishwomen did not write books. Julian breaks through a long history of feminine silence in England, and that breakthrough marks her greatest contribution to rhetorical theory and practice. Probably convent educated as a Benedictine nun of Carrow, near Norwich, Julian lived most of her life as an anchoress in the churchyard of St. Julian at Norwich (for whom she was undoubtedly named), a world of confined, virginal, and intellectual religious experience.

A question of literacy. Writing at a time when relatively few people could both read and write (either Latin or English), when the intellectual standards of most religious women and men were very low, and when society at large conducted its affairs orally, Julian translated her theology into the vernacular. Her theology spoke *to* her audience rather than *for* it; therefore, it purposefully spoke the language of those outside the influence and protection of a religious or educational academy.[64]

By her own account, Julian is "a simple creature unlettered" (*Julian,* L, ch. 2). Yet given our current understanding of medieval literacies, she could well have been "unlettered" and still have had a measure of literate behaviors from which to choose. In *Listening for the Text,* Brian Stock assures us that medieval texts did not have to be written: "oral record, memory, and reperformance sufficed. Nor did the public have to be fully lettered. Often, in fact, only the *interpres* had a direct contact with literate culture" (37). The strong oral component of medieval popular literacy meant that "the masses of people read by means of the ear rather than the eye, by hearing others read or recite rather than by reading to themselves" (Crosby 88)—those who could decipher print mediated writing to the *illitterati*.[65] The use of memory, the persistent habit of reading aloud, and the preference, even among the educated, for listening to a statement rather than scrutinizing it in script comprised popular literacy practices. The issue of Julian's ability to comprehend or produce print, then, is mitigated by the pervasiveness of popular literacy practices during the Middle Ages.

Whether Julian possessed a wide range of rhetorical and linguistic capabilities is a matter of debate; her term *unlettered* "most certainly means knowing no Latin and probably also no French" (Riehle 29); she may not have been a scholar, but she probably knew Latin and was "strongly original" (Molinari 10); the "internal evidence of her book" clearly indicates "a woman of profound intellect; and her book . . . shows such meticulous organization and literary skill that she has been ranked with Chaucer as a pioneering genius of English prose" (Janzen 15). Julian's most recent editors—Edmund Colledge and James Walsh—were led to the "inescapable conclusion" that Julian had been formally educated even before she began to compose the short text (Julian, *Julian*, S, 43). They mention her deep familiarity with "all four gospels, the Pauline and Johannine epistles and Hebrews, the Psalms, the sapiential books and Deutero-Isaias" (43). They only conjecture about "how she acquired her Latin and learning" (43).

Whether she received her textual knowledge aurally, whether she dictated her revelations to an unmentioned and educated amanuensis, or whether she received extraordinary academic training, Julian, nevertheless, demonstrates her

> knowledge of such great masters as Augustine and Gregory; and she seems to have become deeply influenced, as she composed the "second edition" of the long text, by William of St. Thierry, not only through his *Golden Epistle*, but also by other of his works, in her day known only in learned circles. Furthermore, her writing, in the long text especially, constantly displays remarkable congruity of both thought and language with contemporary English writings: notably *The Treatise of Perfection of the Sons of God*, *The Cloud of Unknowing* and *The Scale of Perfection* and their ancillary treatises, and Chaucer's *Boethius*. (Julian, *Julian*, S, 44–45)

Whatever her background, Julian composes two versions of her visionary experience that inform a rhetoric of inclusion, a rhetoric of theology that widens the circle of purposeful Christian participation.

Entering the rhetoric of religion. A rhetorical precept of great importance in the development of *ars praedicandi* was rhetorical judgment, a distinction between levels of audience capability. Jesus himself had used the parable, a narrative followed by a moral lesson, for it was not given to all people to know his message directly: "with many such parables he spoke the word to them as they were able to hear it; he did not speak to them without a parable, but privately to his own disciples he explained everything" (Mark 4.33–34). Thus, even Jesus resorted to audience analysis for the successful dissemination of his beliefs and gauged his speech accordingly.

Julian followed in that tradition; she analyzed her audience and presented herself and her information accordingly. But most important of all, she wrote in the vernacular, reaching an unlettered audience that had theretofore been neglected. Julian's decision to write both versions of her mystical material in her mother tongue was influential in yet another way: she provided an early and masterful example of vernacular prose. Like the *Ancrene Wisse* and the Katherine Group, Julian's "homiletic and devotional writings helped keep English prose alive during the years following the Norman Conquest, when French became the official language and, with Latin, threatened to squeeze out English entirely" (R. Stone 12). That French and Latin were the official languages of power—of government, religion, and education—thwarted the education of all people, particularly women.

Showings and tellings. *A Book of Showings* charts the development of Julian's assurance, understanding, and presentation of her sixteen "showings," her mystical material: "Know it well, it was no hallucination which you saw today, but accept and believe it and hold firmly to it, and you will not be overcome" (Jesus to Julian, in *Julian*, S, ch. 22).

Paul and Augustine had laid the groundwork for Julian's mystical revelations, their own relationships with God having already validated the visionary medium and supported such individualistic interpretations as Julian's. Both men had experienced the supernatural suspension of physical law central to mystical experience; both had experienced Christophanies and thus realized "the immanence of the temporal in the eternal, and of the eternal in the temporal" (Inge 5).[66] For Paul, nothing separates the soul from God; nothing "shall be able to separate us from the love of God, which is in Christ Jesus our Lord" (Rom. 8.39). In his *Confessions*, Augustine would recount his own Christophany: "What is that light whose gentle beams now and again strike through to my heart, causing me to shudder in awe yet firing me with their warmth? I shudder to feel how different I am from it: yet in so far as I am like it, I am aglow with its fire. It is the light of Wisdom" (11.9).

According to Julian's compelling accounts, she was stricken with a severe illness that peaked (on 13 May 1373) in an intensified, rather typical mystical experience. Sixteen dramatic visions (or showings), cascading for five hours, centered on the corporeal sufferings of a crucified Jesus and his silent, grieving Mother. Within the tradition of affective piety, Julian concentrated on the Passion, the physical sufferings of a human Jesus and the emotional reactions of those witnessing the prelude to and culmination of the Crucifixion. As a mystic within that tradition, she demonstrates, with naturalistic physical and emotional details, her mind's kinship with those spiritual realities:

> And suddenly it came into my mind that I ought to wish . . . that our Lord, of his gift and of his grace, would fill my body full with recollection and feeling of his blessed Passion, . . . for I wished that his pains might be my pains. . . . And at this, suddenly I saw the red blood trickling down from under the crown, all hot, flowing freely and copiously, a living stream, just as it seemed to me that it was at the time when the crown of thorns was thrust down upon his blessed head. Just so did he, both God and man, suffer for me. I perceived, truly and powerfully, that it was himself who showed this to me, without any intermediary. . . . This everything God showed me in the first vision, and he gave me space and time to contemplate it. And then the bodily vision ceased, and the spiritual vision persisted in my understanding, and I waited with reverent fear, rejoicing in what I saw and wishing, as much as I dared, to see more, if that were God's will, or to see for a longer time what I had already seen. (*Julian*, S, chs. 4–5)

In her initial version, she presents herself as a devout Christian woman with slow-burning religious fervor—validated by the Holy Spirit. Yet she evinces twinges of disquietude regarding her right to speak of her union with God. Julian prudently assesses and explains her rhetorical situation as a woman writing:

> I pray you all for God's sake, and I counsel you for your own profit, that you disregard the wretched worm, the sinful creature to whom it was shown, and that mightily, wisely, lovingly and meekly you contemplate God, who out of his courteous love and his endless goodness was willing to show his vision generally, to the comfort of us all. . . . And I am sure that anyone who sees it so will be taught the truth and be comforted, if he have need of comfort. But God forbid that you should say or assume that I am a teacher, for that is not and never was my intention; for I am a woman, ignorant, weak and frail. (S, ch. 6)

Both versions express Julian's mystical union with God and move from the initial, detailed transcript of her insecurity with her new position and anxiety about her material to an enriched version, written after some twenty years' brooding and reflection. The second, longer version promotes her meditative assurance in eternal mysteries and in her oneness with all people and with God:

> And for the great endless love that God has for all mankind, he makes no distinction in love between the blessed soul of Christ and the least soul that will be saved. For it is very easy to believe and trust that the dwelling of the blessed soul of Christ is very high in the glorious divinity; and truly, as I understand our Lord to mean, where the blessed soul of Christ is, there is the substance of all the souls which will be saved. (L, ch. 54)

Julian, "ignorant, weak and frail," continues on her course of developing a theology, claiming her rightful place as God's messenger: "But because I am a woman, ought I therefore to believe that I should not tell you of the goodness of God, when I saw at that same time that it is his will that it be known?" (S, ch. 4).

Julian's rhetoric of theology. Rightfully, then, Julian joins the established tradition of religious mysticism in England. Yet her religious disclosures take her further than membership in that tradition: the understanding, interpretation, and precise recording of her mystical revelations entitle her to join the ranks of Christian rhetors (Augustine's teachers, preachers, and movers), particularly as she develops a rhetoric of theology. Besides providing the earliest extant English writing by a woman and contributing distinctly to the rise of the vernacular as a literary language, the religious rhetoric Julian develops expressly modifies the patriarchy made sacred in prevailing Christianity and ensures the rhetorical possibility of a Margery Kempe.

After some twenty years' contemplation of her showings and initial version, Julian began to revise her understanding of her experience, as Jesus would have her do, into a second, longer version. Denise Nowakowski Baker reminds us that such "affective meditation on the humanity of Christ . . . initiates a process of moral reform that prepares the meditator for the more spiritual contemplation of Christ's divinity" (26). Thus, Julian's wish for a connection with a human God permits her to fuse his humanity—and hers—with his divinity and her spirituality: "I saw no difference between God and our substance, but, as it were, all God; and still my understanding accepted that our substance is in God, that is to say that God is God, and our substance is a creature in God" (*Julian*, L, ch. 54).

In terms of her language, her *Revelations* convincingly illustrates the dialectical relationship between humans and God in the process of union, a cornerstone of her theology: "Prayer unites the soul to God. . . . [P]rayer is a witness that the soul wills as God wills" (L, ch. 43). "It is quicker for us and easier to come to the knowledge of God than it is to know our own soul. For our soul is so deeply grounded in God and so endlessly treasured that we cannot come to knowledge of it until we first have knowledge of God, who is the Creator to whom it is united" (L, ch. 56).

The unity of all existence is a fundamental doctrine of mysticism: God is in all, and all is in God. Therefore, Julian's concentration on a human Jesus allows her to identify with his God-man on human terms. And her mysticism, her human connectedness with God, transforms her rhetorical situation: no longer is she a solitary supplicant to an ineffable God; she transcends her earthly condition to reach a dialogic relationship with the human side of her God that culminates in her theological understandings and insights, which she must then share with others. For instance, after witnessing the Passion, Julian writes: "The fair skin was deeply broken into the tender flesh through the vicious blows delivered all over the lovely body. The hot blood ran over so plentifully that neither skin nor wounds could be seen, but everything seemed to be blood" (L, ch. 12). Jesus asks her, "Are you well satisfied that I suffered for you? . . . If you are satisfied . . . I am satisfied. It is a joy and a bliss and an endless delight to me that ever I suffered my Passion for you, for if I could suffer more, I would" (S, ch. 12). Julian is "lifted up into heaven" by his reply. Her dialogue with this human-God is one she wants to open up to all Christians.[67]

Julian's regional reputation as a holy woman was no doubt linked to her ability to deliver a rhetoric of theology her listening audience could readily understand. However, she was probably not well known as an author during her life, for "the small number of extant manuscripts and the late date of most of them indicate that *A Book of Showings* did not circulate widely" (Baker 3). All her eventual readers, though, including us, continue to appreciate her lucid prose style and her theology, as well as her complete ease with being a female interpreter of the divine, her individualistic piety, and her eventual influence. But besides its accessibility, Julian's rhetoric of theology distinguishes itself in yet another way: it transforms traditional medieval Christianity (that masculinist enterprise of male gods and male religious privilege) into a religion of openness and equality for all, male and female, cloistered and lay.

In her earlier version, Julian had revealed herself to be somewhat of a moralizer, flustered by her rivalry with fellow Christians:

> Everything I say about myself I mean to apply to all my fellow Christians, for I am taught that this is what our Lord intends in this spiritual revelation. . . . And you who hear and see this vision and this teaching, which is from Jesus Christ for the edification of your souls, it is God's will and my wish that you accept it with as much joy and delight as if Jesus had shown it to you as he did to me. . . . I am not good because of the revelation, but only if I love God better, and so can and so should every man do who sees it and hears it with good will and proper intention. And so it is my desire that it should be to every man the same profit that I asked for myself." (*Julian*, S, ch. 6)

Her later text—the re-vision—reveals a woman more confident in the significance and application of her showings to the point that, as Augustine would have it, the message overshadows the medium (*On Christian* 4.27.59). Julian skillfully closes the original distance between herself and other Christians to establish Burkean identification with her audience, a vast and tender perception of unity with God and all of humanity.[68] She uses first-person plural to speak in unison with her fellow votaries, moving their oneness toward oneness with God:

> God is our true peace; and he is protector when we ourselves are in disquiet, and he constantly works to bring us into endless peace. And so when by the operation of mercy and grace we are made meek and mild, then we are wholly safe. Suddenly the soul is united to God, when she is truly pacified in herself, for in him is found no wrath. . . . [W]hen we are wholly in peace and in love, we find no contrariness in any kind of hindrance, and our Lord God in his goodness makes the contrariness which is in us now very profitable for us. . . .
> So is God our steadfast foundation, and he will be our whole joy, and he will make us as unchangeable as he is when we are there. (*Julian*, L, ch. 49)

Julian's treatise breathes warmth and humanity into theology, merging the love of God with God's love for all of humanity.

Inclusionary religious rhetoric. Julian writes out of her experiential knowledge and moves toward action that improves the spiritual lives of all men and all women. In the broadest sense, then, she practices a kind of feminist liberatory theology. Now, to say that Julian of Norwich is a protofeminist would be anachronistic. But if being a protofeminist means articulating a "self-consciousness about women's identity both as inherited cultural fact and as process of social construction," then Julian was indeed a pioneering feminist, of a special kind (Nancy K. Miller, qtd. in Heilbrun 18). After all, "the critical principle of feminist theology is the promotion of the full humanity of women. Whatever denies, diminishes, or distorts the full humanity of women is, therefore, appraised as not redemptive . . . [nor] reflect[ive of] the divine or an authentic relation to the divine" (Ruether, *Sexism* 18–19). Feminist theology gives women a place in religion; liberatory theology welcomes them to that place—in language they understand. Julian's theology of inclusion, written in the vernacular, extends specifically to women; it includes all women in the worship of and dialogue with God, as well as including a female representation in the Trinity. As she persuasively urges this theology of inclusion, she enacts an expansion of the medieval rhetorical tradition.

The parabolic and hortatory teachings of Church Fathers and male clerics demanded that Christian women desex themselves. The fundamental maleness of Christian theology regulated the possibilities for female redemption—but not according to Julian. As though she were a twentieth-century feminist arguing that traditional scripture and theology were codified according to male experiences rather than universal human experience, Julian argued for women's place within the spiritual and eschatological sociology of a masculine Church. She quoted Jesus himself, not the Church Fathers, for Jesus had preached equality: "Come unto me, all ye that labour and are heavy laden, and I will give you rest." "For whosoever shall do the will of my Father which is in heaven, the same is my brother, and sister, and mother" (Matt. 11.28, 12.50). Enacting a kind of feminist liberatory praxis, Julian ensures that Christianity neither excludes nor desexes female followers; women are central to Julian's theology.

Julian's theology of inclusion builds on the belief that all of humankind, male and female, are created in God's image. For her, God encompasses both sexes, and she goes so far as to specify the male and female natures of the Holy Trinity. After all, "the deity can be referred to only metaphorically as a person and . . . any assignment of sex or attribution of gender to the Creator projects the conditions of creatureliness onto the ineffable" (Baker 108). Julian writes: "[M]an is blinded in this life, and therefore we cannot see our Father, God, as he is. And when he of his goodness wishes to show himself to man, he shows himself familiar, like a man, even though I saw truly that we ought to know and believe that the Father is not man" (*Julian*, L, ch. 51).

The Father is not only man. According to Julian, the Godhead is both spiritual and human, both male and female—transcendent of all imaginable difference. The relationships among the human-imposed categories are fluid and dynamic: "I saw that God rejoices that he is our Father, and God rejoices that he is our Mother, and God rejoices that he is our true spouse, and that our soul is his beloved wife" (L, ch. 52). "God the blessed Trinity," according to Julian, has three properties: fatherhood, motherhood, and lordship—all in one God (L, ch. 58). Refusing to desex herself as a worthy Christian, Julian nevertheless unsexes the maleness of God, of Jesus, of Christianity, with a feminine and masculine Christology through which women and men could be liberated and redeemed—as women and as men:

> In our almighty Father we have our protection and our bliss, . . . for he is our Mother, brother and saviour; and in our good Lord the Holy Spirit we have our reward and our gift for our living and our labour. . . . [T]he high might of the Trinity is our Father, and the deep wisdom of the Trinity is our Mother, and the great love of the Trinity is our Lord; and all these we have in nature and in our substantial creation. (L, ch. 58)

In addition to making a rightful place for women as worshipers, she also protects their place in the Holy Trinity. Julian had, of course, followed a traditional belief of equating the Holy Spirit with feminine Sophia, or Wisdom, but she goes even further to prepare a place for women in Christianity: she takes Mary's divinity to its ultimate conclusion, uniting her motherhood totally with Jesus. Thus, Jesus becomes our Holy Mother in the Holy Family:

> Our great Father, almighty God, who is being, knows us and loved us before time began. Out of this knowledge, in his most wonderful deep love, by the prescient eternal counsel of all the blessed Trinity, he wanted the second person to become our Mother, our brother and our saviour. From this it follows that as truly as God is our Father, so truly is God our Mother. Our Father wills, our Mother works, our good Lord the Holy Spirit confirms. And therefore it is our part to love our God in whom we have our being, reverently thanking and praising him for our creation, mightily praying to our Mother for mercy and pity, and to our Lord the Holy Spirit for help and grace. . . .
> And so Jesus is our true Mother in nature by our first creation, and he is our true Mother in grace by his taking our created nature. All the lovely works and all the sweet loving offices of beloved motherhood are appropriated to the second person, for in him we have this godly will. . . .
> I understand three ways of contemplating motherhood in God. The first is the foundation of our nature's creation; the second is his taking of our nature, where the motherhood of grace begins; the third is the motherhood at work. And in that, by the same grace, everything is penetrated, . . . and it is all one love. (L, ch. 59)

"All one love" is Julian's description of union among the Trinity and among all human creation. She extends the traditional familiar father-son analogy of the Trinity to include Jesus as mother and brother, her rhetoric enveloping all souls, all creation, and all sexes.

Trusting in the maternal tenderness of Jesus and the Holy Mother, Julian replicates that tenderness. First of all, she assures humans that they can know themselves by knowing God; God is manifested in all creation just as all creation exists in God. Just as God and creation cannot be separated, neither can substance and sensuality—not since Jesus reintegrated substance and sensuality and thus brought a wholeness to the fallen self. God and creation, sensuality and substance, are one, whole, complete. She writes that

> our substance is in God, and . . . God is in our sensuality, for in that same instant and place in which our soul is made sensual . . . exists the city of God, ordained for him from without beginning. He comes into this city and will never depart from it, for God is never out of the soul, in which he will dwell blessedly without end.
>
> . . . The place that Jesus takes in our soul he will never depart from. And all the gifts which God can give to the creature he has given to his Son Jesus for us, which gifts he, dwelling in us, has enclosed in him until the time that we are fully grown, our soul together with our body and our body together with our soul. . . .
>
> And so my understanding was led by God to see in him and to know, to understand and to recognize that our soul is a created trinity, like the uncreated blessed Trinity, known and loved from without beginning, and in the creation united to the Creator. (L, ch. 55)

Second, she transmits that holy tenderness, that "familiar love," in her role as spiritual guide. Visiting and departing from her cell as they wished, people came to "Mother Julian" in search of spiritual advice and consolation. She writes that it is "truly love which moves me to tell it to you, for I want God to be known and my fellow Christians to prosper." "I pray you all for God's sake, and I counsel you for your own profit . . . that mightily, wisely and meekly you contemplate upon God" (S, ch. 5; L, ch. 8). The *Revelations* came to her, but they were for everyone: "I am not good because of the revelations, but only if I love God better; and inasmuch as you love God better, it is more to you than to me. I do not say this to those who are wise, because they know it well. But I say it to you who are simple, to give you comfort and strength; for we are all one in love" (L, ch. 9). Her union with God has allowed her to embody a small portion of his vast tenderness.

For Julian, true peace was impossible without perfect union with God. Through his mercy and grace, she achieves oneness, a goal for all Christians. Any tenderness she shows to Christians is immeasurably small in relation to the tenderness and love of the Creator, who "is to us everything which is good and comforting for our help. He is our clothing, who wraps and enfolds us for love, embraces us and shelters us, surrounds us for his love, which is so tender that he may never desert us" (L, ch. 5).

Although Mother Julian, tender and wise, could not always expect her audience to appreciate the full scope of her rhetorical or theological ability, she could rely on them to recognize her biblical sources and to sense her formidable intelligence. Frances Beer writes of Julian's "clarity" and her "deep humility," two factors that ensure her use of accessible language—and evangelical success (138). Julian's sensitive attention to her projected ethos, her own image as spokeswoman for God in terms of her mostly uneducated, most assuredly mixed audience, is especially impressive. Because she wants to share the significance of her showings, she takes care not to alienate any of her audience, particularly the males, for any reason. She uses the humility topos repeatedly as she invokes God's tenderness, love, and inclusiveness—all to her advantage, the better to secure goodwill and then moralize.

Julian's influence. Julian was much valued for advice and spiritual guidance during her years as a recluse, but once she had finished the longer version of her *Revelations*, she wrote no more, apparently satisfied that she had transmitted as accurately as possible all it was her responsibility to make known. In England, her *Revelations* has had long-term influence as a classic of English piety, establishing as it did a female tradition of religious visionary literature and her own superior literary and theological understanding. She participates in the Christian movement seeking simplicity in preaching and uses rhetorical restraint to underline the sublimity of her feelings.

Julian wrote at a time when the Catholic Church was under attack from the Lollards, who wanted to reform the Church of its clerical and religious abuses. John Wycliffe's followers had a deep devotion to the human Jesus, which Julian came to share. Their push for popularizing the English vernacular and thereby making the entire Bible available to all people was considered heretical, as was their leniency with women preachers. Yet, safely anchored in her cloister, Julian followed their beliefs and developed her own, composing a theology in English, not Latin. She combines an emphasis on unity and love to her singular purpose, effectively adapting rhetorical devices to accomplish what few of her age—and no other Englishwoman—had been able to do. In her production of *Revelations*, she rendered seemingly intractable matter, the *process* of her visions and locutions, into a beautifully balanced and cogent rhetoric of theology.

Julian of Norwich was not the only woman to make a name for herself in English letters, however. But her rhetorical praxis paved the way for Margery Kempe, a bourgeois woman some thirty years her junior, who gave voice to the visionary religious laywoman. Born at about the time of Julian's showings, Margery went to Mother Julian's cell for study and guidance regarding her own mystical revelations:

> Then she was bid by our Lord to go to an anchoress in the same city, named Dame Julian. And so she did and showed her the grace that God put into her soul, of compunction, contrition, sweetness and devotion, compassion with holy meditation and high contemplation, and full many holy speeches and dalliances that our Lord spoke to her soul, and many wonderful revelations which she showed the anchoress to know if there were any deceit in them, for the anchoress was expert in such things, and could give good counsel.
>
> The anchoress, hearing the marvelous goodness of our Lord, thanked God with

all her heart for his visitation, counseling this creature [Margery] to be obedient to the will of our Lord God and to fulfill with all her might whatever he put in her soul, if it were not against the worship of God, and profit of her fellow Christians, for if it were, then it were not the moving of a good spirit, but rather of an evil spirit. . . .

Much was the holy dalliance that the anchoress and this creature had by communing in the love of Our Lord Jesus Christ the many days that they were together. (Kempe 18.20a.5–35)[69]

Margery's testimony about seeking Julian's spiritual guidance is particularly convincing because it echoes Julian's own language and thought.

Like Julian, Margery was a mystic who had communicated with God and who demonstrated typical late medieval longing for the Passion. And like Julian, she was a woman writing prose in the vernacular—a practice reserved exclusively for saving souls or improving morals (for instance, Chaucer's "Tale of Melibee").[70] Margery, however, is both saving souls *and* improving morals with her vernacular prose. Neither woman acknowledged receiving conventional training in Latin rhetoric or composition. In both cases, they documented their mystical experiences approximately twenty years after the fact. And both writers had the same avowed goal: to help others achieve greater knowledge and appreciation of God's ways. Together these women are the most prominent female authors of Middle English devotional prose, devotional rhetoric.

Margery Kempe and a Rhetoric of Autobiography

In her prologue, Chaucer's Wife of Bath tells us, "Experience, though noon auctoritee / Were in this world, is right ynough for me / To speke of wo that is in mariage" (lines1–3). Not a churchman, she had no authority to speak of marriage or of womanhood; not a flesh-and-blood woman, she could tap only fictional experience. Powerful and compelling though they may be, the Wife of Bath and her tale reflect the interest of a man, Chaucer, the artist. Neither Wife nor tale is the creation of a woman, and the Wife herself wishes that "wommen hadde writen stories" (line 693).

Nearly fifty years later (1432–36), a woman wrote a story of marriage and womanhood and religion. Margery Brunham Kempe (1373–c. 1439) of Lynn, a cosmopolitan English town, created both her self and her life story with her spiritual autobiography, *The Book of Margery Kempe*. Daughter of a prominent family, wife of a less-prestigious burgess, and mother of fourteen children, Margery left her relatively comfortable life to answer God's call to weep (her "gift of tears") and to pray for the souls of her fellow Christians—and not to do so in a cell or convent but throughout England, Europe, and the Holy Land. In old age, she dictated to scribes (to one about 1431 and to the other in 1436) an autobiography that recounted the trials and triumphs of her physical and spiritual pilgrimage. Her *Book* would lie neglected but preserved until 1934, when Hope Emily Allen identified it and helped Sanford Brown Meech edit the unique manuscript, long the possession of the Butler-Bowdon estate. And since the 1940 publication of Margery's *Book* by the Early English Text Society (Meech and Allen's literal copy of the manuscript), this historical pilgrim has often been compared with Chaucer's Wife, her literary antecedent. True, both mobile, bourgeois women "hadde passed many a straunge strem" (Chaucer, "General Prologue," line 464): each travels without her spouse; both are outspoken, opinionated, and strong willed; and each speaks frankly about her life.

But Margery Kempe speaks to us on her own, through a character created by herself. She is the first woman to compose her life story in English (although Julian of Norwich seems to have been the first woman to write about herself), and that story is the earliest extant autobiography in English. Her female literary contemporaries were mostly erudite women, writing in Latin or French, enclosed within religious orders. Her male literary contemporaries (Chaucer, the Gawain poet, the mystery playwrights, Malory) immediately gained the support of a public or courtly audience. Margery Kempe, however, gives voice to a largely silent and unsung force, the voice of the middle-class, uneducated woman determined to be understood on her own terms: "I preach not . . . ; I come into no pulpit. I use but communication and good words, and that I will do while I live" (52.60b.5).

Locating a rhetorical space. In *Writing a Woman's Life*, Carolyn G. Heilbrun asserts that "power is the ability to take one's place in whatever discourse is essential to action and the right to have one's part matter" (18). Gaining that power often requires translating one's own opinions into the dominant idiom by employing *dialogism* (a technique I explain below). Despite her lack of formal training, Margery was a skillful and powerful rhetorician, for she located herself within the particular discourse of Franciscan affective piety, where she could self-consciously author and own the story of her life, create her self, record her spiritual development, and, most important, validate her life and her visions to her "authorial audience," the hypothetical audience for whom each author designs her text. Although she makes certain that her "narrative audience," the person each flesh-and-blood reader must pretend to be in order to believe the text is real and to respond accordingly to the narrator, understands and believes that her words and actions actually took place, she does not try to win its approval.[7] In fact, she regularly offends that audience as she composes her self. More important to her seems to be her authorial audience, which she privileges by gauging her ethos to its satisfaction and approbation. That projected ethos—that convergence of spirituality, selfhood, and authorship—which creates antithetical responses, constitutes Margery's unique contribution to rhetorical practice.

Margery did just what the great Cistercian and Franciscan writers had directed the devout to do: within the tradition of affective piety, she freely contemplated the Gospels, meshed her own individual history with the sacred history of the Scriptures, and used her imagination to experience life with Jesus (Despres 3). And as a mystic within that tradition, Margery demonstrated her mind's kinship with spiritual realities. Her divine visions allowed her to communicate with God, love Jesus in his humanity, attend the Virgin, and participate with all her emotions in the joy and grief of the Christian story: "Daughter, I will make all the world wonder at you, and many a man and many a woman will speak of me for love of you, and worship me in you" (Jesus to Margery, 30.36a.35).

Mystics functioned effectively within the whole of medieval life and participated in the customary late-medieval longing for the Passion (Petroff). Women mystics rallied around an all-purpose figure of Jesus as lover, spouse, and teacher, but they were especially attached to Jesus the sufferer.

Composing her self. Referring to herself as "this creature," a fairly common medieval usage, the lively and gregarious Margery opens her *Book* with the life-threatening experience of her first childbed, a scene that relates her first visions and invites the appearance of Christ.

> When this creature was twenty years of age, . . . she was married to a worshipful burgess and was with child within a short time, as nature would. And after she had conceived, she was belabored with great accesses till the child was born and then, what with the labor she had in childing, and the sickness going before, she despaired of her life, imagining she might not live. . . . And anon, for the dread she had of damnation . . . , this creature went out of her mind and was amazingly vexed and labored with spirits for half a year, eight weeks, and several days. And during this time, she thought she saw devils opening their mouths all inflamed with billows of fire as though they should swallow her. . . . And also the devils cried upon her with great threats and bid her to forsake Christendom, her faith, and deny her God, His Mother, and all the saints in Heaven. . . . Whatever the spirits tempted her to say and do she said and did. . . . And, when she had long been labored . . . , Our Merciful Lord Christ Jesus, ever to be trusted, worshipped be His Name, never forsaking His servant in time of need, appeared to His creature which had forsaken Him, in the likeness of a man, most seemly, most beauteous, and most amiable that ever might be seen with man's eye, clad in a mantle of purple silk, sitting upon her bedside, looking upon her with so blessed a countenance that she was strengthened in all her spirits, and He said to her these words, "Daughter, why hast thou forsaken Me, and I forsook never thee?" And anon, as He said these words, . . . this creature became stable in her reason as well as ever she was before. (1.3b.5–32, 4a.19, 21–25, 28–31, 4b.36–37, 8–22, 26–27)

The first of many scholars to discount Margery's spirituality and consider her *Book* an anecdotal curiosity, R. W. Chambers writes that *The Book of Margery Kempe* "may disappoint or even shock the reader" and that we "must come to her not expecting too much" (xviii). A deterrent to taking her narrative seriously seems to have been that she begins her holy revelations postpartum, inviting many scholars to assume she was in the midst of a postpartum depression. Such "hysteria" serves to remind scholars of its origin as God's curse against Eve (Knowles 146; Chambers xv–xxvi; Thurston; Meech liv, lxv, in Kempe; R. Stone 35). And scholars continue to view Margery's spirituality as hysterical. Hope Phyllis Weissman takes Margery seriously; nevertheless, in her "Margery Kempe in Jerusalem: *Hysterica compassio* in the Late Middle Ages," she tells us that "to diagnose Margery's case as 'hysteria' need not be to trivialize her significance or reduce her *Book*'s value as cultural testimony" (202). Indeed, the *Book* provides valuable testimony to religious, cultural, business, and literary practices.

In what is often a moving narration, Margery reveals herself to be a woman who could neither read nor write, dependent upon amanuenses to record her story: "[W]e are probably safe . . . in assuming that the *Book of Margery Kempe* represents the kind of prose that Margery herself would have written had she not been illiterate" (R. Wilson 105). In fact, the manuscript begins with the priest's incipit, in which he recounts his tribulations in attempting to revise the previous priest's transcription of Margery's text:

> Then there was a priest for which this creature had great affection, and so she . . . brought him the [first transcription of the] book to read. The book was so "evil" written that he could discriminate little of it, for it was neither good English nor German, nor were the letters shaped nor formed as other letters were. Therefore, the priest truly believed that no man would ever read it, except by special blessing. . . . [But eventually] he read every word of it to this creature, she sometimes helping where there was any difficulty. (Proem, 2b.12–18, 3a.11–12)

"Evil written" as it may have been, if Margery's *Book* had originally found a broad contemporary audience, it would have contributed to the widespread resumption of English as a written medium in the fifteenth century, to "the triumph of the vernacular" (Szarmach 14). And it might also have played some small part in the drama of the English Reformation. But for us and for now, the book merits attention not only because it seems to be the earliest extant, large-scale narrative written in English prose (verse was, of course, another matter), but also because it introduces unprecedented artistic and rhetorical techniques. Her self-disclosing, candid, direct view of contemporary life gives her text a verisimilitude rarely found in devotional or soul-saving literature. Margery "would seem to be an early, if not the first, example in English prose literature of the skillful use of dramatically appropriate dialogue based on the substantial memory of what had taken place" (Knowles 144). No English writer had committed to writing such an intimate, revealing, and humane account of life and thoughts. Perhaps only a woman (untrained in and unconscious of standard rhetorical and literary practices) would assert her *self* this way.

A rhetoric of autobiography. Like any autobiographer, Margery Kempe was convinced that her life was special, her life story valuable to readers distant in time or space. In service of that significance, she had to shape the raw material of her inner and outer experience—spiritual, emotional, intellectual, and so-cial—into a memorable narrative. And memorable it is, though neither predict-ably coherent nor conventionally chronological. Like many of Margery's con-temporaries, then, her future scholarly audience has often judged her and her book to be incoherent, exaggerated piety, regardless of her circumstances, mo-tivation, or intention. But Margery's mysticism derives its impact from experi-ence of feeling; she offers pathetic testimony, not logical proof. Her visions are in accord with the tenor of her personal faith: Jesus had singled her out among women to suffer, to preach (saving souls and improving morals), to receive his steadfast love, and to be saved.

The absence of chronology in Margery's narrative seems to render it logi-cally incoherent, a problem that not even her second scribe could rectify, as explained in this disclaimer:

> This book is not written in order, everything after the other as it is usually done, but like the matter came to the creature in mind when it should be written, for it was so long before it was written that she had forgotten the time and the order that things happened. And therefore she wrote nothing except what she knew right well for the very truth. (Proem, 3a.12–18)

Instead of being linear, *The Book of Margery Kempe* is cyclical and associational, a record of her spiritual development—the stages exemplified by sickness, con-version, travel, evangelism, persecution, and divine intervention. By associat-ing her own development with incidents in Jesus's life, Margery blurs her the-ology with her autobiography. Although her narrative is loosely organized (akin to the edifying homily structurally but to the exhortative sermon the-matically), she effectively marshals the information within each true-to-life, self-contained vignette, just as the best of fiction writers, commingling homely, even commonplace events with rather self-satisfied descriptions of her great devotion, her intimacy with Jesus, and the gradual routing of those who op-pose or mock her (opposition, mocking, and routing are practices consistent not only with Jesus's life but with saints' lives as well). And her presentation of her created self, what Wayne C. Booth calls the "implied author" (71–75), achieves one of her most important rhetorical effects.

Although Margery unknowingly relaxes conventional distinctions of genre and structure, she deliberately exerts distinctions of audience for calcu-lated rhetorical ends, especially between the authorial audience and the narra-tive audience. Both her story and her character appeal to the authorial audi-ence, though they often perturb the narrative audience. And "this creature" frequently offends the "immediate audience," the other characters within her narrative. Like all authors, Margery would have no guaranteed control over the "actual audience," the flesh-and-blood people who read the text (Rabi-nowitz 126).

The conversion scene illustrates her rhetorical technique. After Jesus's initial appearance to her, which restored her health, Margery returns to her vain, proud, and superficially religious ways. Only after the failures of her brewery and her mill is she humbled enough to turn wholly to God. The circumstances of her conversion serve as a morality tale to her authorial audience, for her visions had led eventually to self-understanding and to a movement from fearful sinner to favorite child of God:

> And, when this creature had thus graciously come again to her mind, she thought that she was bound to God and that she would be His servant. Nevertheless, she would not leave her pride or her pompous array. . . . All her desire was to be worshipped by the people. She would not take heed of any chastisement, nor be content with the goods that God had sent her, as her husband was, but ever desired more and more. . . . [After her business failures,] some said she was accursed; some said God took open vengeance on her. . . . And some wise men, whose minds were more grounded in the love of Our Lord, said that it was the high mercy of Our Lord Jesus Christ that called her from the pride and vanity of the wretched world. And then this creature, seeing all these adversities coming on every side, · thought they were the scourges of Our Lord that would chastise her for her sin. Then she asked God's mercy, and forsook her pride, her covetousness, and the desire that she had for the worship of the world, and did great bodily penance, and began to enter the way of everlasting life as shall be told hereafter. (2.5a.7–10, 2.5a–b.27–30, 2.6a.36–38, 1–10)

"This creature" projects a sense of radical dependency on God for her ongoing creation, a projection grounded in the humility topos. Although Margery's consistent reference to herself as "this creature" is probably in deference to her Creator, this common usage also serves to remind us that this illiterate "creature" was in constant collaboration with her scribes: Margery told her story to men who then wrote it out. Yet this Christian woman—devout/arrogant, humble/forceful, feverish/submissive—actually creates herself, a complicated and sometimes contradictory ("real") self. And these "real" selves—mystic, woman, author—connect in a narrative sequence that sanctions her words and actions. In fact, this nexus of selves, this ethos, subsumes her vernacular evangelical prose to appeal in varying degrees to different audiences.

Margery's implied author, her implied version of her self, shapes the narration and selects the events to present a carefully wrought ethos. From the outset, the ethos Margery introduces is her only means of self-preservation, both within the written text and within the text of her life. Margery the actual author (the flesh-and-blood woman) creates Margery the implied author (a persona that dictates to the scribe) who creates Margery the character ("this creature"). Hence, Margery Kempe is preserved.

The historical Margery, the actual composer of the text, employs what has come to be known in theoretical circles as *dialogism*, a conversation among conflicting intentions, values, claims, opinions—a conversation among her selves. Margery creates a heteroglossic self (Bakhtin 324), stratified by the voices of the implied author, the third-person narrator, and the character—three Margerys in all. Thus, *The Book of Margery Kempe*, presented as nonfiction, subtly implements highly sophisticated fictional techniques—and demonstrates the refinement of her rhetorical method.

What is most impressive—amazing, in fact—about this medieval fictionalized nonfiction is Margery's use of *instabilities* and *tensions*, narrative dynamics with Burkean resonances (Phelan). Burke tells us that form in literature is "an arousing and fulfillment of desires" (*Counter-Statement* 124) and that form is "'correct' in so far as it gratifies the needs it creates" (138). But narrative movement is also shaped by "instabilities between characters [which are] created by situations, and complicated and resolved through actions" and by tensions among values, beliefs, opinions, knowledge, and expectations within the discourse itself (Phelan 15).

The Book of Margery Kempe manifests both instabilities and tensions, and they lead to two results. First, the implied author evokes a sympathetic response in the authorial audience for the historical Margery, who longs for confirmation of her mystic status. (Although the author wants all readers to join the authorial audience, not every reader will want or be able to join that hypothetical group.) Second, the narrator (who was created by the implied author) reveals neither sympathy nor admiration for Margery the character, "this creature." Hence, the response to Margery of the narrative audience duplicates the response of the characters in the story: both her narrative audience and the characters within her story find Margery's single-minded moralizing and constant interference annoying, if not harassing. Such a negative response seems perfectly reasonable given the narrative line. And the implied author, the Margery who dictates her memoirs, ultimately engineers both positive and negative responses to a version of her self.

The following scene between Margery and her husband exemplifies the implied author's rhetorical technique; the scene strikes a sympathetic chord in the authorial audience and dissonance in the narrative and immediate audiences. This scene also typifies the narrator's purposeful use of gossipy anecdotes and fresh dialogue, a striking effect strengthened by her natural and homely figurative language. Margery spends many years of her marriage trying to dissuade her husband from their sexual relationship, and the account of her ultimate success is engaging and homespun.

It befell on a Friday on Midsummer Eve in right hot weather, as this creature was coming from York-ward bearing a bottle with beer in her hand and her husband a cake in his bosom, that he asked his wife this question, "Margery, if there came a man with a sword and would smite off my head unless I should commune naturally with you as I have done before, tell me the truth of your conscience—for ye say ye will not lie—whether ye would suffer my head to be smitten off or else suffer me to meddle with you again, as I did at one time?" "Alas, sir," said she, "why raise this matter when we have been chaste these eight weeks?" "For I will know the truth of your heart." And then she said with great sorrow, "Forsooth, I would rather see you be slain than we should turn again to our uncleanness." And he said again, "Ye are no good wife." (II.12a.9–24)

The implied author commands Margery the character's native tongue for use in her own self-definition and self-defense. Although the implied author is doing the commanding, ensuring that the narrator gives Margery the character a believable "voice," the narrator is telling the story, and the character is doing her own speaking. Yet all this commanding belongs to the flesh-and-blood author, the historical Margery, the artist. The rhetorical style (including tone and voice) of the artist is effectively matched to the implied author's aim: to impress upon her readers (the authorial and narrative audiences) her chastity, a form of spiritual expression that offers psychic freedom. After all, Margery the character's witness to God's love (her contrition and compassion) merited spiritual graces designed to earn and to validate publicly the recovery of her virginal purity, the most valuable of all God's gifts. The implied author is taking full advantage of this opportunity to justify "this creature's" behavior by remaking, re-membering, and re-creating her life to her readers (her authorial and narrative audiences).

Yet this created Margery seems to have no good sense of *immediate audience* (the other characters within her story), for her accounts are replete with her offensive behavior at home and abroad. Not dedicated to the vow of silence, Margery the character reproves even the highest Church officials for what she considers moral lapses: lacking moral courage and shirking responsibility. And although these same Church officials may have questioned her behavior, none of them refuted her doctrine or denied her persistent petitions (to live apart from her husband, wear white clothes, go on pilgrimage, and receive weekly communion). She was permitted to live the life God commanded and she wanted. She also preached to people wherever she found them. Her absolute certainty of her own moral and spiritual superiority, her dizzying intimacy with Jesus, her inconceivable apprenticeship as a saint—characteristics fused to a formidable and flamboyant self-glorification—annoy most of her narrative audience. Her fellow Christians within the immediate audience taunt, harass, molest, and abandon her; she is an especially easy target for their derision because she travels without the protection of her husband.

Her incessant religious harangues, her moralizing, and her sobbing fits (exacerbated by her perpetual neediness) infuriate nearly everyone she meets, especially those on pilgrimage:

They were most displeased because she wept so much and spoke always of the love and goodness of Our Lord, as much at the table as in other places. And therefore shamefully they reproved her and severely scolded her and said they would not suffer her as her husband did when she was at home and in England. . . . And then she said to one of them specially, "Ye cause me much shame and great grievance." He answered again anon, "I pray God that the devil's death may overcome thee soon and quickly." . . . They cut her gown so short that it came but little beneath her knee and made her put on a white canvas, in the manner of a sacken apron, so that she should be held a fool and the people should not make much of her or hold her in repute. . . . And, notwithstanding all their malice, she was held in more worship than they were, wherever they went. (26.30a.18–23, 31–34, 30b.14–18, 20–22)

In her witness to God's love, Margery the character's retrospective account answers her critics and explains apparent mistakes and inconsistencies, but in no way does her account, especially of her degrading attire, mitigate the response of the other characters within the immediate audience.

Margery's rhetorical purposefulness translates into her creation of herself as character: "Things might have been easier for Margery, if she had been a recluse. At large in the world, people found her a nuisance. In a cell, where people could come and speak to her when they wished, and depart when they liked, Margery would have fitted better into medieval life" (Chambers xix). For instance, when her visions transport her to the scene of the Christ's interment (according to Franciscan participatory meditation, the penitent should envision or re-create scriptural events), Margery treats the mournful Blessed Mother as though she were just another to-be-helped Christian, giving Mary unsolicited care and advice:

Then the creature thought, when Our Lady was come home and was laid down on a bed, that she made for Our Lady a good caudle [a warm, medicinal beverage] and brought it her to comfort her, and then Our Lady said unto her, "Take it away, daughter. Give me no food, but mine own Child." The creature answered, "Ah! Blessed Lady, ye must needs comfort yourself and cease of your sorrowing." (81.95a.5–12)

But such behavior—appreciated or no—establishes the Margery character's ethos; she wants to present herself and be recognized as a religious woman, one singled out above all other humans, to be saved at once (without the pains of purgatory). Margery is determined not only to be "worthwhile" but also to be "recognized as such," to be a respected mystic (Leuba 121). Despite their profession of humility, obedience, and long-suffering, the great mystics should not be categorized as meek and purposeless. On the contrary, "Their light shall not shine under a bushel. They show the firmest purpose and accept no influence that does not lead where they want to go" (121). Far from being an incoherent hysteric, Margery the implied author is, instead, a careful artist, fashioning a character who behaves consistently within a well-established social and spiritual context.

In addition to her good works and witnessing, the Margery character is also intensely interested in her weeping fits and her clothes (an interest that makes the sacken apron episode even more humiliating). All these concerns emerge as features of female authorial consciousness. The implied author determined that these concerns best reflected the Margery character's ethos in terms of her successful evangelizing. (Always in the balance, however, is the relationship of the implied author's ethos to the Margery character's ethos.)

In the Holy Land, Margery receives her "gift of tears"—a gift of the spirit that is not always comfortable or convenient. Margery copiously manifests her gift of tears every day for ten years and at less frequent intervals over an additional fifteen, whenever reminded of Jesus or the Passion. The implied author skillfully creates a devout weeping spell in such a way that the authorial audience sympathizes with Margery, delights in her eccentricity, all the while understanding why the Margery character vexes the characters within the immediate audience:

> On Purification Day, or otherwise Candlemas Day, when the said creature beheld the people with their candles in church, her mind was ravished into beholding Our Lady offering her Blissful Son Our Savior to the priest. . . . Then was she so comforted by the contemplation in her soul that she . . . could hardly bear up her own candle to the priest . . . but went wavering on each side like a drunken woman, weeping and sobbing so sore, that scarcely could she stand on her feet for the fervor of love and devotion that God put into her soul through high contemplation. And sometimes she could not stand but fell down among the people and cried so loud that many men wondered and marvelled what ailed her; for the fervor of the spirit was so great that the body failed, and might not endure it. (82.96a.1–23)

Margery's gift of tears was a physical token of her special sanctity, akin to St. Francis's gift of the stigmata. Thus, Franciscan ethos and pathos color her dramatic piety, her unqualified, unconditional, and fearless love of God.

Although Margery the flesh-and-blood author, Margery the implied author, and Margery the character wanted to live chastely with her husband, Margery was, indeed, a married woman. Her decision to dress as the bride of Christ, completely in white wool, and to wear a gold ring engraved *Iesu est amor meus* was an effrontery to her townspeople, her immediate audience. White clothes could indicate either chaste living or salvation without time in purgatory, and Margery wore them for both reasons. The townspeople, however, were offended by her attire, and instead of accepting her sainthood, they often accused her of being a hypocrite. In Lambeth, for instance, a townswoman came forward to curse Margery: "I would bring a faggot to burn thee with; it is a pity that thou live" (16.18a.15–16). Since Margery had a newborn son and a living husband, her behavior was considered anomalous, if not scandalous.

Several passages underscore Margery's recurring concern for her attire as a reflection of her spiritual status. In the following passage, she has just been abandoned by her irritated fellow pilgrims, who refuse to travel with this overbearing evangelist; providentially, Jesus appears to the frightened Margery with advice:

> "Dread thee not, daughter, for I shall provide for thee right well and bring thee in safety to Rome and home again into England without any villainy to thy body if thou will be clad in white clothes and wear them as I said to thee while thou were

in England." Then this creature, being in great pain and despair, answered Him in her mind, "If Thou be the spirit of God that speak in my soul, and I may prove Thee for a true spirit with the counsel of the Church, I shall obey Thy will; and if Thou bring me to Rome in safety, I shall wear white clothes, though all the world should wonder at me, for Thy love." (30.37b.5-16)

Although the authorial audience can be amused or even impressed by Margery's willingness to bargain with Jesus with regard to her costume, rarely does her narrative support or her immediate audience appreciate her spiritual confidence, her self-proclaimed holiness, or her costumes.

In the opening chapters, the young, proud, attention-seeking Margery dresses in the gayest new fashions for the sole purpose of outshining the other merchants' wives. And she knows full well "that men said of her much villainy, for she wore gold pipes on her head, and her hoods, with the tippets, were slashed. Her cloaks were also slashed and laid with divers colours between the slashes, so that they should be the more staring to men's sight, and herself the more worshipped" (2.5a.13-18). Throughout her life, the Margery character offends many people with her choice of dress, a physical expression of her ethos: before her conversion, she is garishly stylish; after her conversion, she wears the powerfully symbolic white; and when her white attire becomes too controversial, she resorts to the later, safer black. When a German priest commands her to wear black, she feels "that she pleased God with her obedience" (34.41b.1-2). The Margery character's costume changes reflect her spiritual condition.

The reactions of the other characters (the immediate audience) and the narrative audience to the Margery character are most often perplexity and exasperation, depending on her behavior (leaving her husband and children for pilgrimage, insisting the pilgrimage conversation be limited to her pontification). Occasionally, they appreciate her "good works," her nursing and serving the poor and the sick, or counseling the bereaved and insane. At the same time, the authorial audience, in response to the author's artistic design and intentions, consistently delights in the antics of Margery (presented by the narrator as told by the implied author) and applauds her decisions. The authorial audience fully understands the negative reactions of the characters in the text, yet it remains sympathetic to Margery the implied author. By fashioning a proleptic ethos for her authorial audience, Margery attends to the expectations of that audience, yet, simultaneously, she meets her own demands as a character before a narrative audience. The artistry of her self-presentation, her ethos, is a major rhetorical accomplishment.

Inscribing the rhetorical tradition. Margery Kempe is one of the most important Englishwomen who participated in the medieval rhetorical tradition, although the males who controlled that tradition did not recognize her participation. A rhetorician who joins her narrative audience but does not join her authorial audience has no means of recognizing Margery's rhetorical sophistication; that reader cannot do otherwise than pronounce her work unimportant in terms of rhetoric. Margery Kempe is not so much practicing rhetoric in its traditional sense as she is inscribing it in a *different* way.

Although never before recognized by rhetorical scholars for its contributions to rhetoric, her fifteenth-century *Book* has rightfully enjoyed special attention from scholars of other stripes attracted to her ability to elaborate with considerable sophistication her theological convictions and practices. Margery represents a unique strain in the most important literary activity by women in the Middle Ages: the flowering of religious writing into the writing and dictation of mystical treatises. Our medieval literary foremothers, such as Julian of Norwich, Hildegard von Bingen, and Margery Kempe, participated in the Continental mystic tradition, beginning with after-illness visions. This tradition of dramatic piety could provide women a socially acceptable and respected medium of religious expression and personal assertion, especially if they were attached to religious orders and, hence, educated in the intellectual tradition. Julian and Hildegard are considered valid mystics because they belonged to this world of confined, virginal, and intellectual religious experience. A bourgeois laywoman like Margery simply could not meet the traditional requirements of mysticism, yet mysticism provided her with the means of composing her life.

Mystics in any period, however, are vulnerable to charges of heresy and disobedience because their direct communication with God bypasses the services and sacraments of the Church. Margery was especially vulnerable, not only because she was an outspoken woman and layperson without formal education, but because she lived at a time of serious disruption in the Church at home and on the Continent:

> Her spiritual independence in seeking the difficult balance between the active and contemplative lives . . . baffled her contemporaries and caused many to question her orthodoxy. . . . Both men and women remarked with hostility on the impropriety of Margery's wandering, as well as the presumptuousness of her teaching. A frustrated intolerance surfaced most frequently in the attitudes of her tormentors. Unable to "define" Margery's behavior by placing her in those roles appropriate for either religious women or laywomen, her contemporaries felt threatened by her. (Despres 87)

But we must understand that Margery's teaching, her blending of personal and scriptural history, was Franciscan in spirit and orthodox in its origins and that her visions gave her a *public* language and a visible office in the world, despite her position as a woman.

The works of the female mystics spoke to religious communities and struck chords in the developing popular piety, a piety seeking emotional and rational stimulation. Moreover, these works were accessible to the populace: works such as Margery's were generally written in the vernacular; and these writings were akin to the sermon, the central dramatic participatory event in Christian corporate life. The themes, structure, and didactic purpose of sermons would have been readily familiar to Margery, for the Church was her primary source of lifelong teaching and comfort, a basic constituent of her worldly, as well as her "ghostly," life and an essential framework for her calling. But most important, the Church provided Margery the language and the opportunity with which to use that calling.

The fragmented nature of her autobiography may, indeed, demonstrate her ambiguous role as an effective Christian and layperson—especially in a society where her gender deprived her of the authority to teach or preach. But this fragmented story corroborates the conclusion of recent scholars: women's autobiographies tend to be less linear, unified, and chronological than men's autobiographies. (Consider the autobiographical works of Adrienne Rich, Mary McCarthy, Maxine Hong Kingston, and even Carolyn Heilbrun.) Women's autobiographies are often novelistic, women's novels autobiographical. And because of the continual crossing of self and other, the continual conversation among the voices, women's writings often blur the public and the private—just as Margery's writing does. Margery's autobiography, her rhetoric, inscribes the feminine conversation rather than the masculine dialectic.

Although presented as nonfiction, Margery's account implements other highly sophisticated fictional techniques besides dialogism. Hers is the timeless, quintessential woman's story of irreducible and irreconcilable gendered-language limitations. Yet, in other ways, her story is a morality tale about asserting those language differences and seeking appropriate—though nontraditional—forms of fulfillment. The conversational quality of Margery's discourse depends on human connections: her discourse relies on others to come into its existence, whether others are scribes or those to whom she testifies.

Margery Kempe would be recognized—and heard. Although she lacked the necessary skills for transcribing her own story and had no guarantee that her story would ever reach an audience, this religious mystic was, nonetheless, determined to record her spiritual autobiography. She used her inner voice for knowing and then turned to "correct," or public, voices for composing and speaking. And in Margery's case, as in the case of so many other women, the same mind can live in several voices.

This first English autobiographer provides us a powerful example of successful double-voiced discourse, articulating her private, disenfranchised experience through the public discourse of religion. It is an inherently interesting text that is also a resounding response to religious instruction. Yet most remarkable of all is Margery's ability to introduce and balance an ethos with dual effects: she faithfully presents the annoying and believable Margery character, who costs her the respect of her narrative audience; but at the same time, she writes the life of the implied author with a disarming and utterly convincing sincerity that gains her the admiration of her authorial audience. *The Book of Margery Kempe* not only redefines the rhetorical tradition, making it inclusive of such female works, it also contributes an innovative example of purposeful and persuasive feminine inscription.

Medieval Rhetoric

CONCLUSION

Julian of Norwich and Margery Kempe lived within a narrow sphere of cultural constraints, under strict religious and societal rules of feminine conduct, yet they found a place to speak their femininity (between the lines of Holy Scripture, perhaps) and move into a religious vocation in the larger world. Theirs are stories of endurance and purpose—and also of an extraordinary kind of transcendent inclusiveness, theological and linguistic inclusiveness. Like Julian, Margery argued for the woman's rightful participation in religion. These early women of faith spoke to limitations of social location and gendered identity within a culture of masculine privilege and religious power that read: "The head of every man is Christ, the head of woman is her husband" (1 Cor. 11.3).[72]

Rather than employ the conventional, misogynistic, exclusionary discourse of the medieval Church, Julian and Margery turned to inclusionary Holy Scriptures (Gal. 3.28; Acts 2.17–18; John 14.2–3). Such biblical texts fortified Julian and Margery to speak to other women and men in the inclusionary and feminine language of mysticism—a "(m)other tongue, a language that is accessible, concrete, real, an embodiment of the feminine" (Frey 507).

The mystical religious experiences of Julian and Margery provide alternative visions of religion and of rhetoric. Each carefully wrought ethos presents ideas we can all understand, even if they take us to an androgynous ideal of Godhead, a truly human Jesus and Virgin. These alternative visions offer Christian equality among and redemptive opportunities for all humankind, regardless of sex, social or religious status, or education. As Julian explores the all-encompassing nature of God, as Margery describes "sucking on Christ's breast" (5.9b.35), they complement the traditional male images of the Father and Son with the analogy of Jesus as Mother Church, nurturing the faithful. God is not exclusively male, and God's word will not be interpreted exclusively by males. By emphasizing the humanity of Jesus, both Julian and Margery displace the age-old emphasis on women as matter and men as essences, on feminine bodies and masculine minds. Julian and Margery are represented in, one with, God, and they know also that God is one with them—one with everyone. They will not be excluded from Christianity; they have feminized their Christian faith.

Theirs was a female-centered translation of the divine into the rhetorical *ought* of moral action; they make space for women's participation and rewards in Christianity—in markedly different ways. Yet each of them seeks the empowering center of her own personhood; when fused with God, each woman can liberate herself from the strictures of silence and passivity of patriarchal religion.

Julian of Norwich and Margery Kempe are the most important Englishwomen who participated in the medieval rhetorical tradition. They represent the most important literary activity by women in the Middle Ages, the flowering of religious writings into the composition of mystical treatises, available to all in the vernacular. But perhaps more impressive is their ability to elaborate, with considerable sophistication, their theological convictions and social practices. To that end, each woman developed a rhetorical discourse, of theology and of autobiography. If rhetoric is the perfect union of thought and word, then each of these women is a consummate rhetor, for her rhetoric blends perfectly her genuine human emotion with her literary craft.

FOUR

Inscribed in the Margins:
Renaissance Women and Rhetorical Culture

INTRODUCTION

The English Renaissance reached full bloom during the reign of Elizabeth, a queen who was arguably the most powerful woman who ever lived. In the first full biographical account of the queen, she is described as the quintessence of the English Renaissance, a trope for her state: "The all-glorious, all-virtuous, incomparable, invict [unconquered] and matchless pattern of princes, the glory, honour and mirror of womankind, the admiration of our age, ELIZABETH, Queen of England, was by the father's side truly royal, being daughter to Henry VIII, grandchild to Henry VII, and great-grandchild to Edward IV" (W. Camden sig. C). Superbly educated by Christian humanist principles and standards, accomplished and prolific in rhetoric and poetics, politically keen and shrewd, devoted to her people (and they to her), Elizabeth ruled her kingdom successfully and wisely, ranking second only to King Philip of Spain in terms of lands, treasury, and power. Elizabeth was an aureole of inspiration for poets and authors, and she illuminated Renaissance literature, a golden age of female-patronized, male-produced literature.

English vernacular, long associated with the uneducated and with hearth and home—with women—triumphed during this era. The great victories of the English early on in the Hundred Years' War (1337–1453) had aroused an English linguistic nationalism that eventually led to the 1362 Act of Parliament declaring English the language of all legal proceedings. The reign of Henry V (1413–22) established English as the language of all court correspondence, another move toward the Englishing of England. As the Norman French dwindled in numbers, English established itself in homes, as well as in schools, and by the early 1500s, English writers and thinkers were exploring the versatility and poetry of a language readying itself for competition with Latin and French as the public language of power and influence.[1]

The scholarly, literary, and political desire to compete with Continental intellectual feats led to widely distributed (thanks to William Caxton) English translations that introduced the Continental Renaissance to England. The insistence of Protestant groups that the Bible be translated into language available to English Christians eventually led to the English language masterpiece: the 1611 King James Authorized Version of the Bible. These translations not only stabilized English, they enriched an English tongue that would achieve further richness and vitality under the influence of Sir Philip Sidney, Richard Hooker, Francis Bacon, Sir Walter Raleigh, Ben Jonson, John Lyly, Edmund Spenser, and, of course, William Shakespeare.

This vernacular literary movement could have afforded women the opportunity to participate in the dominant discourse of politics, religion, and literature. But, for the most part, it did not. The Renaissance Englishwoman continued to be marginalized from the body of linguistic performance. The literary participation of even the most erudite and talented was limited to patronage, religious writing, and translation. And even these restricted literary and rhetorical contributions could be received with condescension. Women were urged to read Church Fathers and to translate sermons, but the measure of their worth remained tied to their chastity, their beauty, their modesty, their demureness, and the extent to which they submitted themselves to the control of men and men's words. Despite Queen Elizabeth's magnificent public example outside such ideological containment, Renaissance women lived and wrote in the margins.

In "Shakespeare's Sister," Virginia Woolf asks "why no woman wrote a word of that extraordinary literature when every other man, it seemed, was capable of song or sonnet" (qtd. in Gilbert and Gubar 1376). Women are a powerful presence in Renaissance literature, in drama and verse, but Woolf, aware of no evidence to the contrary, wrote that women seem to have had "no existence save in the fiction written by men" (1377). Even now, women's rhetorical accomplishments in translation, argument, oratory, literary rhetoric have gone mostly unnoticed, but as Richard Hooker wrote, "Posterity may know that we have not through silence permitted things to pass away as in a dream" (1:77).

This chapter follows the patterns of the previous ones: it opens with a brief overview of the Renaissance, its cultural and intellectual dynamics, before moving to woman's literary and historical place within that historical construct. Then it explores Renaissance rhetoric, which flourished as a male-dominated practice that connected at various points with literature, education, religion, science, and politics. The last section charts the rhetorical activities and contributions of three women who inhabited these rhetorical interstices.[2] Margaret More Roper, Anne Askew, and Elizabeth I personify Christian humanism, the Protestant Reformation, and English imperialism, respectively, the three major cultural movements comprising Renaissance England and invigorating Renaissance rhetoric.

THE GENDERED CONSTRUCTION OF RENAISSANCE CULTURE

The English Renaissance marked a time of enthusiasm for expanding literary, scientific, educational, and political boundaries and for masculine accomplishments in those areas. The emphasis on individualism and human destiny gave rise to great inventions and discoveries: the printing press, telescope, and gunpowder would change the world forever; Nicolaus Copernicus, Johannes Kepler, and Galileo dislodged the earth from its traditional place in the center of the universe and placed it in orbit around the sun; Ferdinand Magellan, Christopher Columbus, Vasco da Gama, and Amerigo Vespucci showed all of Europe the rest of the world. But despite the pervasiveness of intellectual and geographical explorations, half the population—women—were at no time encouraged, let alone invited, to join these various expansions. Like every Western culture preceding it, Renaissance society was gendered to the advantage of the adult male, who served as the template for all of humankind, women and children having been misstamped for other uses.

Law

Thus it comes as no surprise that English laws during the Renaissance favored males; the principle and practice of primogeniture, hardly distinguishable from patriarchy, affected all families at the financial expense of females: "Women have nothing to do in constituting Lawes, or consenting to them, in interpreting of Lawes or in hearing them interpreted at lectures, leets or charges, and yet they stand strictly tied to men's establishments, little or nothing excused by ignorance" (*Lawes*). Financial, and therefore legal, power tended to drift into the hands of the eldest males, with every family member constantly trying to win the approval of or gain a reciprocal claim upon whichever male had been entailed the purse strings and the land.

The law, then, protected the eldest son financially; younger sons were expected to serve the Church or to marry well, a situation by which the bride's family transferred a significant amount of real or personal property to the groom's family. Both unwilling girls and stubborn boys could be physically subdued or financially threatened into a marriage agreement, the dividends of such unions (money, lands, social status) being greater than the temporary discomfort of the participants, who might naively wish to hazard romantic love: "Children are so much the goods, the possessions of their parent, that they cannot, without a kind of theft, give away themselves without the allowance of those that have the right in them" (Allestree 291). When the fictional Juliet refuses to marry Paris, for example, Capulet is well within his nonfictional parental and legal rights to assert his authority in the marriage of a minor daughter, going so far as to threaten to abandon her socially and financially (Shakespeare, *Rom.* 3.5.176–85, 191–94). The gentry and yeomanry also practiced marriage as an investment to protect their lands and wealth, but the propertyless had little to gain or lose by arranging marriages.

Marriage held few guarantees for a woman, regardless of her class. In the best financial circumstances, and in return for the investment of her dowry, the wife might be guaranteed a financial settlement—an annuity or jointure—from the husband's family in the event that she survived her husband. She could, as could a widower, remarry and reinvest, but a woman's legal right to hold and dispose of her own property was limited to the details of her marriage contract (akin to our contemporary prenuptial agreement). In *The Family, Sex, and Marriage in England 1500–1800*, Lawrence Stone writes,

> By marriage, the husband and wife became one person in law—and that person was the husband. He acquired absolute control of all his wife's personal property, which he could sell at will. By a judicial interpretation, a husband's debts became by law a prior charge on his wife's jewels and other personal property, although it is fair to add that the husband also became responsible for his wife's debts. A husband always had full rights during his lifetime over his wife's real estate, and by an act of 1540 he was empowered to make long leases for three lives or twenty-one years and to pocket the fines. (195)[3]

Marriage, in fact, deprived women of all legal rights. Like their children, women were denied the vote and were legally subjected to their husbands, who controlled all family property, money, and members.

Work

Inheritance, lands, dowries, and jointures could not support the entire Renaissance populace; many people worked on farms, in homes, in trades, and in businesses. And that daily work life unfolded within the frame of enduring gender and social hierarchies, for, regardless of her work, a woman was expected to be the economic dependent of the man—the father or husband or employer—who controlled her life.

The large number of working women belied the common expectation that women always had financial protection from a male relative. Fathers who could support their daughters until marriage did so; those who could not sent their daughters to work, thereby sparing the family the dual expense of keeping daughters at home and marrying them off. Building up a dowry was vital to a woman's marriage prospects (as well as to ensuring her economic welfare in the event of widowhood); therefore, these daughters worked in the hope of accumulating enough wages for a dowry and the work skills necessary for attracting a husband. Husbands of all ranks, but especially those with low or middling status and wages, needed wives who could contribute to the family income. A wage-earned dowry could stake the couple in establishing a business, shop, or workshop (if he were a master).[4] A husband took full control of whatever money a woman brought into a marriage, investing her dowry, using her weekly wages, and taking for granted her working alongside him in the family business. Given the absolute financial necessity of living within a sphere of masculine financial leadership, women at the very lowest levels of society were scarcely able to survive outside the limits of marriage or long-term employment.[5]

Regardless of their socioeconomic station, many Renaissance women had to demonstrate continued resourcefulness in weaving together their domestic and economic duties, adjusting their work duties outside the home to those inside to keep the household fed, supplied, and clothed. And her work would be further regulated according to her role in life: as daughter, unmarried woman, wife, or widow. Perhaps the best working situation for a woman was alongside her husband in his guild activities. She might work in production, distribution, or billing. Upon his death, she might receive permission from the other guild members to continue production in his name, permission crucial to her livelihood because it allowed her to retain apprentices already indentured by her husband. With that permission, she could continue to pay her dues, clear her debts, and participate in guild activities, but she rarely could take on new apprentices, the very cheapest form of skilled labor.

If permitted by the local guilds, girls as young as twelve might apprentice themselves to the traditional occupations of fabric and clothing production or embellishment.[6] The best-off females often worked outside all guild restrictions, using their earnings (or the family's pooled savings) to set up a tavern, a cabaret, or a refreshment stand. Other young girls or women might seek work as domestics (the largest occupational group in urban society).[7] Or they might become barmaids, farm laborers (particularly residential work at dairy farms), road workers, or manual workers (in menial occupations related to fishing, selling wares, prostitution, or wet-nursing). Manual workers—male and female alike—faced physical neglect, harassment, and overwork on a daily basis, as well as threats to their financial and bodily welfare. For example, a woman might spend her life nursing other women's children. If she were lucky, she might be paid (at varying rates, with varying fringe benefits) to take in a child of a wealthier family, but very often she found herself nursing orphans and foundlings, putting her health and her livelihood at the risk of transmitted venereal diseases. A woman working at the lowest of occupations had little chance of building a dowry; her only financial hope was marrying another laborer with whom she could pool her wages and eke out subsistence for their family.

In addition to their work outside the home, women also worked at housewifery, an occupation far more formidable than contemporary notions of cleaning, dusting, cooking, and doing laundry: without housework, "society would have been hungry, naked, and without remedies against sickness" (Bell, *Women* 2).[8] Duchesses and goodwives alike supervised the factorylike production of a family's needs: bread, butter, cheese, storable vegetables, fruits, pottage, and meats; ale, eggs, candles, linens, and clothing.[9] Women who could somehow afford not to work outside the family structure did not, for housewifery was in itself an endless cycle of obligations and physical labor. Outside the family and the allotted roles of daughter, wife, and mother, then, only the wealthiest women from the best of circumstances could beat the considerable odds against independence.

Medicine

Medicine and science, closely related, also played out the culturally gendered differences between males and females, intersecting as they did on issues of genital differentiation, obstetrics, and gynecology. Not surprisingly, Renaissance women were scientifically proven to be physically inferior to men.[10] Just as it had informed medieval thought, Aristotle's theory of sexual hierarchy (which had been so successfully forwarded by Galen) influenced Renaissance study as well, his influence providing the basic orientation for nearly two thousand years of embryological thought, particularly regarding the influence of masculine "heat" on the perfection of male genitalia: "man is more perfect than the woman, and the reason for his perfection is his excess of heat, for heat is Nature's primary instrument" (Galen 2: 630); "turn outward the woman's, turn inward, so to speak, and fold double the man's [genital organs], and you will find the same in both in every respect" (qtd. in Laqueur 25). Heat makes man an active, formative agent in reproduction, a fully human true parent; conversely, lack of heat keeps woman from ever reaching the true measure of humanness. Woman's role is merely to contain and nourish the male-implanted fetus.

This scientific bias against women continued throughout the Renaissance, with some modification. University of Padua professor of medicine and science Allesandro Benedetti (1450–1512) argued that women did, indeed, play a role in generation: "[T]he members of the foetus are formed from both the male and the female and the spiritual life is produced from both, but the principal members are constituted from the male seed and the other more ignoble ones from the female seed, as if from purer matter, just as the spiritual vigor is created" (99). Even scientists who performed dissections continued in the same vein: Spanish anatomist Andres de Laguna (1499–1560) wrote of woman's seed being produced in her left testis, the source of impure blood; Belgian anatomist Andreas Vesalius (1514–1564) confirmed this misunderstanding with his anatomically "correct" sketches of female reproductive organs.[11] Regardless of the explanation, each points back to the one-sex model of humanity, with men the model and women a weaker, imperfect version of manhood.

The one-sex model of humanity might have been—but was not—challenged by Matteo Realdo Colombo's "discovery" of the clitoris. Successor to Vesalius as professor of surgery in Padua in 1543, Colombo extolled the virtues of empiricism (of dissection, viewing, touching), the only means by which scientific truths could be established. Colombo's scientific discovery of the clitoris, which he referred to as "Venus," could have unsettled the belief that the female was an inverted male, that the vagina was a penis in reverse, but it did not.[12] Thus, the Renaissance woman continued to be considered a misstamp of man, whose external penis ensured his privileged social status.

RENAISSANCE INTELLECTUAL DYNAMICS

Individuality, spiritual morality, and worldly accomplishment marked the Renaissance, or rebirth, of classical values. To recapture the intellectual and cultural glories of their ancient heritage, the Continental literati acquainted themselves with Greek and Latin authors, as well as classical art; their English counterparts acquainted themselves with ancient and contemporary Continental literature, either in the original or in translations. The literati venerated the ancients as superior beings with supreme utterances and used them and their literary and artistic legacies. Classical art and literature provided expert, yet attainable, even surpassable, models for Renaissance artists of every kind, who shared the ancients' passion for harmonious arrangement and instructive realism. By the time the Renaissance reached England, however, this rebirth of classical arts and learning had become serious, practical, and moral. For the English, the Renaissance would not be so much a rebirth as a new beginning for themselves, particularly among the great English writers who would stake their reputations and livelihoods on the artistry of their native tongue.

Renaissance literary scholars were like their medieval predecessors in their reverence for the ancient and the traditional. But they soon realized that medieval understanding of the ancients had been badly flawed, their understanding limited by incomplete, missing, or mistranslated manuscripts. The medieval grasp on antiquity was revealed to be much less certain than Thomas Aquinas and the scholastics had supposed.[13] The invention of the printing press had made possible the duplication and dissemination of these ancient texts and some startling and disquieting revelations about medieval literary study: in their passage across the centuries, many classical and religious texts had been corrupted through mistranslation, additions, deletions, and forgery. The 1416 discovery of the complete and true texts of Quintilian served as a case in point.[14] Therefore, newly reconstructed ancient texts assumed their rightful status in the Renaissance intellectual tradition as Renaissance scholars methodically ferreted them out in numbers. The turn from medieval to "true original sources"—Greek, Latin, and Hebrew (which would include God's original words)—was imperative.[15]

Humanism

The Renaissance tendency to celebrate individual genius, achievement, and discovery in all the arts and sciences was somewhat tempered by Renaissance humanism. The discovery of Quintilian's complete works had ushered in tremendous enthusiasm for the *studia humanitatis*, a cultural and educational program that emphasized and developed a specific core of literatures: grammar, rhetoric, history, poetry, and moral philosophy, the five *studia* that would come to define humanism (Trinkaus 19).[16] The intensive and extensive study of each of these subjects was understood to include the reading and interpretation of its standard ancient writers in Latin and, to a lesser extent, in Greek (Kristeller 23).[17]

Humanism was never a mass social movement; its influence was felt only by well-bred, well-established males. Young girls of all social classes were systematically excluded from this course of study; the study of classical literature (which could tend toward the bawdy and violent) was of no practical use to the domesticated Renaissance lady, who, as companion to her husband and as household manager, would have no time for such recreational study.[18] Only the later progression, Christian humanism, advanced by Desiderius Erasmus, Juan Luis Vives, and Sir Thomas More, would provide some women admittance into the ancient worlds. But even this movement, which enthusiastically joined religion and education, aimed no further than the production of learned women who could harness their intellectual and religious potential to the domestic sphere. Regardless of the version, though, rhetoric was the cynosure of humanistic studies, for the literary and practical aims of the rhetorician were rarely if ever separated.

Christian Humanism

Scholars who included religious and theological problems in their course of classical and rhetorical studies and writings came to be known as Christian humanists. A central issue to Christian humanism was the availability of biblical texts for lay piety, part of a larger movement to normalize religion and religious belief while educating males and females of all social classes.[19] Erasmus and More, in particular, intended that their writings be used broadly as practical handbooks of daily piety; they both emphasized simple piety and the ethical demands of the gospel, which would lead to proper social conduct.[20] Literacy would be the key to Christian knowledge, for all.[21]

Thus, as the Renaissance moved from medievalism to the new age, women gradually moved out of the religious-education milieu in which they had been contained by the Church for many centuries. Besides finding ways to continue the work of Augustine, in combining classical rhetorical studies with religious instruction, Christian humanism provided the means for (upper-class) women to achieve intellectually—but never the means to achieve as much as men were achieving.[22] Both More and Erasmus insisted that "learning and morals go together," a persuasive claim for women's education being that it made them better women. However, the phrase carried both praise and limitation. By claiming that learning would increase women's virtue (i.e., their chastity, obedience, humility), the Christian humanists and their successors reassured society that women's knowledge was (still) under control and directed to enhancing only their womanliness—and their piety.

RENAISSANCE EDUCATION THEORY, PRACTICE, RESULT

Renaissance thought focused on a liberal artistic and political education that would be as important to the cloister as to the world at large. Learning, progress, and the overall quality of a nation were interdependent. The ancients themselves had set the pattern for combining education with politics: Isocrates, Socrates, Cicero, and Quintilian had all argued for the education of good and useful citizen-rhetors; Augustine had argued that secular government should join the Church in ensuring that people be good citizens. But it was Quintilian who specifically directed Renaissance thinkers to the original source of what would become known as Renaissance pedagogy: Cicero, who exemplified Roman civic consciousness and the active (vs. contemplative) life.

Cicero's fundamental impact on Renaissance writing was his connection of individual eloquence with individual moral goodness as its source, means, and measure. The cult of Cicero, praising eloquence and goodness (both moral and civic), celebrated the individual's God-given faculty of reason, which separated *man* from beast. This Ciceronian-based celebration of the individual became the mainstay of English Renaissance culture and education. The Renaissance cognoscenti designed a system of schooling that fused political, moral, and religious instruction, a formal system of intellectual training that prepared students for service to society, to the state.

In his 1531 *Book Named the Governor*, Englishman Thomas Elyot extols the relevance of classical learning and goodness to the higher calls of citizenship and public service, principles Italian Baldesar Castiglione advanced soon after.[23] Elyot sought to mold the complete gentleman—provident, industrious, temperate, just, virtuous, learned, courteous, responsible, and efficient—and through him, a flourishing society. "Sound learning," according to Elyot, would be the understanding and application of the wisdom of Athens and Rome to contemporary needs.[24]

Writers of educational theory and practice, such as Castiglione, Elyot, and Princess Elizabeth's own Roger Ascham (*The Scholemaster*), were among those concerned with the education of the elite, the leaders of the state, the art of governing (and the arts of literature as they might be practiced in courtly poetry). In sum, theorists and students alike embraced the idea of the self-fashioning of individual gentlemen. The real work of fashioning Renaissance gentlemen was done in the grammar, or petty, schools or by private tutors, situations that limited the concept of *self-fashioned ladies* to terms of adornment and devotion. The seeds of such fashioning, however, did sift through the masculine cultural screen: some of the humanists' educational ideas filtered into the chambers of privately educated gentlewomen, as well as into the cloisters of educated churchwomen.

Women's Education

Access to sacred truth and the new learning was, in general, monopolized by those men who had been "properly" schooled as youths and properly born. Grammar schools offered those boys a classical education, untainted by a female presence. For young women, though, the primary routes to education were tutoring at home (by their brothers' tutors if they were to learn Greek, Latin, or Hebrew), schooling in convents (before the dissolution), and, occasionally, participation along with the boys in a local petty school.[25] University was closed to female students.[26]

Education did not create queens, princesses, or gentlewomen—not even a Christian humanist education. Study and formal training might enable them to develop their intellectual potential, but the future of that potential was predetermined at and by birth. Women of the middle and lower estates lacked such opportunities, and neither group was free unidirectionally to pursue learning and scholarship.[27] Contemporary literature of edification advised Renaissance women to learn the homely—and womanly—arts of domestic fiscal management and material production, self-adornment, and Christian devotion, equating women's daily work with women's education.[28]

Even at a time when "the majority of Tudor women lacked any academic training beyond elementary instruction in conversational English and in religious exercises" (Warnicke 3), Christian humanism managed to inspire another kind of ideal woman, the educated Christian woman. But her education would be controversial. Although an advocate of female education, Vives advised against women's use of humanistic training in speaking with men publicly or in arguing with anyone anywhere: "a woman needeth [eloquence] not, but she needeth goodness and wisdom" (qtd. in Watson 53). Further, in *The Instruction of a Christian Woman*, Vives explains that "It neither becometh a woman to rule a school, nor to live amongst men, or speak abroad, and shake off her demureness and honesty [all that is worthy of her honor]" (qtd. in Watson 53), "which if she be good, it were better to be at home within and unknown to other folks, and in company to hold her tongue demurely and let few see her, and none at all hear her" (55). "I give no license to a woman to be a teacher, nor to have authority of the man, but to be in silence" (56). Advice such as Vives's aggravated the question of women's place in intellectual society. Even when educators and theologians argued for women's equality or even superiority in certain respects (virtue, for instance), many continued to advocate submission to masculine authority.

Erasmus, friend to both More and Vives, argued that Vives was too severe with women; after all, Latin literacy and classical learning were the two sources of practically all human knowledge, and the Christian humanists were wise to make them available to noble daughters, as well as noble sons. More's home life was living proof of Vives's unwarranted conservatism: More's three daughters and their kinswoman, Margaret Giggs, were profiting from a liberal and classical education, in which "women were treated as men's peers in conversation and where knowledge and wit passed to and fro" (Neale, *Queen* 10). Margaret More Roper, his eldest daughter, would be renowned as first of the learned English ladies of the sixteenth century (see below). "Such women were the pattern of the age, and humanists boasted of them in their letters to foreign scholars." (10). The linguistic and literary talents of such highly accomplished women could scarcely be matched by their contemporaries; they were exceptional, hardly "the pattern."

Even though Erasmus, More, and Vives actively supported the education of women, they did so within private and domestic terms. For the most part, the educated Renaissance woman was silenced and marginalized, deprived of all but a few limited outlets for her intellectual abilities.

WOMAN'S PLACE IN RENAISSANCE ENGLAND:
HISTORICAL AND LITERARY

Individuality, spiritual morality, and worldly accomplishment—those dynamics of Renaissance culture that also constituted the ideal Renaissance man—were not expected of nor extended to Renaissance women, that is, of course, except for the cultural dynamic of spiritual morality. Had it not been for the Christian humanist movement, laywomen would have had little intellectual opportunity at all.

The quintessential Renaissance man is the widely informed man of the world, a Sir Philip Sidney, perfect courtier and gentleman by birth and by nature, soldier, diplomat, scholar, literary critic, patron of poets and the arts, and poet himself. But who is the ideal Renaissance woman, and how does she fit into that seemingly exclusive picture of Renaissance accomplishment? In the opening scene of Thomas Heywood's *Woman Killed with Kindness* (1602), the newly wed Lady Anne is introduced as exemplifying the Renaissance ideal of the wellborn, beautiful, intelligent, and educated woman:

> . . . a wife
> So qualified, and with such ornaments
> Both of the mind and body. First, her birth
> Is noble, and her education such
> As might become the daughter of a prince;
> her own tongue speaks all tongues, and her own hand
> Can teach all strings to speak in their best grace,
> . . . .
> To end her many praises in one word,
> She's Beauty and Perfection's eldest daughter . . .   (1.1.15–22)

Woman's beauty and perfection might counterbalance man's endowments of wit, judgment, and a mind almost divine. But she always "must needs prove / Pliant and duteous [to her] husband's love" (1.1.39–40). Beauty and perfection—not intellect or schooling—were paramount to ideal womanhood, but cheerfulness, contentment, and modesty could give beauty to a soul.[29]

The Tudor Women

During the Tudor period, the women of the court were celebrated for their beauty, their modesty, and their education: "charming and by nature so mighty pretty as I have scarcely ever beheld"; "of marvellous beauty and wonderfully clever"; "the greatest beauties in the world, and as fair as alabaster"; "cheerful, courteous and of good address" (Samuel Kiechel, Francesco Ferretti, Étienne Perlin, and anonymous, qtd. in Plowden 3). From Catherine of Aragon to Catherine Parr, each queen articulated her place in history, though, more often than not, her articulation was recorded (or invented) by a man. Henry VIII's 1509 ascension to the throne had brought a king responsive to the new learning, as well as a queen imbued with the Renaissance spirit.

Queen Catherine of Aragon (1485–1536), Henry's first wife, had come from a family of daughters who read and wrote Latin as well as their well-educated mother, Queen Isabella of Castile.[30] For Princess Catherine herself, Vives had written his *Instruction of a Christian Woman*.[31] Thought to be the model for Zenobia, the virtuous, obedient, wise, and strong governor in Thomas Elyot's *Defence of Good Women* (c.1535), Queen Catherine also served as the catalyst for the More circle, owing to her own learning, piety, and intense interest in educating her own daughter, Princess Mary. Like her mother, Queen Catherine invited the best Renaissance scholars to tutor Mary. After serving as Erasmus's assistant, the Spanish Vives traveled to England to supervise the education of the young princess, for whom he wrote his *Plan of Study for Girls*.[32] After studying in Italy, Englishman Thomas Linacre taught the princess, for whom he wrote a Latin grammar.

The example of the Tudor court gave aristocratic parents license to educate their own daughters. Anne Boleyn (1507–36) in Norfolk and Catherine Parr (1512–48) in Westmoreland (second and sixth wives, respectively, of Henry VIII) were both educated according to the new learning, Catherine having been educated by Vives alongside Princess Mary. The letters of both women indicate their versedness in Latin, Greek, and other languages (Green, vol. 2).

Lady Jane Grey (1537–54), who rose to the throne for nine days in 1553, also had a reputation as a well-educated young woman, a reputation established by her loving tutor, Roger Ascham, who contrasts his student's enthusiasm for the new learning to her parents' old-fashionedness. In *The Scholemaster*, he writes that while her parents were hunting in the park, she was in her room reading Greek with as much delight, as some gentlemen would read a merry tale in Boccaccio. After our greeting, . . . I asked her why she would leave such pastime in the park? Smiling, she answered me: "I believe all their sport in the park is but a shadow to that pleasure I find in Plato. Alas, good folk, they never felt what true pleasure meant." "And how came you, Madam," I asked, "to this deep knowledge of pleasure, and what chiefly allured you unto it? Not many women and very few men have attained such a level." "I will tell you," she said, "and tell you a truth, which perchance you will marvel at. One of the greatest benefits that ever God gave me is that he sent me such sharp and severe parents and such a gentle schoolmaster. For when I am in the presence of either father or mother, [whatever I do] . . . I must do it . . . ever so perfectly, as God made the world, or else I am so sharply taunted, so cruelly threatened . . . with pinches, nips, and bobs that I think myself in hell, till the time comes that I must go to M. Elmer, who teaches me . . . gently, . . . pleasantly, and with . . . fair allurements to learning. . . . And when I am called from him, I fall on weeping because whatever I do except learning is full of grief, trouble, and fear. . . . And thus my book has been so much my pleasure and more, that in respect of it, all other pleasures, in very deed, are but trifles and troubles to me." I remember this talk gladly, both because it is so worthy of memory and because it was the last talk I ever had and the last time I ever saw that noble and worthy lady. (100–10)[33]

Nevertheless, a measure of parental interest and control must have been necessary to encourage or enforce the long hours of study that alone could not have produced young women as precocious as Lady Jane Grey, Catherine of Aragon, the More sisters, and even Princess Elizabeth herself. Ascham goes on to praise his former student, the queen, for her extraordinary literary and linguistic accomplishments:

[T]he best gentlemen of this court . . . show not so much good will, spend not so much time, bestow not so many hours, daily, orderly, and constantly for the increase of learning and knowledge, as does the Queen's Majesty her self. . . . [B]esides her fluency in Latin, Italian, French, and Spanish, she reads . . . more Greek every day, than some Prebendaries of this Church read Latin in a whole week. . . . [M]ost praiseworthy of all, within the walls of her privy chamber, she has obtained that excellency of learning, to understand, speak, and write, both wittily with her head, and fair with her hand. . . . I count this the greatest, that it pleased God to call me to be one poor minister in setting forward these excellent gifts of learning in this most excellent Prince. If the rest of our nobility would follow her example, then England might be a spectacle to all the world, for learning and wisdom in nobility. (140–41)

Ascham's praise of these two women identifies a radical shift in the conduct of a small number of aristocratic women that took place during the middle of the sixteenth century. Until these women began to read and write with educated intelligence, the pioneering educational efforts of the Christian humanists had borne little fruit except for excellent, in-house translations and other religious writings. Betty Travitsky accounts for some one hundred compositions or translations of Englishwomen during this time alone, most of which have, until recently, been neglected by scholars.[34]

Not surprisingly, women of aristocratic and gentry origin published more than any other socioeconomic group of women, sometimes paying outright for their works to be published, sometimes circulating their manuscripts until admiring male relatives had them published. Still, books and writing were considered a male prerogative, particularly the kinds of scholarly writings that depended upon classical learning. In fact, of all the male-authored publications regarding women's education, only Robert Vaughan's *Dyalogue Defensyve for Women* (1542) encourages women to translate their learning into writing:

> In our countrey natyve, women thou mayst se,
> In both tongues experte, the Latyne and the Greke
> In Rhethorycke and Poetrye, excellent they be
> And with pen to endyte [write] they be not to seke
> If women in youth, had such educacyon
> In knowledge and lernynge, as men use to have
> Theyr workes of theyr wyttes, wolde make full probacyon
> And that of men counceyll, they nede not to crave. (qtd. in Benson 209)

In those lines, Vaughan incites Renaissance women to write and then study their own works—not only for their edification and pleasure but for their benefit and empowerment as well.

But given Renaissance orthodoxy, writing and femininity seemed incongruous, despite the best efforts of humanists and reformers. If the educated woman was exceptional, the writing woman might be absurd. Regardless of their education, women were still, *by nature*, timid, passive, and tender of heart; those who were immodestly publishing their scholarly or political writings were simply unnatural.

Even a queen would have to explain herself as a writer. Each of Henry VIII's queens, even the most erudite, retained her definition as his property: each queen was an economic cipher and social possession. Powerful as they may have been in the social hierarchy, they were nonetheless women, supposedly powerless in the gender hierarchy. But when Elizabeth became queen, she had to be ungendered, to be made an exception to the rules of gender. Otherwise, she might come to represent the capacities of any woman given the chance. Elizabeth I willingly played the gender game, publicly performing her ability to transcend the limitations of her ordinary woman's body and act with the spirit of a king. In her successful speech "To the Troops at Tilbury," she says: "I know I have the body but of a weak and feeble woman, but I have the heart and stomach of a king, and of a king of England too" (qtd. in G. Rice 96). Elizabeth adroitly and continuously manipulated the paradoxes inherent in her role as female monarch.

Elizabeth is often glorified as the feminist heroine, yet her reign actually did little to affect the opportunities for contemporary women. On the stage of public life—and she liked to call it that—the queen ruled with a king's identity. Her princehood underlay her obvious femininity and lent her alone of all English-women authority and privilege. Social and gender categories collapsed to make her the most powerful person in England—male or female.

Literary Images of Women

During Elizabeth's reign, literary images of women might have ranged from the hyperbolic Petrarchan lady to a reflection of historical reality, the queen, an all-powerful female energy tempered by masculine sensibility. After all, "Queen Elizabeth's lofty stature as revered monarch, embodiment of the national destiny, and epitome of chaste virtue might suggest that English authors would fill their poems and plays with similarly heroic female characters" (Beilin 151).[35] But that would not be the case. Even within the most liberal of educational and social milieux, the ideal Renaissance woman, whether fictional or historical, remained essentially unchanged since classical times: she was chaste, silent, and obedient. Little wonder, then, that beyond the obvious exaggerations of Elizabeth herself, of exceptionally brave and long-suffering women, or of exceptionally ruthless women (literary villians), "most writers only exalted women as paragons of private virtues" (151).

Paradoxically, then, Renaissance literature characterized historical womankind as weak and timid, but an infinite number of female performances, beginning with that of their queen, were offered as sturdy and aggressive.[36] Yet despite the truly spectacular number of assertive women in Renaissance literature, female courage and tough-mindedness—both actual and fictitious—continued to be widely regarded as exceptional and "unnatural": "if a vast majority of women had failed to conform to expectations about timidity, passivity, and tenderness of heart, that would have proved only that a good many women were unnatural nowadays" (Woodbridge 214).

This condescension of Renaissance writers toward women is surprising given that their monarch was a queen, but their queen's position was a divinely ordained exception to natural rule. Therefore, the writers who ventriloquized feminine speech in literary, pedagogical, advisory, and popular accounts tended to reinforce women's traditional and essential virtues, their imaginations incapable finally of bridging the gap between the literary and the actual.

Assertive female characters. Renaissance textual images of women, for the most part, transcribe cultural presumptions of women's "naturally" subordinate status in the social hierarchy, for even those female characters who articulate their own power do so while participating in the rule of patriarchy. Still, these characters transform the margins into spaces of potential or actual (textual) strength. For instance, Edmund Spenser's epideictic *Faerie Queene* casts Britomart in the "new mold," a truly powerful female character: "O, Goddesse heavenly bright." Britomart (along with Gloriana and Belphoebe) is one of the "great sexual personae" in the work, personae who "flood the verse with a strange golden light" of principled morality (Paglia 177). Like Spenser's queen: "light seems to penetrate [their] blonde forms, so they seem midway between matter and spirit" (177).

Indeed, Spenser seems to have had a specific reason for creating his female knight of chastity, who, without losing her ardor, overcomes all who oppose her. Spenser glorifies Britomart in ways inspired by Elizabeth I. Like the virgin queen herself, Britomart looks forward to honorable marriage, which is a spiritual rather than a mere fleshly union; after all, Britomart is "pure from blame of sinfull blot" (3.2.23) and is "the flowre of chastity" (3.10.6). Beauty is a moral principle, and it is her beauty (or to the Renaissance mind, the beauty of her chastity) that overpowers people. Thus his encomium of Elizabeth can be read as a political act, epideictic, always containing a didactic function in its praise (or blame). The queen is the source of instruction rather than its object. Queen Elizabeth draws strength, power, and influence by simultaneously inhabiting two roles: that of *virgo* and mater (never *mulier*).[37] Akin to the queen, Britomart is beautiful, young, and powerful; she is drawn with such nobility and inviolable virtue that she stands out as Spenser's example of perfect womanhood: "That peerelesse paterne of Dame Natures pride, / And heavenly image of perfection" (4.6.24). Furthermore, Britomart uses her strength to alter the structure of female rule (Amazonian society), reinstating male authority:

> She there as Princess rained,
> And changing all that forme of common weale,
> The liberty of women did repeale,
> Which they had long usurpt; and them restoring
> To men's subjection, did true Iustice deale.   (5.7.42)

Britomart is Spenser's stylization of Elizabeth, just as the queen herself is a stylization of the flesh-and-blood Elizabeth; neither speaks the voice of a real woman.[38]

Another powerful—and exaggerated—female character is Shakespeare's Lady Macbeth, not as powerful as a queen but powerful enough to orchestrate the death of a king. Like Britomart, though, she is another "not-woman." She is ruled by ambition—an intense, overmastering, self-indulgent passion that is gratified at the expense of justice, kin, and sacred hospitality. But Lady Macbeth's behavior does not really raise questions about women's tenderheartedness, for she has had to be unsexed before she can divest herself of tenderness.[39] Lady Macbeth so terrifies and cows her husband with her hypermasculinity that he responds "I dare do all that may become a man; / Who dares do more is none" (Shakespeare, *Mac.* 1.7.46–47). She out-mans him, but in doing so, she loses her threat to men, for she is unnatural and misogynistic as well.[40] Like Britomart, Lady Macbeth lacks verisimilitude and serves as no example of female power. Both Britomart and Lady Macbeth speak male author's words and perform his deeds. Neither is a threat to public sensibility, no more than

Thelma or Louise are; they are entertainment. Because they are presented by males as androgynes, because they so blatantly transgress the feminine, their characterizations in no way narrow—or threaten—the distance between the literary and the actual.

Ben Jonson's *Epicoene, or The Silent Woman* presents yet another kind of female power. The Collegiate Ladies—Madam Haughty, Madam Centaure, and Mrs. Mavis—combine the negative stereotypes of Renaissance women who overstep gendered boundaries, particularly the boundary of the play's title, silence. These women are "a new foundation . . . of ladies," "that live from their husbands; and give entertainment to all the wits, and braveries [gallants] o' the time"; "cry down, or up, what they like or dislike in a brain or a fashion, with most masculine, or rather hermaphroditical authority" (1.1).

Sporting with sexual identity, this play reflects the entrenched and over-drawn idea that, once a woman violates one convention of her traditional domestic role (silence, confinement, or obedience), she automatically falls into orgies of lust and vanity (and violates the third convention, chastity). In violating any of these cultural restrictions, Collegiate Ladies are "rather hermaphroditical," *epicoene*, in fact, monstrously unnatural. They are lusty, loud, amoral, bossy, intellectually pretentious, overpowering—and thus they threaten masculine authority. These Collegiate Ladies look like women—but they act like men. So for Jonson, androgyny can be the only acceptable explanation for autonomous women. And misogyny is the only solution: such female characters are ultimately silenced.

All these female, not-woman characters are unrealistic in their possibility, unrealistic as actual threats. Forceful, public, and articulate, they are anti-Petrarchan, with character every bit as unattainable as that of the Petrarchan lady. None, in short, would inspire the songs or sonnet sequences of Spenser, Sidney, or Shakespeare, for none is "more lovely and more temperate" than a summer's day (Shakespeare, *Son.* 18). But then few living, breathing women ever were. That *Epicoene*, for instance, is burlesque, an exaggeration of lusty attitudes, suggests that at least some actual Renaissance women fell markedly short of the Petrarchan ideal.

Dissipated female strength. Other strong female characters squander their power in their own willfulness. The insubordination of the fictional Juliet, Desdemona, and the Duchess of Malfi might have rung true to Renaissance ears. After all, despite the social and economic mechanisms that reinforced arranged marriages, it was in marriage that actual parents were most often challenged. Each young woman defies her family and patriarchal authority to marry her husband of choice. But they do not threaten the structure of that authority because they all are hushed and immobilized in death. They may initially appear ungovernable, but their characters are manipulated until they pay for their obstinance and nonconformity with their lives—as they should, according to Renaissance sensibilities.

The young and beautiful Juliet, Desdemona, and the Duchess of Malfi invest everything (including their lives) in their husbands of choice. Dissembling Juliet, already married to young Romeo, goes so far as to promise her parents that she will prepare herself for her wedding to the older, better-situated Paris, "a gentleman of noble parentage, / Of fair demesnes, youthful, and nobly train'd" (3.5.180–81). But instead of preparing for a wedding that will merge family fortunes and social power, Juliet arranges for her feigned death.[41] Her deathlike trance presages her eventual suicide, the playwright's solution for her impossible situation.

O that Capulet could have learned from Brabantio, who cries when he learns that his precious Desdemona has eloped with the Moor: "O heaven! How got she out? O treason of the blood! / Fathers, from hence trust not your daughters' minds / By what you see them act" (*Oth.* 1.1.170–73). Only paternal authority could ensure that the purpose of marriage, the transfer of property from one male to another, would endure. Children (read, "daughters") who ignored their fathers undermined this reproduction of social relations. But it was the husband in these unions who ventured the greater loss: he endangered his own claims to paternal power. Little wonder that Brabantio could incite Othello with "Look to her Moor if thou hast eyes to see, / She has deceived her father and may thee" (1.3.292–93).

Older than either Juliet or Desdemona, John Webster's high-spirited, high-minded duchess, too, depends upon the blessings of her kinsmen. A widow, her dependence falls on her brothers, both of whom forbid her to remarry. "Will you hear me," she announces to her controlling brothers, "I'll never marry." But she does, for she is "the Duchess of Malfi still" (4.2). She could not be trusted by her kinsmen in terms of marriage, for like the other women, she marries secretly—as well as far beneath her station. When her marriage to her steward is discovered and she is about to be murdered along with her children, she courageously cries out that she "could curse the stars" (4.1). Even a brave duchess pays for her sins.

In these three plays, death is largely a containment of female transgression. All three women are doomed, suffering death because of circumstances that grew out of their initial disobedience, their insubordination to the men in their lives.[42] Juliet's death is a matter of fortune: Romeo does not receive the friar's explanatory letter; Friar Lawrence is too late at the vault. Desdemona's death too is determined by fortune: she is a double victim, a victim of Iago's lies and of her husband's capacity to believe them. And as for the poor duchess: she is a victim of her high estate, an estate her brothers will not have contaminated. Unlike Queen Elizabeth in her estate, the duchess remains gendered female and thus is subjected to male rule. Feminine women not kept under control, willful women like Juliet, Desdemona, and the duchess, eventually face avoidable dilemmas that transcend boundaries of rank, place, and time. Their tragedies lay not so much in ill-starred romance as in the way they brought destruction upon themselves by violating the norms of their society. Female disobedience does not go unpunished.

Masculine gaze and the fictional feminine. In the celebrated literature of the Renaissance, male writers placed their versions of women on center stage, providing those fictions a place to think, speak, and activate their male-conceived experience.[43] That same male-written literature did little to transform women's apparently private and passive virtues into the public, active attributes that were so valuable to the conduct of the commonwealth and to participation in civic life. Women's literary voices, then, were dubbed. Men were doing the actual speaking.

Regardless of her rank, whether she were fictional or flesh and blood, any woman who spoke publicly breached all three of the "cardinal and synonymous feminine virtues": chastity, silence, and obedience. Any real Renaissance woman, then, who wanted to surpass the domestic sphere struggled in a double bind: she would not only have to break through cultural-social restrictions and expectations but resist the models and worldview of various fictional stereotypes as well. Her resistance would be read against the gendered threat of female monstrosity, which could only end badly, and her efforts would be continually undercut by a woman ruler's efforts to personate masculinity. The social system simply did not allow for actual women to achieve public success or fame.

THE RENAISSANCE RHETORICAL TRADITION

During the English Renaissance, rhetoric occupied the public sphere of politics, law, diplomacy, education, the Church, and the court—the marketplace of successful men. The crucial characteristic of any ambitious man, whether entering civil administration or one of the learned professions, was facility with language. After all, eloquence shaped the individual gentleman and produced both the articulate male citizen and the artist; rhetorical expertise enhanced one's ability to overpower, gain power, or gain control by using language.[44] Rhetorical study, practice, and performance came to permeate the culture of individual improvement and achievement.[45] Believed to be central to the development of all mental capacities and to be critical preparation for all professional positions, rhetoric informed not merely styles of expression but also ways of thought and world outlook: "from typographical usage to court manners, from drama to Bacon's reform of science" (Ong, "Tudor" 40).

Consequently, the backbone of Renaissance rhetorical studies was Ciceronian belief: "the primary task of man is action and service for the community; and the contact of the spirit with the active life does not distract his powers but stimulates his highest energy" (Baron 91). Serving his society would be the ideal rhetor—a good man. In spirit, then, rhetorical study was linked, as both Cicero and Quintilian would have it, with all things good. Cicero's orator, a man broadly experienced and educated, employed his wisdom to win an audience. Quintilian's good man fused his good speech with his good morals to the point that they were indistinguishable.[46] The ethical feature of the rhetorical inheritance enabled humanists to move beyond the apparent conflict between the life of philosophical and religious contemplation (*vita contemplativa*) and that of active citizenship (*vita activa*) to practice public, political, agonistic oratory.

Practicality is perhaps the most distinctive feature of the Renaissance rediscovery of classical rhetoric, particularly rhetoric's practical application to the public, active life: "the individual's duties should go first to the country that has given him citizenship and a language, then to his fellow-citizens, his family, and friends, and lastly to himself" (Vickers, *In Defense* 271). Of course, ever-evolving definitions of the "public good" constantly supplied a demand for rhetorical performances and reinforced the Ciceronian idealism that teaching and writing allowed men to "apply their own practical wisdom and insight to the service of humanity. And for that reason also much speaking (if only it contain wisdom) is better than speculation . . . ; for mere speculation is self-centred, while speech extends its benefits to those with whom we are united by the bonds of society" (Cicero, *On Duties* 1.4.156, in *Brutus, On*).[47] Renaissance writers were to use language to bring people together, not to amuse their individual selves. Language use was social, not solitary: to think or write or speak for oneself alone was anathema to the Renaissance intellectual ideal of the active life, active citizenship for the common good.[48]

But as Renaissance rhetors actually employed their art, human practicality naturally overcame the idealism of human goodness: "[E]loquence for many Tudor writers [and speakers] was not—could not have been[—] . . . the golden language of the good and wise man . . . , but the manipulation of words in a country where eristics was respected and daily practiced" (Kinney 387). Because classical oratory had taught forceful argument and taking sides, even the most diverse discursive genres took on an oratorical cast that reflected the classical pattern—that is until rhetoric turned away from agonistic display to persuasive style and delivery.[49]

Rhetoric and Style

If Ciceronian belief was the backbone of Renaissance rhetorical studies, then style was the flesh and blood: "style is to thought as clothes are to the body," wrote Erasmus; "Just as dress and outward appearance can enhance or disfigure the beauty and dignity of the body, so words can enhance or disfigure thought. Accordingly a great mistake is made by those who consider that it makes no difference how anything is expressed, provided it can be understood somehow or other" (10.4–6). Indeed, style made the rhetorical man, for eloquence was the greatest human achievement. A man's language or style was the "social indicator both of [his] individual character and his way of communicating with his fellow beings. Wherever the question of style was debated, the larger issues of anthropology, sociology, and politics were sure to be involved," because theories of style evoked theories of man's individual motives, rhetorical, oratorical, and poetic (Plett 357).

Stylistic rhetorical study flourished during the Renaissance, merging with humanist education to contribute to and influence the incredible output of spectacular literary works in the vernacular.[50] The long-practical art of rhetoric came to focus on the study and improvement of style. In doing so, rhetoric subsumed the productive art of poetics, recognizing it as a particular case of persuasion, just as Aristotle had originally envisioned: "This is what, in the speeches in Tragedy, falls under the arts of Politics and Rhetoric; for the older poets make their personages discourse like statesmen and the moderns like rhetoricians. . . . [Thought] is shown in all they say when proving or disproving some particular point, or enunciating some universal proposition" (*Poetics* 1450.b.7–13, in *Rhetoric*). The rediscovery of Aristotle's *Poetics* in the second half of the sixteenth century made clear his deliberate crossovers: he repeatedly uses persuasive (poetic) speeches taken from epic and drama in his *Rhetoric*, and he addresses questions of audience and stylistic analysis (grammar, metaphor, and rare words) in his *Poetics*.

The coincidence of rhetoric and the poetic is in style, a convergence that provided "the humanists with the kind of synthesizing approach for which they yearned" (Murphy, *Rhetoric* 360). As poets and rhetors and poet-rhetors, the humanists worked to move beyond the careful arrangement of words: they looked beyond those individual words to an appreciation of their divine inspiration and civilizing, didactic power.[51] Thus, nearly every account of the art of Renaissance poetry or drama or culture exhibits a corresponding appreciation of the art of rhetoric and vice versa (Mohrmann).[52]

In his *Apology for Poetry*, Sidney explains the rich irony of uniting these sister arts:

> But what? methinks I deserve to be pounded for straying from Poetry to Oratory: both have such an affinity in this wordish consideration, that I think this digression will make my meaning receive the fuller understanding— . . . acknowledging ourselves somewhat awry, we [writers] may bend to the right use both of matter and manner: whereto our language giveth us great occasion, being indeed capable of any excellent exercising of it. (52)

Sidney's "right use both of matter and manner" exemplifies the course Renaissance literary, religious, and political writings would take, with self-conscious delight in words, rhetorical technique, and stylistic experimentation—all in English.

Thus, Sidney, in the true spirit of *sprezzatura*, focused on the defense of what was becoming the national *poesy*. John Lyly's rather early (1578) vernacular attempt on the public literary stage had not been wholly successful; the prose style of his *Euphues: Anatomy of Wit* was stilted, dull, and extremely artificial, especially given his deadening overuse of rhetorical schemes and tropes.[53] In a style reactionary and antithetical to that of Lyly, then, Sidney worked to establish a new literary vernacular: one of purely English idiom, yet versatile in syntax; one free from gaudy and fantastic embellishments, yet reminiscent of its predecessors in its fanciful personifications and antitheses; and one of clear and ingenious arguments, yet playful and exuberant.[54]

Sidney's theory of style forms the link between rhetoric and poetics. His apology rests, as does his understanding of a successful and worthwhile poetics, on its rhetorical ability to move men (and women) to particular virtuous actions. He calls for responsibility in language use, by both those who produce texts and those who process them. He wants his audience to be rhetors, to judge—just as they would any other rhetorical work.[55]

Rhetoric and Texts

As English intellectuals became more comfortable with using English as their professional language, they offered up a number of English rhetorics, of various quality, the earliest of which is Leonard Cox's *The Art or Crafte of Rhetoryke*, which first appeared in London around 1530. Although his is not the first mention in English of Cicero's five rhetorical divisions, Cox's rhetoric is the first systematic attempt to acquaint English readers with the original rhetorical content of the Ciceronian doctrine of invention in English.[56] Cox, a grammar school master at Reading, writes that his "professyon" was "to make some proper worke of the ryght pleasunt and parsuadyble art of Rhetoryke" (qtd. in Nelson 125).[57] Whether his students become "aduocates," "proctoures in the law," "Ambassadores," or "techars of goddes worde," they should be able to use language "in such maner as may be most sensible and accepte to theyr audience" or to "any companye, what someuer they be." Hence, it is a milestone on the long road towards the vernacularization of classical learning.

In his 1550 *Treatise of Schemes and Tropes* and in his 1555 *Treatise of the Figures of Grammar and Rhetorike*, Richard Sherry fosters eloquent expression and oratory among both the general population and grammar school boys.[58] Sherry divides his work into a study of grammar (mostly the figures, tropes, and modes of amplification) and a study of oratory, with the idea that proficiency in the former would automatically transfer to the latter. His vernacular rhetoric met with less success than Cox's, but it, nevertheless, managed to push forward the Englishing of stylistic rhetoric and literary ornament.

Thomas Wilson's *Arte of Rhetorique* (1553), the first complete Ciceronian rhetoric in English, was much more influential than Cox's had been, for not until Wilson had any Englishman accounted fully for the "five great arts" nor demonstrated the whole process of Ciceronian oratory. Believing that an excessive preoccupation with style could easily damage the content, Wilson focused on invention rather than style. He realized that persuasion may not rest with the truth of statements alone but with the right impressions of the speaker's character on the audience. His *Arte of Rhetorique* overlays rhetorical study with a general pride in English culture (many of his examples are from an Englished Erasmus, for example) and with the learning being published in English. More pronounced is his purpose of improving English itself, as a written and oral language. His famous attack on "inkehorn termes" shows his concern for the purity of the language and for style: "What wise man readyng this letter, will not take him for a very caulfe, that made it in good earnest, a thought by his inke[horn] termes, to get a good personage" (3.86–88). Wilson's emphasis on careful choice of words, amplification, and effective use and order of vivid language demonstrate his aim to make *English* as expressive, eloquent, and persuasive as the ancient tongues.

If rhetoric were ever to harness the English language, then the schemes and tropes would have to tame it. Henry Pe[a]cham offered up *The Garden of Eloquence, Conteyning the Figures of Grammer and Rhetoric* (1577), a program of *elocutio* directly connected to the thoughtful use of rhetorical figures. Convinced of the Ciceronian belief in the necessary connection of wisdom and eloquence, Peacham deliberately chooses English as the language to reach the broadest possible audience, so "that their Eloquence maye be wise, and their wisdome eloquent" (A.ii). In writing for anyone who could read English, Peacham fulfills a special need.[59] Disappointed to find "many good bookes of Philosophy and preceptes of wysedome, set forth in english, and very few of Eloquence," he was suddenly moved "to take this little Garden in hande, and to set therein such fyguratyue Flowers, both of Grammer and Rhetorick, as doe yeelde the sweete sauour of Eloquence" (dedication to *The Garden*). For Peacham, then, rhetoric provided men an opportunity to wield eloquence and wisdom simultaneously.

His work was soon followed by George Puttenham's *Arte of English Poesie* (1589), another attempt to teach persuasive style, this time in terms of poetry rather than oratory. Puttenham was convinced that poetry was a nobler form of persuasion than prose, for verse is a

> maner of vtterance more eloquent and rethoricall than the ordinarie prose, which we vse in our daily talke: because it is decked and set out with all maner of fresh colours and figures, which maketh that it sooner inuegleth the iudgement of a man, and carieth his opinion this way and that, whither soeuer the heart by impression of the eare shalbe most affectionatly bent and directed. (1.4)

Although the art of rhetoric could ornament either, poetry was more persuasive than prose, both psychologically and historically: "the Poets were . . . from the beginning the best perswaders and their eloquence the first Rethoricke of the world" (1.4). Although it concentrates on verse, *The Arte of English Poesie* raises issues of style for both vernacular verse and prose, for in either genre, the English language must be elevated, beautiful, and rhythmic to be memorable and persuasive.

Rhetoric, Eloquence, and Influence

Renaissance men began to feel that English was theirs to form into any style they wished. And they began to celebrate English *as language*. Consequently, they ranged in style from the purest simplicity of Ascham's hero John Cheke (who along with Wilson promoted anti–"inkehorn" terms) to the extravagant rhetoric and vocabulary of Lyly's Euphues. The development of English oratory so complemented the development of English poetry that all wordsmiths—poets and orators alike—recognized their persuasive power even if they did not always embrace their responsibilities. No longer necessary to prepare students for the career of orator in a democracy, "where major political decisions hinged on one effective speech in an open assembly" (Vickers, "Some" 84), rhetoric survived as a practical application to invigorating the English language itself, in all its stylistic uses, both private and public, across the genres.

The union of rhetoric with poetics—eloquence—brought to the fore an exuberant, forceful, and confident English language. In fact, "as the Tudors continued to develop their own high age of rhetoric, they drew more and more on what we should call imaginative or creative techniques to attract their listeners and persuade their audiences. As ambassadors, they needed oratory: as orators, they became, in Lucian's words, actors. And as writers they became poets" (Kinney 387). This Renaissance of style enjoyed great prestige—in spite of the controversies it was subjected to (e.g., inkhorn terms vs. pure English; Ciceronianism vs. Senecanism; the use of the vernacular vs. "learned" languages)—because language, the English language, was thought to be a social indicator both of man's individual character and of his way of communicating with his fellow beings. Except for comparing beautiful language to a well-bred woman's beautiful clothes, neither a woman's rank nor her character is ever mentioned in the rhetorical treatises. Rhetoric, in the most traditional sense, remained the province of men, the product of teaching and practice, a means of achievement and power. Rhetoric is the vehicle by which the male writer or speaker dramatizes his social awareness, experiments boldly with the flowering of the English language, and represents himself to his audience. For the Renaissance gentleman, then, rhetoric was indispensable, the capping of wisdom and good argument with eloquence.

For the Renaissance man, erudition and rhetoric (wisdom and eloquence) were the means to an end, whether social position, power, or persuasion. For Renaissance women, however, wisdom and chastity formed their reputations. Any rhetoric and erudition they might obtain would be used as ends in themselves, not as public display. Even so, a number of women followed alternative routes into the rhetorical tradition of learned discourse, with its persuasive wisdom, art, and eloquence.

MARGINAL VOICES: WOMEN IN THE RHETORICAL TRADITION

In his 1952 *Elizabethan Woman*, Carroll Camden assured us that women participated in the rhetorical tradition of wisdom and eloquence: "cultural interests became quite fashionable for women, so that the educated woman became a kind of ideal, and the principles of her education were those of the humanistic scholars. . . . [T]he status of women was even more improved by Queen Elizabeth, who . . . was looked upon as a paragon of learning" (56). Now, many of his assertions regarding the rising status of Renaissance women rhetors seem debatable; however, his catalog of well-educated Renaissance women remains irrefutable: Elizabeth I, the Cooke sisters, Jane Howard, Jane of Somerset, Jane and Mary of Arundel, Lady Jane Grey, Marie Stuart, Elizabeth Fane, the More sisters, Mary Sidney, Margaret How Ascham, Jane Fox, Dorothy Leigh, Mary and Jane Maltravers, Elizabeth Hane Weston, Arabella Stuart Seymour, Esther Inglis, Catherine Tishem, and Elizabeth Legge (57–58).

Camden goes on to gauge Renaissance women's contributions to the intellectual atmosphere, statistically: "Over fifty women wrote some eighty-five compositions during the years from 1524 to 1640" (58). More recently, Betty Travitsky has accounted for over one hundred works written by women who were "stimulated to write by the thinking and writings concerning women of Renaissance humanists and Reformers" (3). Humanists and reformers had not changed women's legal status in any discernible way, nor had they opened up the world of affairs to Renaissance Englishwomen. Nevertheless, the writings of both these groups stimulated women's intellectual pursuits that could be undertaken privately, particularly in terms of religious work and translations.

Outside wealthy homes (and a few remaining convents), the literacy rate for women was extremely low, most usually limited to reading from the vernacular Bible, prayer books, psalters, homilies, and other religious books, which were available in churches.[60] The ability to write, let alone compose, was not automatically linked to an ability to read. After all, "teaching women to read the words of men without teaching them to write their own was one effective means of silencing them" (Hannay 8). Women's writing was restricted in other ways as well: their lack of education excluded them from the language of particular learned groups, those that used Latin, for instance, in their professional and theological discussions. Given their small measure of literacy and given that women were socialized to keep their intellectual accomplishments within their private sphere, Renaissance women's publication rate is amazingly high:

> Fifty-eight of these [eighty-five] books were printed separately, while the others appeared in anthologies, liturgies, and other collections. The nature of these printed pieces is rather interesting: they include three translations of non-religious works, sixteen translations of religious works, thirty original non-religious compositions, and thirty-six original religious compositions. . . . [M]ore than sixty percent of their printed efforts are given over to religious subjects. (C. Camden 58)

Clearly, most women's writing related to religious concerns or to translations.[61] Religious writings remained a suitable venue for women to explore in the shadow of God (as they searched for their own spiritual perfection); translations permitted them to produce derivations in the shadow of the original male author. Still, at a time when publishing was not considered a suitable goal for either men or women of good rank, Camden's publication numbers cannot begin to reflect the amount of writing and intellectual exchange actually taking place, the number of intellectual, writing women who will remain unknown to us.[62] Camden's numbers, then, support the sad probability that only a small percentage of the female population was active in intellectual circles. And for these relatively few women, who emigrated slowly from the domestic sphere, public articulation came gradually—over generations.

Even an English queen tread softly on rhetorical territory. The first woman to publish her work in English with the sole intention of influencing the public was Queen Catherine Parr, author of the 1547 *Lamentacion, or Complaynt of a Sinner* and *Prayers, or Meditacyons.*[63] She repeatedly invoked the humility topos when she published *Lamentacion*, writing that she was motivated entirely

> by the hate I owe to sin, who has reigned in me, partly by the love I owe to all Christians, whom I am content to edify, even the thexample [sic] of mine own shame, forced and constrained with my heart and words, to confess and declare to the world, how ingrate, negligent, unkind, and stubborn, I have been to God my Creator: and how beneficial, merciful, and gentle, He has been always to me His creature, being such a miserable, wretched sinner. (qtd. in Travitsky 39)

Queen Catherine, the last wife of Henry VIII, devised and commanded a specific rhetorical situation—but with hesitation. Extremely well educated and erudite in her day, Queen Catherine, nevertheless, wrote within the traditional constraints of women's deliberate and systematic marginalization from rhetorical activity.

In his widely circulated *De studiis et literis* (c. 1405), liberal educator Leonardo Bruni celebrated women's learning, but he expressly prohibited the study of rhetoric to women. In a letter to an about-to-be-married countess to whom he directed his tract, Bruni writes,

> subtleties of Arithmetic and Geometry are not worthy to absorb a cultivated mind
> . . . and the great and complex art of Rhetoric should be placed in the same category. My chief reason is the obvious one, that I have in view the cultivation most fitting to a woman. To her neither the intricacies of debate nor the oratorical artifices of action and delivery are of the least practical use, if indeed they are not positively unbecoming. Rhetoric in all its forms—public discussion, forensic argument, logical fencing, and the like—lies absolutely outside of the province of woman. (qtd. in Jones 75)[64]

According to Bruni, then, rhetoric "lies absolutely outside of the province of woman" and remains the rightful province of men. No woman could enter the rhetorical sphere representing herself as a woman, not even a queen. Instead, a woman had to be swept into the public sphere on a wave of intellectual support, so that her rhetorical endeavors could be read through a masculine screen of male words, male religion, or male rule.

The intellectual women of the Renaissance fall into three generations: those supported by the initial wave of Christian humanism, those encouraged by the reformists, and, finally, those supporting the literary rhetoric of the late sixteenth century. Those relatively few Englishwomen can be represented by three: Margaret More Roper, who, in successfully uniting her erudition and her domestic vocation, exemplified the ideals of the new humanist learning and translated male words; Anne Askew, who implemented the rhetoric and dialectic of the Protestant reformers to understand and propagate her beliefs and to defend herself, using the masculine religion of Christianity; and Queen Elizabeth I, whose patronage of individual literary rhetorical endeavors was overshadowed only by her own private literary and public rhetorical accomplishments presented behind the guise of a male ruler, a king.

These representative women are like those in Christine de Pisan's *City of Ladies*: female intellectuals of a privileged elite, not representative of women in all walks of life yet representative of a type. And in each case her "feminine voice" reflects a measure of individuality, as well as a measure of internalized male aesthetic norms. And in each case, her best work was in the vernacular.

The Margins of Christian Humanism

Profound though its influences on educational and rhetorical practices were, Christian humanism did not open up the full range of intellectual opportunities for women, not even for upper-class women. Those female rulers and aristocrats renowned for their erudition never entertained humanism as a profession, necessary for the male-only careers of politics, teaching, and the court. Aristocratic men might be educated to serve the state, but women would be educated to serve and honor men. A woman's intellectual accomplishment was considered an end in itself, like fine needlework or musical performance. Her education prepared her to patronize further humanistic studies and to be virtuous, all the time keeping her hands and mind busy. Sir Thomas More reinforces this point, writing to daughter Margaret that her studies prevent her from being "idle and slothful," that he had never found her "idling" (qtd. in Stapleton 100, 108). For Margaret More Roper, then, her erudition would keep her busy, as well as please the men in her life, her husband and father and their male friends: "Erasmus, for her exquisite learning, wisedome and vertue, made such an accompt of her, that he called her the flowre of all the learned matrones in Inglande. . . . [H]e . . . dedicated his commentaries made vpon certaine hymnes of Prudentius. / And to say the truth, she was our Sappho, our Aspasia, our Hypatia, . . . our Cornelia" (Harpsfield n.p.).

One of the leading proponents for the education of women and known for the education of his favorite child (Margaret), More, nonetheless, considered learning in gendered terms. In a letter to his children's tutor, he writes,

[Men and women] both have the same human nature, and the power of reason differentiates them from the beasts; both, therefore, are equally suited for those studies by which reason is cultivated. . . . If it be true that the soil of woman's brain be bad . . . (and on this account many keep women from study), I think . . . on the same grounds a woman's wit is to be cultivated all the more diligently, so that nature's defect may be redressed by industry. (qtd. in Reynolds 17)

And industrious Roper would be: "A perfect master of Greek and Latin, some knowledge of philosophy, astronomy, physic, arithmetic, logic, rhetoric, and music—these were the accomplishments of Margaret More" (Neale, *Queen* 10). Thomas Stapleton, More's earliest biographer, describes Roper as attaining, "in literature and other branches of study," "a degree of excellence that would scarcely be believed in a woman. . . . She wrote very eloquently prose and verse both in Greek and Latin. Two Latin speeches . . . are in style elegant and graceful" (103). More himself would write to Roper regarding the impressive, yet very private, success of her intellectual investment. Writing from prison (c. 1534), he reminds her of one of his bad jokes:

> It was to the effect that you were to be pitied, because the incredulity of men would rob you of the praise you so richly deserved for your laborious vigils, as they would never believe, when they read what you had written, that you had not often availed yourself of another's help: whereas of all writers you least deserved to be thus suspected. Even when a tiny child you could never endure to be decked out in another's finery. But, my sweetest Margaret, you are all the more deserving of praise on that account. Although you cannot hope for an adequate reward for your labour, yet nevertheless you continue to unite to your singular love of virtue the pursuit of literature and art. Content with the approbation of your conscience, in your modesty you do not seek for the praise of the public, nor value it over much even if you receive it, but because of the great love you bear us, you regard us—i.e., your husband and myself—as a sufficiently large circle of readers for all that you write. (qtd. in Stapleton 105)

Her learning is a private matter, intended for *no other audience* than her father and her husband. Instead of public articulation and acclaim, both of which would be indecorous, she must work for the approval of the men who love her and whom she loves. In another letter, her father writes: "I send only [the amount of money] you have asked, but would have added more, only that as I am eager to give, so am I desirous to be asked and coaxed by my daughter, especially by you, whom virtue and learning have made so dear to my soul" (qtd. in Stapleton 102).

Even though humanism brought Latin and Greek literacy, classical learning, and rhetorical educational practices (stylistic not oratorical) to noble daughters, as well as to noble sons, those young women were to use and enjoy their learning privately—and silently. Roper was expected to speak Latin on demand, for her fluency reflected glory on her father. But any public demonstration of learning initiated by women themselves was problematic, and strong psychological constraints were exerted against producing any original written work displaying this learning. To speak in public was deemed unseemly. Besides, an assertively intelligent woman was thought to be self-indulgent and licentious. Only a saint could neutralize that suspicion.

Translating from the Margins: Margaret More Roper

A paragon of Renaissance educated woman was saintly Margaret More Roper (1505–44), eldest daughter and first child of Jane Colt More and Sir Thomas More, the child who most "resembled her father . . . in stature, appearance, and voice, . . . in mind and in general character" (Stapleton 103). Fully accommodating to the male-inscribed currency of thought, she, nevertheless, became recognized as a fine scholar, perhaps the finest Renaissance scholar relegated to the margins of discourse. From secondary sources, we know that Roper wrote poetry, entertained her father and his scholarly clique with her emendations of a corrupt Cyprian manuscript, performed (with her sisters) a disputation before Henry VIII, translated Erasmus from the Latin and Eusebius from the Greek, surpassed her father's composition on the Four Last Things (death, judgment, hell, and heaven), composed an argumentative oration on the rights of a rich man to poison the poor man's bees, and penned many Latin letters.[65]

Even though her literary output far exceeded even her father's view of the proper bounds of women's activity, Roper's intellectual boundaries were circumscribed by timeless, male-imposed tradition. Like the perfect humanist woman she was, she patronized her in-home school and limited her writing to dedications of translations, letters, private devotional meditations, diaries, and translations—except for a few surviving letters and her published translation of Erasmus, her works have unfortunately been lost or destroyed.[66]

That so many intellectual women limited their work to translations is not coincidental: composition was the masculine art, the articulated original; translation was feminine—derivative, defective, muted, and "other." Although men might offer translations to patrons as evidence of their capacity for public service, women could not.

> [T]his low opinion of translating perhaps accounts for why women were allowed to translate at all. . . . The dynamics underlying this way of thinking are transparent. Translation, especially translation of works by males, was allowed to women because it did not threaten the male establishment as the expression of personal viewpoints might. Perhaps more importantly, however, translation did not threaten the male ego. By engaging in this supposedly defective form of literary activity, women did not threaten perceptions of male superiority; any competence they displayed could be dismissed by denigrating the task of translation itself. (Lamb 116)

At the heart of the differences between male and female writers, then, is the decorum of language. Women's language must reflect the traditional feminine virtues (chastity, modesty, and, ironically, silence) and is thus constricted in a way that men's language is not. For example, in a letter to William Gunnell, More family tutor, More writes: "Renown for learning, when it is not united with good life, is nothing else than splendid and notorious infamy: this would be specially the case in a woman" (qtd. in Stapleton 94). The educated Renaissance women were silenced, deprived of nearly all outlets for their intellectual abilities—except for their primary outlet, translation.

Learned women from aristocrats to queens were socially encouraged to translate. Translation provided the educated woman an outlet for her rhetorical skills, as well as a voice and an identity as a writer, decorously concealed in the work of a known and accepted male author. Translation deprived those women of any original voice; their originality overlay a man's literary creation.[67]

Despite her father's earlier admonition against seeking fame, Roper published her translation of Erasmus's *Devout Treatise upon the Pater Noster* (1524), which was exceptionally good, meeting with much acclaim, including that of her father.[68] Not only was she entrusted with translating work by Erasmus, one of the finest minds of her time, but her translation is itself a major work. One of the earliest examples of the Englishing of Erasmian piety, her translation initiated a broad campaign directed at the English-reading public in that it domesticated and disseminated Erasmus's original thoughts on the paternoster. But perhaps more important to her contemporaries, Roper's translation does nothing to detract from her womanly modesty, piety, and humility. Richard Hyrde wrote the introduction to her translation and describes Roper thus:

> this gentlewoman, which translated this little book, hereafter following: whose virtuous conversation, living, and sad [serious] demeanor may be proof evident enough what good learning does, where it is sure rooted: of whom other women may take example of prudent, humble and wifely behavior, charitable and very Christian virtue, with which she has, with God's help, endeavored herself, no less to garnish her soul than it has liked his goodness, with lovely beauty and comeliness, to garnish and set out her body: and undoubted is it that to the increase of her virtue, she has taken and takes no little occasion of her learning, besides her other manifold and great commodities, taken of the same; among which commodities, this is not the least, that with her virtuous worshipful, wise and well learned husband, she has by the occasion of her learning and his delight therein, such especial comfort, pleasure and pastime, as were not well possible for one unlearned couple, either to take together or to conceive in their minds, what pleasure is therein. (qtd. in Watson 167–68)

Hyrde's encomium vindicates women in general as students of the humanities and justifies Roper in particular, for "she has shown herself not only erudite and elegant [in both English and Latin], but has also used such wisdom, such discreet and substantial judgment, in expressing lively the Latin" (171). Her first-rate translation, a manifestation of her rhetorical training and skills, appeared as an act of piety, as an extension of her studies, as a tribute to her father, and as an integral part of her family's interests. And her prose seems markedly more steady than Hyrde's own.

Roper's translation, one of the earliest publications by a woman, is remarkably smooth, idiomatic, metaphorical, personal, and poetic—especially considering that English syntax was still in an unsettled state, neither so rich in resources nor so carefully standardized as it has become. Her naturally gentle rhythm, straightforward diction, and logical placement of phrases and clauses (depending on their relationships to the other parts of the sentence) suggests an expertise in English composition not frequently found in the English prose of the early sixteenth century. The following is a typical passage from the meditation on the third petition:

> And that we may be able every day more and more / to perform all this / help us O Father in heaven / that the flesh may ever more and more be subject to the spirit / and our spirit of one assent / and one mind with thy spirit. And likewise as now in diverse places thy children / which are obedient to the gospel / obey and do after thy will: so grant they may do in all the world beside / that every man may know and understand / that thou alone art the only head and ruler of all things / and that in likewise as there are none in heaven / which mutter and rebel against thy will / so let every man here in earth / with good mind and glad cheer obey thy will and godly precepts. (Roper 116)[69]

Her unpretentious yet sensitive and poetic translation was only to be expected, her father having provided her with rigorous and vigorous translation exercises.

Roper's translation far surpassed schoolgirl exercises and suggests that she had undergone "a considerable apprenticeship in the art of vernacular translation," for it is immediately apparent that "the translation proceeds straightforwardly from one clause to another of the often long and somewhat involved sentences of the original," and yet

> it rarely follows the Latin ordering and structure to the extent of being slavishly literal. . . . In general the Latin construction is treated with felicitous freedom which combines scholarship and art. The diction is also praiseworthy, a Latin word being seldom expressed by its English derivative. Likewise observable now and again is a pleasing rhythm, attained in part by skillfully transposing the Latin order . . . the translation is to be regarded as a mature achievement of its kind. (Gee 264–65)

Erasmus's own influence is apparent in Roper's translation; her tendency toward amplification is resonant with *De copia*. Roper's careful balance of linguistic daring and confidence is expressed in her addition, expansion, or reversal of phrases, clauses, and ideas and in her doublings and couplings of Erasmus's singular words. For instance, she uses "know and understand" for *intelligant*; "head and ruler" for *Monarcham*; and "mutter and rebel" for *repugnet* (Verbrugge 40).

While Roper is clearly aware of Erasmus's elegant parallelism, she often softens it, thereby achieving an easier and more expansive English rhythm. And her amplification reveals her perception of Tudor life: Erasmus's *ambitio* becomes "ambitious desire of worldly promotion." At least twice she slightly expands a potentially dramatic scene involving a relationship between God and man, which allowed her to reflect upon a relationship between child and (heavenly) father. In fact, "the most striking aspect of her Englishing . . . is how she heightened this relationship: by position of vocatives, by an increased number of 'father's' [sic] or 'good father's' [sic]" (McCutcheon 462). Her syntactic and semantic choices render Erasmus's already meditative and conversational work even more so. But such an impressive translation was only to be expected of one trained in both rhetoric and poetics, sister arts thought to provide the rules for writing well in prose and verse, respectively. .

This particular translation is an outstanding example of an interim stage in the development of modern English, a stage that did much to establish modern English literary prose. Yet because women were discouraged from creating their own original works, her translation is also representative of women's derivative works. In some instances, religious devotion could both liberate women as writers and simultaneously hobble their intellectual confidence. But in Roper's case, her devotion may well have inspired an unequaled translation that was richly supported by her magnificent intellectual background.

Roper's Greek and Latin letters, her *ars dictaminis*, were additional proof of her splendid gift of powerful language, no doubt a direct result of her rhetorical training and academic exercises. Unfortunately, however, the few of her letters that have received special study do little to bring out any sense of her individuality. The exchange of letters with her father during his imprisonment are thought to be so alike in style and substance (and in "rather little" punctuation) that the problem of specific authorship surrounds them, especially one important letter. But questions of authorship are not the only problems for those of us interested in calibrating the full measure of her rhetorical power. Most of her work remains lost.

Despite the loss, enough of her work remains to establish Margaret More Roper as a practitioner of rhetoric. She is best known as a sensitive translator and exceptional grammarian, as a rhetor of learned rather than creative tracts. But lest anyone think her first-rate mind and education were put to second-rate tasks or that those tasks made little contribution to rhetorical practice, we must remember that by the standards of any century, sixteenth-century Roper was an impressive scholar and skilled practitioner of her rhetorical training. Her translation of Erasmus alone earned her position as the exemplar of the new learning, the "new" educated woman personified. And like most early Renaissance Englishwomen, Roper showed no signs of dissatisfaction with the thinking of Renaissance theorists. For instance, without any complaint, she forbore publishing her own translation from Greek to Latin of Eusebius when she learned that Bishop Christopherson was engaged in the identical task.[70] If Roper ever publicly or privately resisted or questioned male authority in general or her father's in particular, such evidence has not been preserved.

The Margins of the Protestant Reformation

From its inception, the Protestant Reformation incorporated a fundamental paradox. It maintained woman's overall subordination to the patriarchy, be it

God, father, or husband, by manipulating her desire for godliness as a way to silence her. Thomas Bentley's 1583 clichés demonstrate: "There is nothing that becommeth a maid better than sobernes, silence, shamefastnes, and chastitie, both of bodie and mind. For these things being once lost, shee is no more a maid, but a strumpet in the sight of God" (qtd. in Hull 142). Nevertheless, the Protestant Reformation granted women relative autonomy in spiritual matters; it recognized women's right to read and interpret the Scriptures and even to disagree with men's interpretations. Therefore, the silenced Christian woman could breach that silence whenever her voice brought forth her religious convictions.

Central to the Protestant Reformation was, of course, the return to the purity of the early Christian Church in terms of liturgy, scripture, New Testament authority (over mere Church traditions and human inventions), and social practice. But on the margins of the Reformation lay an emphasis on public education for the "priesthood of all believers." Like the Christian humanists, the reformers advocated woman's education as the foundation for her piety, her "sobernes." All Christians should be capable of reading the Bible and other religious literature, and at the core of both disciplines (humanism and reformism) was rhetoric: it permeated the literature, and its aim was the instruction of men and women alike, women being just as important and worthy in the lay piety.

Reformist instruction differed markedly from that of the humanists in essential ways: for the humanists, a broad, multilingual education connoted intellectual and social *cultivation* for upper-class women; whereas, for the reformers, a more narrow, vernacular, biblical education for women of all ranks connoted the moral and social *domination* inherent in the Christianization of society. Although less intensive intellectually than (Christian) humanism, the reformist educational program was broader in one way: it fashioned itself as returning to earliest Christianity, a spiritual movement that not only extended equality to its female followers but also provided the opportunity to address the problems of the Church just as men did:

> [T]here were said to be more women than men in the very first large body of English separatists, in London in 1568. . . . It was of course among the Quakers that the spiritual rights of women attained their apogee. All the Friends were allowed to speak and prophesy on a basis of complete equality, for the Inner Light knew no barriers of sex. (K. Thomas 44–45)

"Women were the first Quaker preachers in London, in the Universities, in Dublin and in the American colonies" (47). Although upper-class and aristocratic women were the first to exercise this right to prophecy, middle-class women soon joined in as outspoken critics of existing religious practices. The sexual equality granted by the sects meant that women, as well as men, could be formally accused of error, heresy, blasphemy—all punishable offenses.[71] Anne Askew was one of those women.

Inscribed in the Margins

Speaking Through God from the Margins: Anne Askew

As much as Christian humanist Margaret More Roper defines the ideal of the learned and virtuous woman as a private, modest, silent being, Protestant reformer Anne Askew (1521–46) seems to diverge from it: she was courageous, disputatious, and strong. One of seventy (only four were women) who succumbed to the fires of Protestant martyrdom during the reign of Henry VIII, the quick-witted, spiritually tenacious, and publicly outspoken Askew set an example just as important as Roper's: she served as a role model for those Protestant women who might not otherwise have viewed themselves as sufficiently important or learned to witness for their faith. Furthermore, she is the only woman to have left records of her religious sufferings, her *Examinations*.[72]

Like Roper, the aristocratic Askew was the daughter of a strong father (Sir William Askew, or Ayscough, of Stallingborough in Lincolnshire) who educated her according to aristocratic humanist principles and promised her in marriage to a suitable partner. But Anne Askew's eventual marriage was not to be as happy as the Ropers', perhaps because she was married in her deceased sister's stead to Thomas Kyme, so that the Askew family could save the money. She reluctantly married Kyme, fulfilled her Christian duty by bearing him two children, and then turned to the reformist movement. When Kyme evicted her from their home for rejecting Catholic doctrine, she moved to London, discarded his family name, and thereafter used her own.

Askew's education, status, and religious convictions earned her the attention of Protestant sympathizer Queen Catherine Parr, whose circle of female friends represented religious reform more extensive than that officially permitted (and whose male friends included religious instructors and preachers whose teachings touched upon widespread Church abuses). Henry VIII's imminent death provided the religious conservatives on his privy council (Stephen Gardiner, Bishop of Winchester; Thomas Howard, third Duke of Norfolk) an opportunity to thwart a reformist ascendance during the reign of Edward VI and a reason to attack the queen's own privy chamber and the more influential and powerful reformist figures with whom she was associated.[73] Anne Askew, tangentially connected with the queen's inner circle, would become a target of the attack.

When Askew was arrested in 1546 on grounds of radical Protestantism (her husband's eviction of her having raised suspicion), she became the first gentlewoman to be judged by a jury. Accordingly, she was forced out of woman's private sphere and thrust directly into public view; she was later that year burned at the stake. What she spoke during her public inquisition and recorded afterwards established her as a public figure, a cause célèbre.[74] Immediately, the public nature of her questionings (and her torture) ensured the wide currency of her words. Her *Examinations* became a matter of public record.

The proceedings of Askew's interrogation, replete with physical torment, were cruel and vicious, as well as entirely illegal; "the law prohibited the rack-ing of women in general, and Askew was a *gentle*woman besides" (Beilin 43). All Protestant propaganda aside, her torture was an unusual technique in reli-gious interrogations and unprecedented when employed against a gentlewoman already condemned to die. To the surprise of her enemies, though, those heated proceedings would purify her as an honest and God-fearing woman and only enflame the reformist movement.

Whether fueled by her reformist beliefs or by the power of her individual personality, Askew was one of the first Renaissance women to stride into the public arena, wielding her rhetorical power for persuasion, exhortation, and self-defense, delivering her rhetorical contributions to the reformist movement. A century after Askew's death, Bathsua Makin would credit the whole of the Protestant Reformation to its courageous women, women such as Anne Askew: "Mrs. Anne Askew, a person famous for learning and piety, so seasoned the Queen and ladies at Court, by her precepts and examples, and after sealed her profession with her blood, that the seed of reformation seemed to be sowed by her hand" (134).

Askew's *Examinations*, allegedly based on her Newgate Prison papers and the public record of her questioning, were widely distributed among reformers and reprinted four times during the reign of Edward VI. In these writings, this "true Christian woman" continually raises her voice in public to bear witness to her faith, in defiance not only of her estranged husband but of the whole hierarchy of Church and state as well. Askew spoke out against forced mar-riages and religious persecution, for in her case, the two were related. But John Bale's enthusiastic elucidations of her *Examinations* clarify the source of her strength and her public voice: God spoke through the purity of Askew's refor-mist beliefs; Anne Askew was not speaking in public as a woman but rather as a spokeswoman for her masculine God: "God's strength is made perfect in weakness" (2 Cor. 12.9). Nevertheless, she eventually suffered cruelly: "this mother of two little children—this sweet young Christian—this wise and noble lady—[was] drawn and stretched and twisted until every cord cut deep into the flesh of wrists and ancles [sic] and the blood spurt forth—until every joint [was] dislocated, and every bone almost . . . broken. *Why?* Because she [would] not lie" (Sharp 12).

Askew's arrest on suspicion of heresy occurred within the context of the Protestant-Catholic controversy over the Sacrament. Specifically, she was charged with denying the Real Presence in the Sacrament of the altar, one of the key theological issues of her day. Although she was rumored to have pro-vided answers to such inane questions as "whether a mouse eating the host received God or not," she writes, "I made them no answer but smiled" (L.i). She did answer, however, the question of whether she believed that "the Sacra-ment hanging over the altar was the very body of Christ really." She replied as she knew Jesus would have her do. She flatly rejected the existence of any priestly miracle in the Eucharist: "As for that ye call your God, it is a piece of bread. For a more proof thereof . . . let it but lie in the box three months and it will be mouldy" (qtd. in Plowden 112). After incriminating herself with this initial answer, which ensured her conviction as a heretic, Askew was, from then on, intrepid and articulate in defending, declaring, and clarifying her strong religious convictions: "And upon these words that I have now spoken will I suffer death. . . . I doubt it not, but God will perform his work in me, like as he hath begun" (qtd. in Plowden 112).

Her inquisitors relied on scholasticism, which stressed adherence to Church doctrine, only to discover that she too could play their game. She resisted all their doctrinal traps, playing upon her lack of formal training, her rhetorical "otherness." Using a time-honored and -tested rhetorical ploy, she responds to their scholastic arguments using her classification as a woman for her explanation. Refusing to speak personally, she speaks categorically, again on the subject of the host:

> [H]e asked me if the host should fall, and a beast [mouse] ate it, whether the beast received God or not: I answered, "Seeing that you have taken the pains to ask this question, I desire you also to take so much pain more, as to explain it yourself. For I will not do it because I perceive you come to tempt me." And he said that it was against the order of schools that he who asked the question should answer it. I told him that I was but a woman, and knew not the course of schools. (qtd. in Travitsky 175)

Not the least source of her power was that she was a woman, "other," alienated from all accepted sources of power but that of God. Her religious convictions empowered her to transcend gender inequality by refusing to interpret Bible passages for her male accusers: "I answered that I would not throw pearls before swine, for acorns were good enough" (L.iii). As her *Examinations* so movingly attest, those convictions also permitted her to penetrate and undermine the masculine view that contained, detained, and eventually executed her. She would speak only for herself—as a Christian woman. But she never allowed herself to comment on her personal, her social, or her domestic life or to respond to her torture; nor could she be forced to speak for or incriminate others, whether reformist or otherwise. All those subjects were extraneous to her religious beliefs.

Anne Askew's rhetoric of silence. In "Expert Witnesses and Secret Subjects," Elizabeth Mazzola writes that Askew was neither marginalized nor repressed; instead, she was a woman who, given the chance, refused to tell her own secrets: "even when she is tortured, Askew never betrays anything but the Protestant faith to which she adheres, reveals no concealed information besides her extraordinary mastery of Scripture, and refuses to share the names of any other members of her sect" (158). Askew is not an object of knowledge—but a subject—and "every occasion to reveal herself serves instead as one to proselytize, to sharpen her doctrine, to elaborate her position" (159). In other words, Askew deploys a purposeful rhetoric of silence: "God has given me the gift of knowledge, but not of utterance. And Solomon says, that a woman of few words, is a gift of God, Proverbs 19" (qtd. in Travitsky 177).

Askew knows how to use silence to her advantage, to "freeze a frame," to keep her listeners "hanging," to command attention, or to indicate disapproval (Gilmore 146–47). When Askew sees the advantage of not speaking, her words are few, but when she does speak, she deflects the question back to her examiners or uses the Scriptures to her disputational (if not mortal) advantage—every time:

> I was asked why I was in trouble. "You tell me," I said. It is "because of that book you have read by a man already burned." I told him that "such unadvised hasty judgment is a token of a slender wit." I showed him the book and he could find nothing wrong with it. The bishop of London told me to bare my conscience. I told him there was nothing to bare. I was asked to interpret a text of Paul. I answered that a woman should not presume to interpret Paul. I was accused of making mock of the Easter communion. "Produce the accuser," said I. I was asked, "If Scripture says that the bread and wine are the body of Christ will you believe it?" "I believe Scripture." "If Scripture says they are not the body of Christ will you believe it?" "I believe Scripture. I believe all things as Christ and the apostles did leave them." I was asked to sign a confession that the body and blood of Christ are in substance in the mass. I said, "in so far as Holy Scripture doth agree unto." (Foxe 5: 537–38)

Her *Examinations* record not only her own spiritual heresy and her inquisitors' unflagging questioning, but they especially emphasize her controlled response. Of special interest to her inquisitors, of course, were questions of her marital state, her court connections (and support), her fellow reformists. Her inquisitors' first point of entry into her religious antagonism was her having left her Catholic husband after her own conversion (or lapse). Askew knew Bible texts intimately enough to dispute them with the best of clergymen and use them for her own linguistic defense, just like the Protestant saint she would become. Instead of revealing anything about her personal relationship with her Catholic husband, instead of giving the prosecution any personal details that they could use against her, she deferred to St. Paul's first epistle regarding the reason a woman could seek a divorce: "If the unbelieving depart, let him depart. A brother or sister is not under bondage in such cases" (1 Cor. 7.15). Although by her example, divorce on such grounds would later become a tenet of the Protestant reformers, it was not acceptable under the rule of Henry VIII, who had set his own precedent for divorce.

When the bishop told her she would be burned, an end she never doubted, she answered that she had searched all through the Scriptures "yet could . . . never find there that either Christ or his Apostles put any creature to death." She writes, "Well, well, said I, God will laugh your threatenings to scorn, Psalms 2. Then I was commanded to stand aside" (qtd. in Travitsky 180).

As a result of her humanist education, Askew knew well the traditionally masculine forms of argument in terms of style and content, and she deliberately resists those forms. In her response to her inquisitor's major proposition, she reveals nothing about herself; instead, she asks for his evidence:

> Then the Bishop's chancellor rebuked me and said that I was much to blame for uttering the Scriptures. For Saint Paul (he said) forbade women to speak or to talk of the word of God. I answered him that I knew Paul's meaning as well as he, which is, I Corinthians 14, that a woman ought not to speak in the congregation by the way of teaching. And then I asked him how many women he had seen go into the pulpit and preach. He said that he never saw any. Then I said that he ought to find no fault in poor women unless they had offended the law. (Askew L.ii–iii)

Her cleverly embedded syllogism stops the bishop's chancellor short. Obedient women do not speak in church. We are obedient women. Therefore, we do not speak in church.

Not only does Askew declare that she understands scripture as well as the chancellor, but she responds by questioning him, exacting an answer, and drawing an appropriate conclusion to discomfit the questioner. Her style suits perfectly her aims, for it is unadorned, understated, and concise; more important, it is also unrevealing, a rhetoric of concealment. And she allows the climactic last sentence to exert its full force: she had broken no law.

The accepted methods of rhetorical argument called for citing past authorities and exempla. While Askew cites the Scriptures at every opportunity, she does so in a directly pragmatic, situational way: Paul said I could and should leave my husband; God will laugh at your conspiracy against me; following Paul's stricture, no women are preaching to a congregation. To Askew the reformer, Scriptures taught her to seek her own salvation and authorized her to speak for her Lord, to bear witness as a true Christian woman—and to conceal her personal life.

Realizing that she is bound for the rack and can gain nothing from her inquisitors by implicating other people, reformist or Catholic, she claimed her secret knowledge for her own. During her interrogation with regard to the queen's reformist sympathizers, she described the substance of her support but not the actual source:

> Then came Riche and one of the counsel, charging me upon my obedience, to show unto them if I knew man or woman of my sect. My answere was that I knew none. Then they asked me about my lady of Suffolk, my lady of Sussex, my lady of Hertford, my lady Dennye, and my ladye Fitzwilliam. I said if I should say anything against them, that I would not be able to prove it. . . .
>
> . . . Then they said that there were diverse gentlewomen that gave me money. But I knew not their names. Then they said that there were diverse ladies which had sent me money. I answered that there was a man in a blue coat who delivered me 10 shillings and said that my lady of Hertford sent it me. And another in a violet coat gave me 8 shillings and said that my lady Dennye sent it to me. Whether it were true or no, I can not tell. For I am not sure who sent it to me, but as the men said. . . .

Then they asked if they were from the counsel that maintained me. And I said, no. Then they put me on the rack because I confessed no ladies nor gentlewomen to be of my opinion, and thereon they kept me a long time. And because I lay still and did not cry, my lord Chancellor and master Riche took paines to rack me with their own hands, until I was nearly dead. (n.p.-M.i–ii)

Askew's understatement—"I lay still and did not cry"—conveys her silent virtue, her strength, and her endurance. She also reveals the depravity of these two religious men, desperate for her confessions. This exchange builds tension that is released in her torture:

Then the lieutenant caused me to be loosened from the rack. Immediately, I fainted, and then they recovered me again. After that I sat two long hours, reasoning with my lord Chancellor upon the bare floor, where as he with many flattering words, persuaded me to leave my opinion. But my good lord God (I thank his everlasting goodness) gave me grace to persevere, and will do (I hope) until the very end. (qtd. in Beilin 43)

The exchange is of rhetorical import, for it illustrates her keen sense of her rhetorical situation. Aristotle's celebrated definition that rhetoric "is the faculty of discovering in any situation the available means of persuasion" (1.1.11–12) held no sway in this immediate situation: Askew realized that she could not use language to change the attitude, modify the behavior, or stimulate a particular course of action on the part of her examiners. Therefore, what she unfolds in this specific section of her *Examinations* is not so much an argument as it is her essential, Christian self. Yet that presentation of argument and ethos (to say nothing of pathos) influenced the thoughts and actions of other reformists, and this self soon became a popular Protestant martyr, the focus not only of her fellow reformists but of other gentlewomen as well.

The significance of self-portrait. This Protestant martyr makes clear her genius for seizing the language of words—and of silence. Askew's *Examinations* are the rarest form of sixteenth-century writing, the self-portrait, one that differs widely from our modern autobiography in that her language does not create an individual (who laments her personal situation or speaks of her associates) but instead creates a participant in the larger community of the Reformed Church. Like the women rhetors who preceded her, she taps (but unlike them, she does not speak to) her personal life for subject matter, but hers is a new purpose: the reformist movement. She presents herself as fully participant in the gifts of the Lord, as a teacher of doctrine, and as a champion of her faith. Her writings movingly document the imprisonment, inquisition, and torture of a Protestant; they provide insight into her individuality insofar as she is able to suffer cruelly and is unwilling to compromise her beliefs or her everlasting soul. In other words, her autobiographical text is entirely shaped to her rhetorical ends as a reformist.

Reasons for the rhetorical power of her self-portrait are readily apparent. The records of her two arrests document her skill at *disputatio* and logical argument, as well as her vast knowledge of the Scriptures. Her humanist education had prepared her well, for soon the time came for her to follow the reformist directive that only those with a proper understanding of the Bible might interpret the Holy Scripture to the faithful (i.e., the reformists). By her own learning, she knew the Bible; as a reformer, she trusted that learning. But her erudition did not please the traditional Christians, the antireformists, who believed in the intellectual inferiority of women. In fact, the most damning charge against her was the accusation that, like other Protestant women, she was violating the biblical admonition that men alone were ordained by God to serve as priests (1 Cor. 14.33–35). Women might be accepted as spiritual equals, but they could hardly be accepted as legitimate expounders of the faith. Thus Askew's disputes with clergymen over biblical interpretation would be particularly controversial.

Her *Examinations* are accompanied by other writings that illustrate her full range of learning and rhetorical ability (persuasive language, use of support, audience awareness): her letters, her confession of faith, her prayer before death, her expert translation of the fifty-fourth Psalm, and an original ballad. The ballad places her among the minor poets of the sixteenth century and marks her as an early, if not the first, woman to have composed original verses in English:

> Like as the armed knight
> Appointed to the field
> With this world will I fight
> And faith shall be my shield. (qtd. in Beilin 44)

Furthermore, all her writings—striking and moving—are informed by her strong faith:

> I am not she that lists
> My anchor to let fall
> For every drizzling mist
> My ship substantial.
> . . . .
> I saw a royal throne,
> Where Justice should have sit
> But in her stead was one
> Of mood cruel wit. (qtd. in Beilin 45)

Not only was she responsive to her rhetorical exigency, but she had a keen sense of her immediate audience (her inquisitors) and of her ultimate audience (her contemporary and future supporters) and was thus readily able to take her rhetorical stance. In fact, her sense of a contemporary audience eager to read her work engenders Askew's careful attention to the nuances of language and to a style not of private revelation of self but of a public celebration of the virtues she values: piety, privacy, constancy, learning, and fortitude. She thus patterns her own life like that of a saint's life, the ultimate model of female virtue.

Askew may seem a volcanic eruption into the public realm of Renaissance literary and political culture, especially when placed in Kenneth Burke's "perspective by incongruity" (*Perspectives* 94–99). Beside Roper, who graciously and gratefully inhabited the private domestic sphere, Askew may seem a firebrand. But her defiance of established Church authorities made her an important example (of a Protestant saint) for the early reformers, an example every bit as important as Roper's was to the Christian humanists. Within a remapped rhetorical tradition, Askew represents a major breakthrough. "As Askew moved from reading and knowing the Bible to quoting it in public [and] to writing it down in the context of her own story, she was breaking down prohibitions against women that had stood for centuries" (Beilin 47). But saints could break through such prohibitions, paving the way for other women to follow. As Roper was their intellectual mother, Askew was their patron saint.

Both Roper and Askew used language to create symbolic narratives that expressed their feelings of constriction, as well as their feelings of community. The participation of these two women pierces the silence and exemplifies the range of rhetorically based endeavors possible for women: from Roper's willing intellectualism (translations, letters) to Askew's resistance (argument, exhortation, analysis), both women established important rhetorical territories on the cultural map. Between Roper's and Askew's two poles of powerful language use and movement into the public domain is a spectrum of women practicing rhetoric in rich and complex ways, the most notable being Elizabeth I, English nationalism incarnate, who seems almost an exaggeration of the public woman.

Women's movement into and acceptance in the public sphere was slow and treacherous. Even Richard Mulcaster (c. 1530–1611), proponent of women's education, compares the public woman with a comet, flashing once across the sky, not a steady beacon of light, guiding other women. Only a woman like Elizabeth Tudor could fully project a compelling voice, a woman who owed allegiance to neither father nor husband, only to her people, a woman with unprecedented power: God's representative on earth. Constantly in public view, Elizabeth I spoke not from the margins of discourse but from its focal point—the throne.

Elizabeth I: Regendering the Throne

Elizabeth I (1533–1603) was the best aristocratic product of her time: deeply religious, refined, richly talented, well-spoken, patriotic, and superbly educated by the best humanists.[75] She would be the best of monarchs, too—despite her sex.

"Elizabeth's rule was not intended to undermine the male hegemony of her culture. Indeed, the emphasis upon her *difference* from other women may have helped to reinforce it" (Montrose 81). After all, a woman considered the political equal of a man could only be culturally alien, a figure relegated to the borders of the culturally constituted community. So Elizabeth self-consciously composed herself as uniquely superior, relegating herself to the very top of a stratified society. To distinguish herself from all the English kings who had gone before, as well as from all other women in the realm, she appeared an androgyne, the perfect trope for an imperialistic, nationalistic state. Elizabeth thereby transformed the feminized margins of political power into a masculinized body of actual strength. Early on, her royal tutor would praise the accomplished young princess in androgynous terms:

> The constitution of her mind is exempt from female weakness, and she is endued with a masculine power of application. No apprehension can be quicker than hers, no memory more retentive. French and Italian she speaks like English; Latin, with fluency, propriety and judgment; she also spoke Greek with me. . . . The beginning of the day was always devoted by her to the New Testament in Greek, after which she read select orations of Isocrates and the tragedies of Sophocles, which I judged best adapted to supply her tongue with the purest diction, her mind with the most excellent precepts, and her exalted station with a defence against the utmost power of fortune. (Ascham, *English* 219)

But Elizabeth's abilities of transcendence extended beyond gender and her "masculine power of application." She also transcended England's competing Catholic and Protestant religious forces: "Being a queen and a prince sovereign, I am answerable to none for my actions, otherwise than as I shall be disposed of my own free will, but to Almighty God alone" (qtd. in G. Rice 33). Catholicism might have been the state religion at the moment of her accession, but, clearly, a Protestant God had saved Elizabeth to rule the nation and to usher in the new age of faith in 1558:

> When first I took the scepter, my title made me not forget the giver, and there [I] began as it became me, with such religion as both I was born in, bred in, and I trust, shall die in; although I was not so simple as not to know what danger and peril so great an alteration might procure me—how many great Princes of the contrary opinion would attempt all they might against me, and generally what enmity I should thereby breed unto myself. Which all I regarded not, knowing that He, for whose sake I did it, might and would defend me. (Neale, *Elizabeth* 2: 128)

Elizabeth would be God's representative on earth. The Protestants would owe their very existence to her rule, and she, having renounced the pope, would be dependent upon them. Paradoxically, the pope helped Elizabeth achieve absolute sovereignty, for only after a papal condemnation of 1570 excommunicated her and thus released her subjects from their allegiance to her rule were her subjects able to pledge their loyalty willingly.

Immediately recognized as the symbol of English nationalism, Elizabeth ascended the throne just in time to be the unintended target of John Knox's grossly mistimed, antigynecocratic *First Blast of the Trumpet Against the Mon-*

strous Regiment of Women (which had been aimed at Mary Tudor): "to promote a woman to bear rule, superiority, dominion, or empire above any realm, nation, or city, is repugnant to nature, contumely to God, a thing most contrarious to his revealed will and approved ordinance; and finally it is the subversion of good order, or all equity and justice" (qtd. in Pringle 18). The queen's sex was a weakness; she owed her throne to the failure of the male line not to her inherent power or skill. Any defense of her, then, must transcend such earthly details: hers was a divine right.

Blasting back, John Aylmer argued that, "when God chuseth him selfe by sending a king, whose succession is ruled by enheritaunce and lyneall discent, no heiris male: It is a plain argument, that for some secret purpose he myndeth the female should reine and governe" (qtd. in Benson 241).[76] Eventually, even to the exiled Puritan Knox, Elizabeth I would be a godsend, for she reformed the social, religious, political, and financial unrest of England with her incredible strength, power, wit, and cunning. This queen/king would not only fashion herself to be the firstborn son and absolute authority of a patriarchal state but also the selfless and bountiful mother of her subjects.

Elizabeth was arguably the most powerful monarch of her day, as well as the most articulate. To say that her rhetorical power stemmed from her royal prerogative to command rather than persuade, that her linguistic power lay in her office rather than in her being would be off the mark; after all, had she not been queen, this woman would have had little if any opportunity to display publicly either her intellect or her persuasive abilities. As queen, she need not, of course, produce a steady succession of speeches in the first rank of eloquence, but necessity dictated and custom required that she employ language to meet the challenges of her rule. Her office did not automatically guarantee her continued security; the unnatural deaths of previous monarchs were proof.

"*Video, et taceo.*" Even as a young girl, Elizabeth could be politically uncertain, given questions of her legitimacy and her place in succession. But she seems always to have been if not rhetorically certain then rhetorically adept, living her childhood by the motto she would adopt as queen: "*Video, et taceo*"—"I see and hold my tongue." At fifteen, she toyed with the literary rhetoric (the patterned cadences of Oxford school prose) so prevalent in the Renaissance, limiting herself (just like a nonroyal) to the feminine intellectual activity of translation. Her translation of Queen Margaret of Navarre's *Godly Medytacyon of the Christen Sowle* is competent, and the tone of her prefatory letter is appropriately humble:

> If thou do throughly reade thys worke . . . marke rather the matter than the homely speache therof, consyderynge it is the studye of a woman, whych hath in her neyther conynge nor science, but a fervent desyre that yche one maye se, what the gifte of God the creatour doth whan it pleaseth hym to justyfye a h[e]art. . . .
>
> Therfore gentyll reader, with a godly mynde, I besyche the[e] paciently this worke to peruse whych is but small in quantyte, and taste nothynge but the frute

therof. Prayeng to God full of all goodnesse, that in thy harte he wyll plante the lyvely faythe. Amen. (qtd. in Travitsky 142)

Yet a few years later, when her younger half brother, Edward VI, was ill, the nineteen-year-old Elizabeth would write to him with rhetorical astuteness, both theoretical and practical, striking a modest, submissive tone. Her poetic letter, beautifully executed both in terms of graphology and content, deploys a salutation and closing that recognize his role as fifteen-year-old king and hers as his relatively powerless sister:

To the most Noble King Edward the Sixt

What cause I had of sory when I harde first of your maiesties siknes al men migth gesse, but none but my selfe could fele, wiche to declare wer or migth seme a point of flatery and therefore to write it I omit. But as the sorow could not be litel, because the occasions wer many, so is the joy gret to hire of the good escape out of the perillous diseases. And that I am fully satisfied and wel assured of the same by your graces owne hande I must nides give you my most humble thankes assuring your Maiestie that a precious iewel at a nother time could not so wel have contented as your lettar in this case hathe comforted me. . . . Moreover I do considar that as a good father that loves his childe derely dothe punis him scharpely, So God favoring your Maiestie gretly hathe chastened you straitly, and as a father dothe it for the further good of his childe, so hathe God prepared this [illness] for the bettar helthe of your grace. And in this hope I commit your Maiestie to his handes, most humbly craving pardon of your grace that I did write no soner desiring you to attribute the faute to my ivel hed, and not to my slothful hande. . . .

Your Maiesties most humble
sistar to comande. Elizabeth.[77]

Early on, then, Elizabeth demonstrates her genius at presentation of self, delicate balance, and transcendence—as well as rhetorical sensitivity. Ascham reports that the young princess favored Latin and Greek readings, especially the disputatious chestnut: the opposing orations of Demosthenes and Aeschines concerning the latter's embassy to Philip of Macedon (Ryan xxi). Even as a girl, Elizabeth's mind turned to oral defense, to what was known as the "Tudor play of mind." Few, if any other, Renaissance women would be included in that play, for it was an exercise in the rhetorical tradition that posed abstract questions and argued answers on both sides of a topic. But Elizabeth was not like any other Renaissance woman: she was a royal, trained in the use of rhetoric to assert authority.

The Tudor play of mind. In fact, Mary Thomas Crane explains Elizabeth's unique motto, *Video, et taceo*, as revealing the royal's political acumen rather than any measure of actual submission. She goes on to write that the motto is "ambiguous," implying both "silent judgment, the informed consideration of a person who must, and can, advise herself," as well as the queenly decision to "maintain the silence thought suitable for a woman" (2). By regendering the throne, however, Elizabeth could keep silent as a queen yet pronounce, decide, and rule as the mightiest of kings, always playing gender to her own advantage.

When, in 1558, the Parliament began petitioning her with the vexing questions of her marriage and the succession, she turned their arguments to her own favor by rendering herself devoutly Christian and patriotic and by gendering herself feminine:

> I have made choice of such state as is freest from the incumbrance of secular pursuits and gives me the most leisure for the service of God. . . . [N]ow that the care and weight of a kingdom lies upon my shoulders, to add these the incumbrance of the married state would be no point of discretion in me: but that I may give you the best satisfaction I can, I have long since made choice of a husband, the kingdom of England. . . . I beseech you, gentlemen, charge me not with the want of children, forasmuch as every one of you, and every Englishman besides, are my children and relations. (qtd. in G. Rice 117)[78]

From the beginning of her reign, then, she was already translating the political liability of her gender to her advantage. She was a true child of her father, realizing that by remaining single she could maintain both her authority and her autonomy; being unattached could only strengthen her political position. Chastity, that highest of womanly virtues, would allow her to devote herself to her kingdom. She cites Pauline doctrine for authority: "The unmarried woman careth for the things of the Lord, that she may be holy both in body and spirit; but she that is married careth for the things of the world, how she may please *her* husband" (1 Cor. 7.34). When she spoke to Parliament a year later, the first point she made was that her spinsterhood was the way of life "most acceptable unto God" (qtd. in Teague 525).

In general, the will of the ruler formed public opinion; the head of the body politic told the feet what to do and think, not the other way around. Yet the feet did not always oblige. In 1566 the Parliament once again confronted her with marriage and succession; she responded as their womanly prince:

> I sent them answer by my council [that] I would marry although of my own disposition I was not inclined thereto. But that was not accepted nor credited although spoken by their prince. . . . I will never break the word of a prince spoke in a public place for my honor's sake, and therefore I say again I will marry as soon as I can conveniently, if God take not him away with whom I mean to marry or myself, or else some other great let happen. I can say no more except the party were present and I hope to have children. Otherwise I would never marry.
>
> A strange order of petitions that will make a request and cannot otherwise be ascertained but by their prince's word and yet will not believe it when it is spoken. . . .
>
> The second point was the limitation of successions of the Crown, wherein was nothing said for my safety but only for themselves. A strange thing the foot [the Parliament] should direct the head [the monarchy] in so weighty a cause, which cause [has] been so diligently weighed by us for that it toucheth us more than them. . . .

. . . [T]hough I be a woman I have as good a courage answerable to my place as ever my father had. I am your annointed Queen. I will never be by violence constrained to do anything.

. . . [A]s soon as they may be in convenient time and that [they] may be done with less peril unto you, although never without great danger unto me, I will deal therein for your safety and offer it unto you as your prince and head without request, for it is monstrous that the feet should direct the head. (qtd. in G. Rice 78–81)

Fortunately, Elizabeth had the traditional Tudor ability to discern and interpret a popular trend; she also had the courage to mold it to what she, as prince, held to be the needs of the kingdom. And like her courageous father, she would not be bullied. Elizabeth's political success lay in her ability

to convert her unprecedented weakness as a celibate queen into a powerful propagandistic claim that she sacrificed personal interests in the name of public service. Her maidenly chastity was therefore interpreted not as a sign of political or social deficiency, but rather as a paradoxical symbol of the power of a woman who survived to govern despite illegitimization, subordination of female to male in the order of primogeniture, patriarchy, and masculine supremacy, and who remained unwed at a time when official sermons favored marriage and attacked the monastic vow of celibacy and veneration of the Virgin Mary. (J. King 30)

After the death of her sister, Elizabeth spoke and wrote herself as a prince and a queen, using deliberative, forensic, and panegyric speaking; *ars dictaminis*; and literary rhetoric to self-fashion herself as the best prince of Henrician lineage. She wrested "the power to impose a shape upon [her]self" and "the more general power to control [her own] identity—[and] that of others" (Greenblatt 1). Her self-fashioning refused the popular concept of woman as conduit for male rule, legitimacy, or power. The rhetorical situation of her accession demanded that, for her own safety, she quell the tensions arising from her "unmastered" womanhood and fashion for herself the authority associated with males: a self-mastered (wo)man, answerable only to God.

"Fit for a king": the queen's rhetoric. Distinct from but related to the notion of the body politic (monarch as head; subjects as body) was the Tudor concept of "the king's two bodies," which was devised during the reign of young Edward VI and deployed by the queen:

For the King has in him two Bodies, viz. a Body natural, and a Body politic. His Body natural (if it be considered in itself) is a Body mortal, subject to all Infirmities that come by Nature or Accident. . . . But his Body politic is a Body that cannot be seen or handled, consisting of Policy and Government, and constituted for the Direction of the People, and the Management of the publick-weal. (qtd. in Axton 17)[79]

Thus, Elizabeth presented her body natural as feminine and her body politic as masculine whenever she appeared in public to exercise her rhetorical power, an imperial image that was appropriate for a woman yet invited obedience. She took care with her ceremonial and occasional speeches to assert that her body politic outranked all other men and women, yet she openly acknowledges her body natural, her inferior sex, thereby rendering that topic "unavailable to her subjects" (Marcus 139):

> My Lords the Law of Nature moveth mee to sorrowe for my Sister, the burthen that is fallen upon me maketh me amazed, and yet considering I am Gods Creature, ordeyned to obey his appointment I will thereto Yelde, desiringe from the bottom of my harte that I may have assistance of his Grace to bee the minister of his Heavenly Will in this office now commytted to me, and as I am but one Bodye naturallye Considered though by his permission and Bodye Politique to Governe, so I shall desyre you all my Lords/Chiefly you of the nobility euery one in his Degree and Power to be assistant to me, that I with my Rulinge and you with yo[r] Service may make a good accompt to Almighty God and leave some comfrote to our posteritye in Earth. (qtd. in Heisch 33)[80]

Her oratory might well have been a product of her classical education in terms of style and ideas, but her political instincts were purely Henrician: "[W]e hope to rule, govern and keep this our realm in as good justice, peace and rest, in like wise as the king my father held you in" (qtd. in Orlin 88). When speaking to her subjects (who differed in religion and levels of education), she had the good sense and taste to avoid quotations from the Scriptures or from the Greeks and Romans and to use a simple style. Her brief coronation address might best illustrate the essence of her style—aptly addressed, simple, direct, self-assured, and reassuring:

> I thank my lord mayor, his brethren, and you all. And whereas your request is that I should continue your good lady and queen, by ye ensured that I will be good unto you as ever queen was to her people. No will in me can lack, neither do I trust shall there lack any power. And persuade yourselves, that for the safety and quietness of you all, I will not spare, if need be, to spend my blood. God thank you all. (qtd. in G. Rice 63)

"No will in me can lack, neither do I trust shall there lack any power." Had her parliamentary auditors paid better attention to her from the start, they might have been less sanguine about their own ability to rule their queen on questions of marriage and succession. But because she initially worked to please her audience, couching what she wanted to say in words and ways they wanted to hear, neither the Parliament nor privy council seemed to notice her resolve until much later, their deafness lasting long enough for "Elizabeth to complete her political apprenticeship and to develop a genuine sense of identity as monarch" (Heisch 33).

Elizabeth was a first-rate epideictic orator, especially when she gave her ever-authorized advice or direction. Speaking as a king ruling his subjects, as a "father over the children" (qtd. in G. Rice 127), as wife of England, as mother to her people, as monarch, she had no need to deliver deliberative or forensic rhetoric, except to justify, or perhaps disguise, her own already conceived, unbending decisions. In fact, Elizabeth's rhetorical performances are more informative and declarative—mimetic, in the sense of "this is the way things are"—than rhetorically persuasive, except, of course, in the Burkean conflation of "meaning" and "persuasion."[81] Elizabeth transforms nearly every recorded rhetorical occasion into an epideictic one that creates and sustains a mood, a decision, an action: hers.

Elizabeth's ultimate attitude toward her audience is as benevolent despot, confident in her political powers and skills; yet, simultaneously, she is sensitive to each rhetorical situation and rhetorical exigency. When she visited Cambridge, she found herself addressing the best-educated men in her kingdom—in the Latin that she loved and knew they would admire. Well aware that these men were expecting the usual Tudor financial endowment, she had to find a way to balance her keen interest in their scholarship with her unwillingness to follow the Tudor tradition of supporting that scholarship financially. In the tradition of her rhetorical foremothers, then, the queen taps the feminine humility topos, using her self-effacement ("[my] rude, off-hand remarks"; "[my] barbarous . . . oration") to offset her kingly and forthright pronouncement of their present "sumptuous" circumstances. Her "Latin Oration at Cambridge University, 1564" exemplifies her special blend of self-deprecation, acute perception, candor, and rhetorical power:

> Although my feminine modesty might deter me from making a speech and uttering these rude, off-hand remarks in so great an assembly of most learned men, nevertheless the intercession of my nobles and my own goodwill toward the University have prevailed upon me to say something. . . .
>
> As to what concerns the advancement of good letters, I recall this statement of Demosthenes: "that words of superiors take the place of books among inferiors, while the sayings of leaders are regarded as legal authority among the subjects." I would have all of you bear this one thing in mind, that no road is more adapted to win the good things of fortune or the goodwill of your prince, than the pursuit of good letters. . . .
>
> Now I come to the University. This morning I saw your sumptuous buildings, which were erected by my ancestors, most distinguished princes, for the sake of letters. And while looking at them, grief took possession of me and those sighings of the soul which are said to have gripped Alexander the Great, who, when he had surveyed the mighty deeds of his fathers, turned to a friend or counsellor and grieved deeply because he had not done anything of this sort.
>
> This common maxim cheers me a little, and although it cannot remove my pain, at least it lessens my sorrow. It is this: "Rome was not builded in a day." And while the thought of Alexander disturbs me a great deal, I hope, before rendering up my account to nature (if Atropos [the Fates] do not cut off the thread of my life too quickly) to accomplish some work of importance. . . . And if it should happen . . . that I must die before I am able to complete this thing which I promise, nevertheless, I will leave behind after my death some monument of distinction, by which my memory may be renowned and by which others may be incited by my example. And I will make all of you more diligent in the pursuit of your studies.

. . . Now it is time that your ears, detained so long by this barbarous kind of oration, be released from boredom. I have spoken. (qtd. in G. Rice 71–73)

Like all her speeches, the preceding reveals Elizabeth's fine sense of timing and her careful appraisal of her audience. For her, speechmaking is a social tool more than a stylistic exercise. In this particular case, she wins the goodwill of her learned audience by speaking in Latin, by invoking her femininity and her Tudor heritage, and by addressing their concerns about her financial support. She charms them with allusions to Demosthenes, Alexander, and Atropos and with hints of financial support to come. Yet woven into the fabric of her text is the strong thread of kingly prerogative: if death does not somehow intercede, she has plans to give financial support eventually (although not just now); she has definite plans that a memorial to her be erected upon her death, one that will induce continued financial support. Her words transform the occasion of financial expectation into one of implied promises and hope. But, it is interesting to note, she ultimately exercises her magisterial prerogative: Cambridge received nothing from the queen either during her lifetime or upon her death.

Because of her accomplished leadership and her fabled erudition, the successful military voyages of exploration, and her crafty handling of her court, Elizabeth embodied, however uneasily, the epitome of Renaissance *virtù*; she was a living example of a "great man." She was also a great queen—mother, teacher, and leader of her people. As such, she was not often called upon to win support by stirring their emotions: she had the authority to expect her every decision and command to be obeyed.

But Elizabeth could easily take her people further than obedience; she could inspire unflinching loyalty. During the final stages of England's war with Spain, Elizabeth appeared "full of princely resolution and more than feminine courage . . . as she passed like some Amazonian empress through all her army," the twenty-two thousand troops encamped on the Thames at Tilbury, who were anticipating the Spanish invasion by the duke of Parma's troops (qtd. in Neale, *Queen* 308).

In the matter of striking the right tone (rather than saying exactly the right thing), Elizabeth was a genius. Her speech to the troops at Tilbury provided visible and audible proof of her appreciation and admiration for and trust in her people. She assured them of receiving back pay (though the parsimonious queen made them wait weeks for it), and she spoke of her responsibility for and loyalty to them. Thus, "To the Troops at Tilbury, 1588" is one of Elizabeth's most successful and felicitous exhortations:

My loving people: We have been persuaded by some that are careful of our safety to take heed how we commit ourselves to armed multitudes for fear of treachery. But I assure you I do not desire to live to distrust my faithful and loving people. . . And therefore I am come amongst you, as you see, at this time, not for my recreation and disport; but being resolved in the midst of the heat of battle to live or die amongst you all; to lay down for my God and for my Kingdom and for my people my honor and my blood even in the dust.

I know I have the body of a weak and feeble woman; but I have the heart and stomach of a king, and of a king of England too, and think foul scorn that Parma or Spain or any prince of Europe should dare to invade the borders of my realm; to which, rather than any dishonor should grow by me, I myself will take up arms; I myself will be your general, judge, and rewarder of every one of your virtues in the field.

I know already, for your forwardness you have deserved rewards and crowns; and we do assure you on the word of a prince they shall be duly paid you.

In the meantime, . . . by your concord in the camp, and your valor in the field, we shall shortly have a famous victory over those enemies of my God, of my kingdoms, and of my people. (qtd. in G. Rice 96–97)

In this powerful statement of courage and national pride, Elizabeth once again employs the humility topos thought appropriate to a woman, particularly a queen who so successfully wields and asserts power in a man's world of wars and troops. But she has also put in place her long-standing appeal to her composite nature as monarch: the body natural that of a frail woman; the body politic that of a king, carrying the strength and masculine spirit of the best of her male forebears.

However, scholars remind us that "the speech [also] gains force from its subtle suggestion that the men present are effeminate. . . . If Elizabeth really has to fight, her taking up arms will have been in some way caused by the male soldiers' inadequacies. The speech provokes them to desire to fight so that she, so patently unable to do so, will not need to" (Benson 232, n. 6). And furthermore, the "queen herself was too politic, and too ladylike, to wish to pursue the Amazonian image very far. Instead, she transformed it to suit her purposes, representing herself as an androgynous martial maiden, like Spenser's Britomart" (Montrose 79). By keeping to the image of an androgyne (rather than the never-popular Amazon), then, she deflects any criticism that could be aimed at her womanly outspokenness, and she appeals to her people as a *monarch* rather than as a queen.

Certain features of all her speeches remain constant: the Anglo-Saxon diction, the balanced sentences, the insistent reverence for God and love of her people, and the regendered sexuality. A product of her educational moment, she created the highly valued Renaissance style, comprising carefully balanced clauses and strings of coordinate elements, as many of the preceding passages indicate. But on occasion, she uses short, blunt sentences for emphasis: "As for my own part, I care not for death, for all men are mortal and though I be a woman I have as good a courage answerable to my place as ever my father had. I am your anointed Queen" (qtd. in G. Rice 81).

The fuller, quasideliberative speech (to the troops) recounts again her argument for remaining single, as well as the necessity of her integrated sexuality.

It is gender play she seems to enjoy. She presents herself to her own advantage, as queen, king, husband, wife, mother, father—sometimes on the same occasion: "between Princes and their Subjects there is a most straight tie of affections. As chaste women ought not to cast their eye upon any other than their husbands, so neither ought subjects to cast their eyes upon any other Prince than him whom God hath given them"—Elizabeth herself (qtd. in Orlin 89). In reference to her own husbandly "understanding and courage" and her subjects' wifely "steadfastness not to offend or thwart, but to cherish and obey," Elizabeth tells the wife of Sir John Harington (her godson) that "after such sort do I keep the good will of all my husbands, my good people; for if they did not rest assured of some special love toward them, they would not readily yield me such good obedience" (qtd. in Orlin 89). Thus, Elizabeth is both husband and wife to her people, and sometimes she is godlike. To a grieving mother, Elizabeth writes, "Call to mind, good Kate [Lady Paget], how hardly we princes can brook of crossing of our commands; how ireful will the Highest power be . . . when murmurings shall be made of his pleasingest will? Let Nature therefore not hurt herself, but give place to the giver" (qtd. in Crane 11).

All through her career, Elizabeth regularly employs the androgyny trope, right up through her valedictory to Parliament, regarding the glories and responsibilities of her rule, her " 'Golden' Speech of 1601." "Great actress" that she was, Elizabeth saw these parliamentary occasions as "the supreme opportunity of projecting upon the nation, through its assembled deputies, her personality and affection, her discipline, her will and unrivalled gifts of leadership" (Neale, *Elizabeth* 2: 432). As it had always been, rhetoric remained, until the last, her instrument of regal power.

In the last of her quasideliberative (she had already decided in favor of the Commons to reform the monopoly system) and ceremonial speeches, she refers to herself first as king and then as queen, playing out the familiar gender topos as her rhetorical strategy, particularly since her body politic was much stronger and vital than her body natural. She then moves ahead to the trope of both her divine authority and her divinely inspired love for the English people. The following excerpt exemplifies her technique:

> I know the title of a king is a glorious title, but . . . the shining glory of princely authority hath not so dazzled the eyes of our understanding but that we well know and remember that we also are to yield an account of our actions before the Great Judge. To be a king and wear a crown is more glorious to them that see it than it is pleasure to them that bear it. For myself, I was never so much enticed with the glorious name of a king or royal authority of a queen as delighted that God hath made me this instrument to maintain His truth and glory, and to defend this kingdom, as I said, from peril, dishonor, tyranny, and oppression. There will never [a] queen sit in my seat with more zeal to my country or care to my subjects, and that will sooner with willingness yield and venture her life for your good and safety

than myself. And though you have had and may have many princes more mighty and wise sitting in this seat, yet you never had or shall have any that will be more careful and loving. Should I ascribe anything to myself and my sexly weakness, I were not worthy to live then, and of all most unworthy of the mercies I have had from God, Who hath ever yet given me a heart which never yet feared foreign or home enemies. I speak it to give God the praise as a testimony before you, and not to attribute anything unto myself. (qtd. in G. Rice 108–9)

Over and above her love and service for her people was her love and service for God—as it should be. Elizabeth wisely attached her self and her reign to the authority of God, thereby transcending issues of her gender, as well as internecine religious struggles. Elizabeth was, until the end, as worried about "overzealous Protestants" as she was about the Catholics, for the Catholics dependably presented an external threat of invasion and of endangering the queen's person; the radical Protestants, however, wanted an ecclesiastical structure that would endanger the queen's government (Heisch 42–43). Therefore, a constant theme in Elizabeth's speeches was her devotion and obedience to God, not to one particular religious cause. Elizabeth tried to comprehend all England in a latitudinarian frame, excluding only recusant Catholics and radical Puritans. And she succeeded.

Queenly expertise. Elizabeth's public rhetoric, whether oratory, official letters, or documents, glorified her as an icon, as a prince transcendent of gender, religion, and strife, a virile monarch authorizing change or stability from the throne. But the more personal rhetoric of Elizabeth inscribed her in other, more traditionally (and "naturally") feminine ways having to do with intellectual rather than political power. The polyglot Elizabeth was vain about her linguistic skills, as translation had been an important part of her education. Paradoxically, however, her private, literary rhetorical skills of translating and composing came to be represented in her public persona, the accomplished queen. Like her female contemporaries, she found herself translating her favorite authors, but in her case they were not all religious: at eleven, she had translated Queen Margaret's *Godly Medytacyon of the Christen Sowle* for Catherine Parr; as an adult, she translated Boethius's *Consolatione philosophiae*, Plutarch's *Curiositate*, a fragment of Horace's *Ars poetica*, a Xenophon dialogue, and epistles by Seneca and Cicero (K. Wilson, *Women* 532). The feminine art of translation offered women the shelter of masculine ideas, concepts, controversies; female translators were most often literal, protected by the male's original words and thoughts. Still, the following excerpted translation of Petrarch's *Triumph of Eternity* speaks clearly to the assertion of her royal self:

> Amazed to see nought under heaven's cope
> Steady and fast, thus to myself I spake:
> Advise thee well—on whom doth hang thy hope?
> On God, said I, that promise never brake
> With those that trust in him.   (Elizabeth 13–14)

But besides her skillful translations, Elizabeth also wrote prayers, meditations, and poems, having learned as a schoolgirl to appreciate the synergy of fusing rhetoric and poetics. And some of her poems are rather good, to wit, "Doubt of Future Foes," which seemingly discloses her political strength in the face of Mary Stuart's threats. The new queen taps her own power base and asserts her aims straightforwardly, as she always would:

> The doubt of future foes exiles my present joy,
> And wit me warnes to shun such snares as threaten mine annoy;
> For falsehood now doth flow, and subjects faith doth ebb,
> Which should not be if reason ruled or wisdom weaved the web.
> But clouds of joys untried do cloak aspiring minds
> Which turn to rain of late repent by changed course of winds.
> The top of hope supposed the root upreared shall be,
> And fruitless all their grafted guile, as shortly ye shall see.
> Then dazzled eyes with pride, which great ambition blinds,
> Shall be unsealed by worthy wights whose foresight falsehood finds.
> The daughter of debate that discord aye doth sowe
> Shall reap no gain where former rule still peace hath taught to know.
> No foreign bannished wight shall anchor in this port;
> Our realm brooks not seditious sects let them elsewhere resort.
> My rusty sword through rest shall first his edge employ
> To poll their tops that seek such change or gape for future joy.   (4)

The queen's participation in literary rhetoric opened the way, no doubt, for a few other upper-class women to venture into the same arena, even though the English court did not, as a rule, provide a venue for female literary activity made public. Even a queen who had amassed political accomplishments could not permanently stabilize the ideologically precarious position created by her gender. "She could not afford the political cost of a court prompting women to what were considered male pursuits"—writing for the public (Krontiris 15). Still, the English court, Tina Krontiris goes on to explain, did offer a kind of literary training ground for at least three secular women writers—Mary Sidney Herbert, Mary Sidney Wroth, and Amilia Lanyer—who spent time in court service (15).

Did Women Have a Renaissance?

"Living female monarchs who hold power in their own right tend to exclude contemporary women from glory rather than opening the way for them as one might expect" (Benson 29). Female monarchs are no example of woman's capacity and ability; they are special, chosen. Therefore, when Joan Kelly asks if women had a Renaissance, the answer is "yes, but . . . " Women did participate in that brilliant explosion of language we call the Renaissance, but their participation was of a different kind. No woman—not even a queen—could use language without recognizing the prevailing social and literary attitudes toward women as she tried to create her own literary personality, the very voice in which to express her ideas and create her *self*.

From Roper to Askew to Elizabeth, each Renaissance woman writer confronted major obstacles, from the moment she entered the male-dominated world of writing and literature until she apologized for having written and for being a woman. Even the woman who did not write for immediate circulation, a young princess perhaps, was acutely aware that her writings would be overshadowed by the works of such contemporary male artists as Spenser, Sidney, Jonson, and Shakespeare. For the Renaissance woman, then, most emphasis has traditionally been on the writing she inspired or sponsored rather than the writing she produced.

Still, many women composed and wrote in their own right. Through language, Roper presented herself as the domestic professor, speaking through masculine intellects. Askew presented herself as the religious defender, speaking through a Protestant God (surely masculine). Queen Elizabeth, however, presented herself as an androgynous trope for the masculine state: romantic and available—yet constant and powerful. The languages of other Renaissance women wrote them as well; after all, any participation in the shaping of language is social power. Lady Jane Grey composed an impassioned, highly crafted letter to convince an apostate to return to the reformed faith. Catherine Parr was the first woman to publish a persuasive, religious tract in English. Anne Dowriche wrote history, *The French Historie. That Is; a Lamentable Discourse of Three of the Chiefe, and Most Famous Bloodie Broiles That Have Happened in France for the Gospell of Iesus Christ*. Translating from French sources, Dowriche composed—in verse—an account of French Huguenot struggles. Although Isabella Whitney's verse is functional, plodding religious verse, at least she was writing, and perhaps she was expressing herself in those very terms. The Cooke sisters (Elizabeth Cooke Russell, Anne Cooke Bacon) wrote themselves as virtuous, pious, and learned through their religious poetry, their translations, their fine letters, and their prefaces.

The languages of Mary Sidney Herbert, Mary Sidney Wroth, Elizabeth Faulkland Cary, and Catherine of Aragon demonstrate their unique contributions to the literary arts. Herbert's translation of the Psalms and her revision of her brother's *Arcadia* demonstrate her rare gift for literary criticism. She was one of few people consciously to grasp and document the literary evolution as it occurred, who sensed the major changes in genres, subjects, and stances as they occurred. Her psalter has been described as "a school of English versification," and it influenced other poets. No collection of lyrics in English had ever been so metrically varied as her 150 poems, and hers are more complex stylistically and more sophisticated in technique than their counterparts by her eminent brother. And her literary reviews evince her understanding that dramatic speeches could evolve with the change in a character. The work of Herbert's niece, Wroth, echoed her own; Wroth's psalter became the model for John Donne and George Herbert. Her *Urania*, a pastoral tragicomedy of disillusioned love, is the first known full-length work of fiction by an English-woman. And she was castigated for this composition, encouraged to follow the example of her pious aunt and re-create (translate) rather than create. The languages of Herbert and Wroth, then, demonstrate their unique contributions to the literary arts.

One can only imagine what the actual, as-yet-undetermined contributions to rhetorical technique, literary rhetoric, and discourse theory these women may have made. And one also wonders what women remain undiscovered in archives and libraries. What we do know for certain, however, is that the gendered social, educational, and religious constraints on Renaissance women contained them in the same way they had contained their foresisters. All these women were proscribed from writing rhetorical treatises. Yes, Roper provides a rhetoric of accomplished translation; Askew provides a rhetoric of fiery religious apologia; and Elizabeth performs a rhetoric of engendered prerogative—and all their discourses reveal an implicit awareness of rhetorical theory, of their respective rhetorical situations. These three women demonstrated their inimitable rhetorics and contributed to the multiple oratorical and literary discourses we call *rhetoric*, speaking across the centuries to the body of rhetorical tradition from their marginalized positions as women, even when the woman was king of England.

FIVE

The Implications of a Regendered, Retold Rhetoric, or Against Conclusions

In *Poetic Closure*, Barbara Herrenstein Smith writes about the pleasures of designed closures: "Our most gratifying experiences tend to be not the interminable ones but rather those that conclude" (1). Indeed. When I initiated this project, I was told that there were no women in the history of rhetoric, but that, if I wanted to do "negative research," that might be OK. When my archival and library research revealed only brief glimpses of women (glimpses that eventually took me several years to bring into rhetorical focus), I was warned that my project might not unfold as anything but a series of cameo appearances. Nevertheless, my work insisted on taking shape, informed by feminism, gender studies, and the inspirational feminist historiographic projects taking hold across the country. My sight lines began to converge; I began to recognize my scholarly investigation as "positive research" that did, indeed, reveal traces of women on the rhetorical landscape.

I am gratified to be concluding this project, but I must resist closure. A regendered, retold rhetorical tradition opens up—not closes down—investigation into rhetorical practices. Even though *gender* is merely a concept borrowed from grammar, it, nevertheless, continues to have far-reaching effects on cultural notions of the relation between the sexed body and its behavior. Gendered experiences continue to be difficult, if not impossible, to separate from human ones. And for that reason alone, the masculine gender, just like every male experience or display, has come to represent the universal. Men have appropriated many public social practices, particularly prestigious practices like rhetoric, as universally masculine; the feminine experience (that of bodies sexed female) has come to represent exceptions, or the particular.

In regendering the tradition, I have not gone so far as to "destroy gender" or even "abolish the category of gender" (Wittig 67). Instead, I have analyzed distributions of power along the axis of gender that have for too long been easily accepted as nature's empirical design for masculine superiority, for patriarchal representations of the universal. This discourse of regendering has allowed me to examine gender(ed) performances within and across cultural constructions of the body, human identity, and power.

To this end, the project of regendering rhetorical history is a feminist performative act, a commitment to the future of women, a promise that rhetorical histories and theories will eventually (and naturally) include women. Of course, gender as a category of analysis contributes to this feminist project, but it is regendering that unsettles stable gender categories and enacts a promise that rhetorical history will be a continuous process of investigating the works of women and men rather than a final product that can be finally or universally represented. As soon as it is written, any historical interpretation—including this regendered rhetorical tradition from antiquity through the Renaissance—becomes an anachronism, for it immediately codes its own investigative site as needing/deserving more attention. As I worked through this project, identified women's bodies, revealed their contributions to and participation within the rhetorical tradition, and, with as much care as possible, wrote them into an expanded, inclusive tradition, I knew full well that "the past is necessarily larger than the sum of even its entire output of documentation" (Belsey 2).

A regendered rhetorical history can never be completed or concluded. We scholars, male and female alike, still have much work to do—that is the feminist premise and promise of this study and the reason for "Against Conclusions," the subtitle of this last chapter. In this spirit, then, I offer four ways that we might work together to realize our performative acts and goals.

First, we might start by recognizing our common ground. Those of us employing feminism in the history of rhetoric share the same deep sense of common purpose: we are working with various openings that provide opportunities to recover, claim, and articulate women's (and men's) contributions to and participation in the ever-expanding histor*ies* of rhetoric. And we are also inhabiting, even if not consciously, postmodern methodologies, for with each of our rewritings, we are reseeing and unsettling rhetorical histor*ies*—at the same time that we (re)compose and reconstitute our scholarly focus, our professions, and our selves.

In the few years I have spent working on this project, I have certainly composed a range of selves, at least one of whom could (re)connect with Sappho, Aspasia, Diotima, Hortensia, Fulvia, Julian of Norwich, Margery Kempe, Margaret More Roper, Anne Askew, and Elizabeth I—and contextualize them within—a rhetorical tradition that shut them out in the first place. These women make strong individual contributions to our collective historical project, but their appearance on the rhetorical map also represents various methodologies for locating and contextualizing *all* rhetorical activity (whether men's or women's, of any class, clan, creed, race, or ethnicity) as we unsettle the margins of rhetoric, as well as its heretofore privileged, masculine, but now-problemized center.

A surviving scrap of Sappho's verse assures us that she knew she would not "be forgotten"—despite the passage of time and the willful attempts to silence the voices of all women. To reconstruct the rhetorical lives of women such as Sappho, women who would not be forgotten, we must work together to continue to develop techniques for listening to their long-silenced voices, so we may want to consider our shared methodologies—or, better yet, methodologies that need to be shared. Provocative secondary accounts assure us that many rhetorical women existed, but all too often only the vibrations of their intellectual endeavors remain, their primary words having been lost, ignored, or destroyed. Therefore, we must investigate those secondary sources; we must find ways to hear these women for ourselves, so we can know, for ourselves, that these women did indeed exist, that they did speak, and that they are speaking to us today.

For too many years, scholars have been throwing up their hands at the thought of women's voices in rhetorical history. But we all know otherwise now: women's rhetorical lives have always existed, among the innumerable, interminable, clear examples of public, political, agonistic, masculine discourse. But the work to locate those voices and listen to them is difficult and not always satisfying, let alone rewarding. If we lament, however, we miss out on many scholarly opportunities, especially the ones that invite us to work together across the disciplines of religion, education, anthropology, art, sociology, feminist theory, gender studies, postmodern theory, law, home economics, philosophy, and medicine (including midwifery), for example. These fields offer "other" (but equally valuable) kinds of rhetorical performances that include women's voices in diaries, journals, poetry, drama, mystical experiences, religious feelings, household accounts, church records, letters, autobiographical sketches, educational treatises, music, translations, and, of course, orations.

Second, we may want to explore various means of collaboration. As we search out more ways to listen to more women—to demystify women's invisibility and so-called silence—our scholarly adventure not only requires our interaction across the disciplines but our collective, mutual assistance based on our varied expertise. We must depend on one another for assistance, support, and direction if we are to perform our feminism, if we are to move ahead to enact and inhabit an integrated rhetorical history. We must compare notes, confess puzzlement and ignorance, report success, pass around information, ask for help and give it (without ever feeling that we *have* to take it, of course). Even *the* history of rhetoric that so many of us read in school can continue to guide us, for we can use that male-centered conceptual tool; we can criticize it, change it, and then pass it along, knowing that it has been all the better honed by and for our feminist analyses. Again, we still have much left to do; we still have traditional, transformative, and performative tasks to undertake.

Third, given the veneration of women's silence, an important transformation for us to consider is the notion of *silence* itself: "It is by writing . . . and by taking up the challenge of speech which has been governed by the phallus, that women will confirm women in a place other than silence" (Cixous 285). Silence is perhaps the most undervalued and *under*-understood traditionally feminine rhetorical site. Silence has long been an unexamined trope of oppression, with "speaking out" being the signal of liberation, especially given the Western tendency to valorize speech and language. But sometimes, some women choose the place of silence. Ratcliffe reminds us that "a woman's silence need not be read as simple passivity. Indeed, her silences may take many forms and serve many functions" (122).

When I turned to Anne Askew, for example, I turned to a woman who, even under torture, purposefully delivered silence rather than the called-for, expected answers; her rhetoric of silence served her own end: to display publicly her stoicism while facing threats to her Christian reformist beliefs. Silence is more than the negative of not being permitted to speak, of being afraid to speak; it can be a deliberate, positive choice. In *Listening to Silences*, Elaine Hedges and Shelley Fisher Fishkin help us understand the expressive, positive powers of silence when it denotes alertness and sensitivity, when it signifies attentiveness or stoicism, and, additionally, when it seeks out and listens to new voices.

Askew is no doubt only one in a tradition of women who have seized public silence to her own end. But without written documents, silence has been nearly impossible to analyze or compare. However, our documentary culture provides us with the recorded silences of contemporary women that may provide us starting points. Until and when they were ready to speak, former Texas governor Ann Richards, University of Oklahoma law professor Anita Hill, and University of Pennsylvania law professor Lani Guinier all demonstrated the various uses of silence; they appropriated and altered spoken rhetorical display and performance to include dialogue, truth telling, and listening. In her public delivery, Richards speaks to, reports on, and listens to her Hispanic, African American, and Anglo constituents. She asks her own listeners to practice inclusion, cooperation, and connection; she proposes that they examine the consequences of their own speech and invites them to consider, instead, the politics of silence, of listening to, of honoring the voices of Others ("Keynote").

Anita Hill seized the national consciousness by testifying that she "could not keep silent" with regard to the unprofessional behavior of Supreme Court nominee Clarence Thomas. But she had remained silent for years. Why? Hill might have been employing the silence of loyalty (to herself, her workplace, her race, her sex); or she might have been employing the silence of incubation that permitted her to make sense out of events; or, perhaps, Hill was employing the silence of working out her own time line, agenda, context, and speaking moment (Ratcliffe 123). Of course, maybe Hill remained silent for so long because she predicted the line of humiliating questioning that she would eventually endure or the kind of capricious reprisals and public dismissals that her publicized, politicized sisters Guinier and Surgeon General Joycelyn Elders would eventually face. Yet when Hill raised her voice to those twelve white men on the Senate Judiciary Committee in October 1991, she helped sensitize

Americans to the pervasiveness and difficulty of sexual harassment—her rhetorical goal.

Guinier soon followed Hill onto the public stage, where she too was expected to negotiate her silencing and her silence to "avoid preempting formal confirmation proceedings" for her appointment as head of the Justice Department's civil rights division (West, "Stolen" 1). The day after President Bill Clinton withdrew her nomination, Guinier broke her silence and achieved her rhetorical goal by speaking directly to her detractors; she encouraged them to silence themselves long enough to listen to others: "I . . . hope we can learn some positive lessons from this experience, lessons about the importance of public dialogue on race in which all perspectives are represented and in which not one viewpoint monopolizes, distorts, caricatures, or shapes the outcome" (qtd. in Guinier 190). Guinier's experience deepened her conviction that "silence is not golden," that we have an obligation to use language "to confront rather than to condemn our problems" (qtd. in West, "Stolen" 2).

Silencing and silence are complicated rhetorical sites most often associated with women, particularly since gender, dominance, language, and silence have traditionally been tidily reduced and divided in terms of male and female, masculine and feminine. In "Women's Silence as a Ritual of Truth," Patricia Laurence writes that, instead of considering women's silences as "passivity, submission and oppression," we might better consider such silence as "enlightened presence," which can be read as "a difference of view, an alternative code of 'truth' or, sometimes, an expression of anger—the only kind that would be socially tolerated. Women's silence, that is to say, may be read as a strategy of resistance and choice—a ritual of truth" (156–57).

Silence is not necessarily an essence; it can also be a position—a choice. We all can deploy silence as a linguistic strategy to demonstrate power or domination, regardless of our gender. We can use silence to make the other person worry, wait, wonder, work harder. Silence can be used to make the other person worry about filling the gap, making peace, starting up the conversation or the negotiations again. Silence can be a presence or an absence, just as purposeful silences can be "cold or companionable" (Lakoff 47). Exploration into silence, silences, and silencing works to remind us of how very much more about women's silence we have to learn, especially when history offers us so very many silent passages.

Much of the past is, of course, irrevocably silenced: gestures, conversations, and manuscripts can never be restored in their original. Still, while most of the female tradition has regrettably been lost, obscured, or maligned, enormous amounts of material survive that can still be used to re-create or re-member a rhetorical situation—which brings me to my fourth and last suggestion. We do not have to compete for bits of female rhetoric, nor do we have to scramble after a few pages of women's letters. Although neither Cicero nor Quintilian are offering up an esteemed female colleague for us to study, the opportunities for feminist work are endless. The "famous" women of history—those exceptional figures, such as Sappho, who refused to be forgotten, or Aspasia, who refused to be ignored, or Queen Elizabeth I, who refused to be silent—have been studied for only a moment (in comparison to the centuries of attention paid to Plato and Aristotle). Just think of the possibilities that lie before us. In every disciplinary field, the neglect of women in the past has been so complete that the opportunities for exploration and experimentation are rich and plentiful for anyone who wants to do the necessary work.

Many of us are choosing to work on not-yet-famous historical women or women's rhetorical practices: Jo Allen's work on women and technical communication comes to mind as do Juanita Comfort's work on African American women researchers; Debra Combs's work on feminine ethos; Cinthia Gannett's work on women and journal writing; Ann Ruggles Gere's work on women's writing groups and on women's use of silence; Karyn Hollis's work on the opportunities at Bryn Mawr; Susan Jarratt and Nedra Reynolds's work on feminisms and ethos; Wendy Johnson's work on antebellum women's writing; Susan Kates's work on women's rhetorical education in alternative educational sites; Gesa Kirsch's ethnographies of women's writing processes; Roxanne Mountford's work on contemporary women preachers and judges; Claudia Myers's cross-disciplinary work on female dramatic characters; Anne Meade Stockdell's work on women and the rhetoric of cyberspace; and Susan West's work on the "non-hearings" of women's political appointments (to name just a few and to leave out far too many). These scholars are all offering up various analyses of rhetorical work that have—until recently—been relegated to the margins of our profession.

All this scholarship—of various women's individual rhetorical endeavors, of processes and methods and movements, on the margins and in the center—has been strengthened by our emotional readiness for it, our ability both to celebrate and to mourn our work. On the one hand, we find ourselves exhilarated by the groundbreaking work that has already been done and has already been extended by other scholars. But we also share an incredible sadness, for the recuperation of past women's voices is a work of mourning. We survivors-scholars-women-men often grieve, especially if we are exploring periods or individuals for whom records are scarce. But we must experience and then move beyond grief over irrevocable loss and move beyond a yearning for the actual person whose remains will never adequately represent her. We must move forward to the mediated, performative pleasures of listening and speaking, both to the dead woman's speech and our own speech and listening.

Susan West's dissertation reminds us all that our notion of *listening* is just as complicated as any notion of *silence*, for listening must be done consciously and purposefully, within a rhetorical situation, if we are to hear, to really hear. Our listening is every bit as important as any spoken or, for that matter, unspoken word. Therefore, that mediated pleasure of listening for—and hearing—the voices of women in rhetorical history, of giving voice to their (perhaps purposeful) silence, allows us to appreciate and celebrate our discoveries and recoveries as only the first traces of hidden conformations, whose power and dimensions are currently inestimable, immeasurable for us.

Whenever we find ourselves entertaining the idea that women have historically internalized the social pressures to be chaste, obedient, and silent, we need to laugh out loud and nudge one another in the ribs. We need to remind ourselves that *some* of them might have been chaste, *some* might even have been obedient (many of them were very brave), but *none* of them were silent. These women still have much to tell us—all we have to do is listen to their voices and their silences.

NOTES
WORKS CITED
INDEX

NOTES

1. MAPPING THE SILENCES, OR REMAPPING RHETORICAL TERRITORY

1. C. Jan Swearingen's *Rhetoric and Irony* provided me this perspective of transition: "Literacy as we have known it may be passing; the literacies of the future await our definition" (19).

2. Mary Ellen Waithe's "On Not Teaching," for instance, reminds us that

Hypatia of Alexandria and Hildegard of Bingen were considered by their contemporaries to be philosophers, but later historians refer to Hypatia as a "mathematician/astronomer," and to Hildegard as a "theologian/medical theorist." Yet what Hypatia and Hildegard wrote fit descriptions of philosophy in their respective eras. We must remind ourselves that the definition of the discipline philosophy has undergone significant metamorphosis over the millennia. If we accept descriptions of philosophy in use at particular periods, we find woman-authored works fitting those descriptions. Women have been philosophers since at least the time of Theano I [600 BCE]. (132–33)

Even given the difficulty of Waithe's access into what she describes as an "essentially male enterprise" of philosophy, such access simply has not been duplicated in rhetoric.

3. In *Public Man, Private Woman*, Jean Bethke Elshtain addresses the issue of women's domination and silencing:

Those silenced by power—whether overt or covert—are not people with nothing to say but are people without a public voice and a space in which to say it.

Of course, years and years of imposed inaction and public silence strangle nascent thoughts and choke yet-to-be-spoken words, turning the individuals thus constrained into reflections of the sorts of beings they were declared to be in the first place. (15)

In *Man Made Language*, Dale Spender writes that, although some women have written, broken the restrictions and been heard, their contributions have been suppressed through a variety of traditionally male-dominated social and political institutions (25). Spender builds on anthropologist Edwin Ardener's "muted-group" theory to argue that

framing questions in terms of the silence of women leads to an examination of the language which excludes and denigrates them, and it also leads to an examination of their access to discourse. When the only language women have debases us and when we are also required to support male talk, it is not unlikely that we shall be relatively silent. When the only language men have affords them the opportunity to encode meanings and to control discourse, when they have made the language and decreed many of the conditions for its use, it is not unlikely that they will use it more and that they will use it more in their own interest; thus they assist in the maintenance of women's silence. (51)

According to Spender, then, women have been doubly dependent on men: for the dominant group's definition of women and women's work and for the dominant group's

183

evaluation of their language use, their expertise in the received male system of expression.

4. Elizabeth Flynn eloquently explores issues of reading and composing as a woman.

5. We talk too often of the territory—rather than the function—of the marginalized. Biesecker helps us understand the function of the marginalized when she writes, "The margin is that which shores up the center and makes *it* visible" ("Towards" 91).

6. As I explain in the following chapters, the one-sex model of gender, with maleness running on a continuum, gives way during the Enlightenment to the two-sex model of gender (male vs. female) that is most familiar to us. Gender theorist Anne Fausto-Sterling, however, deploys a five-sex model, which runs along an axis of male, male-female, hermaphrodite, female-male, and female.

2. CLASSICAL RHETORIC CONCEPTUALIZED, OR VOCAL MEN AND MUTED WOMEN

1. In book 8 of *The Odyssey*, for example, the prerhetorical qualities of Odysseus's speech are easily identified when Odysseus meets the challenge of the defiant Euralyus, using well-chosen words about the power of words:

> Stranger, thou hast not spoken well; thou art like a man presumptuous. So true it is that the gods do not give every gracious gift to all, neither shapeliness, nor wisdom, nor skilled speech. For one man is feebler than another in presence, yet the god crowns his words with beauty, and men behold him and rejoice, and his speech runs surely on his way with a sweet modesty, and he shines forth among the gathering of his people, and as he passes through the town men gaze on him as a god. Another again is like the deathless gods for beauty, but his words have no crown of grace about them; even as thou art in comeliness preeminent, nor could a god himself fashion thee for the better but in wit thou art a weakling. Yet, thou hast stirred my spirit in my breast by speaking thus amiss. . . . [T]hy word hath bitten to the quick, and thou hast roused me with thy saying. (108–9)

And Andromache, Hecabe, and Helen use purposeful, persuasive language for a special occasion as well: the return of the dead Hector. Their epideictic funeral orations, encomia all, revive Hector's memory and deliver Hector unto his people. The exile's lament is the last to echo over Hector's remains; at the end of the *Iliad*, Helen says:

> Hector, best beloved of all by goodbrothers, and dearest to my heart! Indeed my husband is prince Alexandros, who brought me to Troy—but would that I had died first! Twenty years have passed since I left my country and came here, but I never heard from you one unkind or one slighting word. If any one else reproached me, a sister or brother of yours, or a brother's wife, or your mother—for your father was always as kind as if he were mine—you would reprove them, you would check them, with your gentle spirit and gentle words. Therefore I weep for you, and with you for my unhappy self. (24.297)

2. Richard Enos pointed out to me this use of rhetoric, as well as this particular example from the *Iliad*.

3. In her introduction to *The Other Sappho*, Ellen Frye tells us that those excavations brought to light thousands of papyrus fragments—the Oxyrhynichus papyri—that had

been preserved in coffins either as reading material for the deceased's journey to the underworld or as strips of the papier-mâché that shaped the coffins themselves.

4. Alcaeus sang the praises of his male cohort, the very stuff of Homer: "Wine, beloved boy, and truth. . . . " (Frag. Z43, qtd. in Page).

5. Anne Pippen Burnett tells us that

> this fierce sense of clan was reinforced by a system of *hetaireiai*—clubs that associated cousins, brothers and more distant kin in one another's constant society. The almost sacramental experience of drinking together moulded such groups into bands of soldiers bound to courageous performance by a seamless web of pride and shame, self-love and love for one's admired companions. (110)

6. For example, in *Works and Days*, Hesiod writes: "Avoid base gains: base gains amount to losses. / Be friend to friend, companion to companion. / Give him, who gives, and give him not, who gives not" (352–54).

7. Although they were in close proximity to each other, there is no evidence that Sappho and Alcaeus were in contact.

8. In "Women's Time," Julia Kristeva writes that "we confront two temporal dimensions: the time of linear history, or *cursive time* . . . , and the time of another history, thus another time, *monumental time* . . . which englobes these supranational, sociocultural ensembles within even larger entities" (qtd. in Bizzell and Herzberg 1252).

9. For example: "[Why am I unhappy?] / Am I still longing / for my virginity?" (Sappho, *Poems*, Frag. 69); "[I assure you] / I will remain a virgin / for ever" (Frag. 70).

10. Pindar's *First Olympian* is among the most celebrated examples of the comparison of popular subjects leading to a climax.

11. Mulvey's "Visual Pleasure and Narrative Cinema" is the finest explanation of the male gaze.

12. Diogenes Laertius writes that "for five years, [Pythagoras's disciples] had to keep silence, merely listening to his discourses without seeing him, until they passed an examination, and thenceforward they were admitted to his house and allowed to see him" (2.8.10).

13. All the letters are in Holger Thesleff's *Introduction to the Pythagorean Writings of the Hellenistic Period.*

14. Plato would later write that family affection dangerously disrupted corporate solidarity, especially because mating was so emotionally charged. Therefore, he thought that children should be separated from their parents and that sex should serve only for the breeding of children (*Republic* 5.454.d–e).

15. *Areté* is referred to as various manifestations of human excellence, usually associated with the wellborn and wealthy citizen-class: as virtue (the prerequisite to the good human life); as a combination of self-control, courage, and justice; as moral nobility; or as valor (W. Gutherie 3: 235–37).

16. Miletus had relatively large numbers of literate citizens, among them the philosophers Anaximander, Anaximenes, and Thales (Harris 63; Vernant *Origins* 127, *Myth and Thought* 343–45; Kirk and Raven 73–75). In *Myth and Society in Ancient Greece*, Jean-Pierre Vernant writes that, alongside moral thought, "a philosophy of nature starts to develop . . . in the Greek cities of Asia Minor. The theories of these first 'physicists' of Ionia have been hailed as the beginning of rational thought as it is understood in the West" (96).

17. Most scholars (Edmund F. Bloedow, Robert Flaceliere, David M. Halperin, Roger Just, Eva C. Keuls, Hans Licht, Josiah Ober, for instance) have labeled Aspasia a courtesan, schooled in intellectual and social arts. But both Eve Cantarella and William Courtney argue that the Athenian suspicion and misunderstanding of such a powerful, political, non-Athenian, unmarriageable woman living with their controversial leader, Pericles, led automatically to the sexualized and undeserved label of *hetaera*; Nicole Loraux refers to Aspasia as a foreigner and as a nonpolitician (*Invention*); Mary Ellen Waithe calls her "a rhetorician and a member of the Periclean philosophic circle" (*History* 75); and Susan Cole writes only of Aspasia's intellectual influence and measure of literacy (225).

18. Cantarella clearly describes a *hetaera* as "more than a casual companion," "more educated than a woman destined for marriage, and intended 'professionally' to accompany men where wives and concubines could not go," namely, social activities and discussions (30). "This relationship was meant to be somehow gratifying for the man, even on the intellectual level, and was thus completely different from men's relationships with either wives or prostitutes" (31). Robert Flaceliere agrees that, "in practice, if not in law, they [*hetaerae*] enjoyed considerable freedom" (130). He goes on to quote Athenaeus's *DeipnoSophists* (bk. 13) that the *hetaerae* "applied themselves to study and the knowledge of the sciences" (131).

19. Keuls suggests that a female educational underground might have been the source of male anxiety, for the philosopher Democritus wrote, "Let a woman not develop her reason, for that would be a terrible thing" (Frag. 110, qtd. in Keuls 104). And a character in a lost play by Menander pronounced that "he who teaches letters to his wife is ill-advised: He's giving additional poison to a horrible snake" (Frag. 702K, qtd. in Keuls 104).

20. Roger Just reminds us that "Aspasia's notoriety and the popular resentment her supposed influence aroused should . . . be remembered—a resentment transmuted into mockery by comedy" (21). In *The Acharnians*, Aristophanes writes that the Megarians "abducted *two* whores from Aspasia's stable in Athens" (523); Plutarch writes that Cratinus, "in downright terms, calls her a harlot": "To find him a Juno the goddess of lust / Bore the harlot past shame, / Aspasia by name" (*Lives* 201). Flaceliere assures us that "the Athenian comic poets never tired of repeating that Aspasia led a life of debauchery, though apparently she was as well behaved as she was well informed, even a scholar" (131). And Cantarella writes, "It is not surprising that many Athenians hated Aspasia. She was not like other women; she was an intellectual" (54–55).

21. Pierre Vidal-Naquet writes that "the sole civic function of women was to give birth to citizens. The conditions imposed upon them by Pericles' law of 451 was to be the daughter of a citizen and a citizen's daughter" (145). Women of low reputation could be spoken of publicly and freely; for some, Aspasia fit such a category. For others, Aspasia's intellectual and political gifts earned her a measure of public distinction. David M. Schaps asserts that there were three categories of women whose "names could be mentioned freely: disreputable women, opposing women, and dead women" (329).

22. But Hans Licht explains that

the preference for Aspasia shown by Pericles afforded a welcome excuse for his opponents to attack him; people would not hear of a woman having anything to say in political life, especially one who was not an Athenian but was brought from abroad, and even from Ionia . . . , which was notorious for the immorality of its women. . . . Hence she was severely criticized by the comic poets. . . . [A]ccording to a statement in Athenaeus . . . she was said to have maintained a regular brothel. . . . When she was accused of *asbeia* (impiety) and procuring, Pericles defended her and secured her acquittal. (352–53)

23. The tautology of Jean Bethke Elshtain's argument rightly encircles Aspasia: "I am not impressed with the claims made for powerful women who influenced men through their private activities—in Athenian society this claim is frequently made for the *hetaera*. . . . Were such 'women-behind-the-men' to have attempted to enter the public arena to speak with their own voices, they would have been roundly jeered, satirized, and condemned" (14–15, n. 11).

24. A. E. Taylor quotes from the fragments of the *Aspasia* collated in H. Ditmar's *Aeschines von Sphettos*.

25. In her epistolary arguments with Abelard, Héloïse relies on ancient authorities. In one particular case, her crown *auctoritas* is Aspasia. Quoting from the now-missing text of Aeschines, Héloïse argues for the excellence of a good wife and a good husband (Moncrieff 58). In her reading of Héloïse's letters, Andrea Nye challenges the philosophical community to be "informed by Héloïse's and Aspasia's wisdom, their subtle, sensitive, mobile, flexible women's tongues." She also wants us to admit that "a woman can be the teacher of a man" (17).

26. Compare the following passages:

How fine it would be, Agathon, . . . if wisdom were a sort of thing that could flow out of the one of us who is fuller into him who is emptier, by our mere contact with each other. . . . My own is but meagre, as disputable as a dream; but yours is bright and expansive, . . . shining forth from your youth, strong and splendid. (Socrates, in Plato, *Symposium* 175.e)

Love is . . . of most venerable standing. . . . I for my part am at a loss to say what greater blessing a man can have in earliest youth than an honourable lover. (Phaedrus, in Plato, *Symposium* 178.c)

When a man freely devotes his service to another in the belief that his friend will make him better in point of wisdom, . . . this willing bondage . . . is no sort of baseness or flattery. (Pausanias, in Plato, *Symposium* 183.b)

Love . . . which is consummated for a good purpose, temperately and justly, both here on earth and in heaven above, wields the mightiest power of all and provides us with a perfect bliss; so that we are able to consort with one another and have friendship also with the gods who are above us. (Eryximachus, in Plato, *Symposium* 188.d)

27. Plato goes on to write,

But the soul which has lost its wings is borne along until it gets hold of something solid, when it settles down, taking upon itself an earthly body. . . .
. . . The divine is beauty, wisdom, goodness, and all such qualities; by these then the wings of the soul are nourished and grow, but by the opposite qualities, such as vileness and evil, they are wasted away and destroyed. . . . And this is a law of Destiny, that the soul which follows after God and obtains a view of any of the truths is free from harm until the next period, . . . but when, through inability

to follow, it fails to see, and through some mischance is filled with forgetfulness and evil and grows heavy, . . . loses its wings and falls to the earth, then it is the law that this soul shall never pass into any beast at its first birth, but the soul that has seen the most shall enter into the birth of a man [at various ranks, accordingly]. . . . Then a human soul may pass into the life of a beast, and a soul which was once human, may pass again from a beast into a man. For the soul which has never seen the truth can never pass into human form. (*Phaedrus* 246.c–e, 248.c, 249.b, In *Euthyphro*)

28. For instance, in spite of his customary analytic and terminological precision, Aristotle never describes the hymen, nor does he distinguish between the labia and the clitoris.

29. See Fantham et al. 68–69 for further discussion.

30. See also Fantham et al. 69.

31. The *Timaeus* is considered a sequel to the *Republic*.

32. According to Plutarch, Cicero interrupted his career (for the benefit of his health) and spent two years (79–77 BCE) studying rhetoric and philosophy in Athens under Antiochus; in Rhodes under Poseidonius and Apollonius; and in Asia under Xenocles, Dionysius, and Menippus. After working to correct Cicero's stylistic excesses, Apollonius heard his pupil declaim in Greek and allegedly said: "You have my praise and admiration, Cicero, and Greece my commiseration, since those arts and that eloquence which are the only glories that remain to her, will now be transferred by you to Rome" (qtd. in Plutarch, *Lives* 1043).

33. In *De oratore* [*The Making of an Orator*, c. 55 BCE], his biased account of his own rhetorical training, Cicero writes:

We were not only studying such subjects as attracted Crassus, but were also being instructed by those very teachers whom he made his friends, we . . . often perceived . . . that, besides speaking Greek so perfectly as to suggest that it was the only tongue he knew, [Crassus] propounded such topics to our masters in the way of inquiry and himself so handled matters in his discourse, that nothing seemed strange to him, nothing beyond his range of knowledge. But as for Antonius, . . . at Athens and at Rhodes alike, that orator had devoted himself to conversation with the most learned men, yet I myself, in early life, went as far as the modesty natural to my youth permitted, in questioning him time and again on many subjects. . . . The result of my many conversations with him on various subjects was . . . that there was nothing . . . about which he was inexperienced or ignorant. (2.1.2–3)

34. Cicero writes that there is

no more excellent thing than the power, by means of oratory, to get a hold on assemblies of men, win their good will, direct their inclinations wherever the speaker wishes, or divert them from whatever he wishes. In every free nation, and most of all in communities which have attained the enjoyment of peace and tranquillity, this one art has always flourished above the rest and ever reigned supreme. (*De oratore* 1.7.30)

35. Cicero writes:

Some persons have wondered why I so suddenly, and with such enthusiasm turned to philosophy. . . . But my interest in philosophy is nothing new or sudden. From my boyhood I have given to it no small amount of devotion and study; and I was actually occupying myself with it most energetically during certain periods of my career when nobody suspected me of such activity. My orations, packed with philosophical aphorisms, prove the truth of this statement; so does my intimate association with the most erudite men . . . and with those illustrious thinkers Diodotus, Philo, Antiochus, and Posidonius, by whom I was taught. And if it is true that all the precepts of philosophy may be applied to life, I feel that both in public and in private I have conducted myself in accordance with its rules and principles. (*On the Nature of the Gods* 1.3, in *Brutus, On*)

36. These were the most popular rhetoric books of antiquity, and perhaps the most disseminated works of any kind. "More manuscripts of them survive than of any other classical texts, and the total of copies and commentaries originally circulating was probably in the thousands" (Vickers, *In Defense* 28).

37. Barilli goes on to say that "none of [Cicero's] other works rivals its breadth, unity, and thoroughness. . . . The work stands alone" (32).

38. With that change,

rhetoric lost the environment that made it a source of political power. While proficiency in rhetoric continued to be an advantage in legal practice throughout the Empire, . . . rhetoric's educational mission shifted and the pragmatic orientation of Republican schools of declamation correspondingly shifted in emphasis to the appreciation of rhetoric for its aesthetic features. (R. Enos, *Roman* 30)

39. Fictionalized accounts of Cicero's life are many, but recently Steven Saylor has published a number of Roman republic mystery novels in which Cicero plays a major role.

40. During this time, rhetoric shifted "from a source of power through free speech to an educational subject, facilitating learning and synonymous with the acquisition of literacy and subsequently culture" (R. Enos, *Roman* 36).

41. "Perfect eloquence is assuredly a reality, which is not beyond the reach of human intellect. Even if we fail to reach it, those whose aspirations are highest, will attain to greater heights than those who abandon themselves to premature despair of ever reaching the goal and halt at the very foot of the ascent" (Quintilian 1.Pr.20).

42. Quintilian writes,

This is essential, [for] . . . if the powers of eloquence serve only to lend arms to crime, there can be nothing more pernicious than eloquence to the public and private welfare alike. . . . I do not merely assert that the ideal orator should be a good man, but I affirm that no man can be an orator unless he is a good man. . . . Vileness and virtue cannot jointly inhabit in the selfsame heart. (12.1.1, 3–4)

43. Quintilian implored his fellow Romans to moral performances:

Who will teach courage, justice, loyalty, self-control, simplicity, and contempt of grief and pain better than men like Fabricius, Curius, Regulus, Decius, Mucius and countless others? For if the Greeks bear away the palm for moral precepts, Romans can produce more striking examples of moral performance, which is a far greater thing. . . . It is from the thought of posterity that [a man] must inspire his soul with justice and derive that freedom of spirit which it is his duty to display when he pleads in the courts or gives counsel in the senate. No man will ever be the consummate orator of whom we are in quest unless he has both the knowledge and the courage to speak in accordance with the promptings of honour. (12.2.30–31)

44. Marcus Cato argued in terms of prohibitions necessary for women:

Our ancestors refused to allow any woman to transact even private business without a guardian to represent her; women had to be under the control of fathers, brothers, or husbands. But we . . . are now allowing them even to take part in politics, and actually to appear in the Forum and to be present at our meetings and assemblies! What are they now doing in the streets and at the street corners? Are they not simply canvassing for the proposal of the tribunes, and voting for the repeal of the law? Give a free rein to their undisciplined nature, to this untamed animal, and then expect them to set a limit to their own licence! Unless you impose that limit, this is the least of the restraints imposed on women by custom or by law which they resent. What they are longing for is complete liberty, or rather—if we want to speak the truth—complete licence. . . .
. . . You have often heard my complaints about the excessive spending of the women, and of the men, magistrates as well as private citizens, about the sorry state of our commonwealth because of two opposing vices, avarice and extravagance—plagues which have been the destruction of all great empires. (Livy, *Rome* 2.34.2, 4)

45. Valerius writes, "No magistrates, no priesthoods, no triumphs, no insignia, no rewards or spoils of war can fall to them: elegance, adornment, dress—these are the insignia of women; in these is their delight and their glory; these are what our ancestors called 'feminine decoration' " (Livy, *Rome* 2.34.7).

46. A woman and her financial worth belonged first of all to her father (the *agnate*, or father's side, as opposed to the *cognate*, or mother's side), and only secondly to her husband. Any woman who transferred her dowry, or family property, to her husband (thereby leaving her original agnatic descent group to enter that of her husband) transferred her *manus*, the authority under which she lived. With the Roman Empire came the elimination of any such transfer. Changes in agnatic guardianship and inheritance and in matrimonial law reflected the belief that women should retain their former status and family membership after marriage. On the surface, these legal decisions appear to emancipate a woman from her husband's authority. Had they been in response to previous unfairness or to supposed inequalities of women, these laws might have effected practical changes. But instead, these laws kept a woman within the legal sphere of her father's family, trapped for life. No longer could widowhood or death offer an opportunity to gain freedom from her agnate of origin.

47. Although she was

legally more enslaved than the Greek, the woman of Rome was in practice much more deeply integrated in society. At home she sat in the atrium, the center of the dwelling, instead of being hidden away in the gynaeceum; she directed the work of the slaves; she guided the education of the children, and frequently she influenced them up to a considerable age. She shared the labors and cares of her husband[;] she was regarded as co-owner of his property. The matron was called *domina*; she was mistress of the home, associate in religion—not the slave, but the companion of man. (Beauvoir 104–5)

48. Not to be confused with Cornelia, last wife of Pompey the Great, mentioned earlier.

49. To the advantage of small farmers, Cornelia's sons introduced procedures by which land could be distributed and corn could be priced more equitably. Their attempts to translate their political idealism to social reform brought immediate violence and prolonged political change. Both their lives ended during political upheaval.

50. Quintus Valerius Maximus writes of Hortensia's father:

Quintus Hortensius thinking there was very much to be ascribed to a decent and com[e]ly motion of the Body, spent more time in practising that, than in studying for Eloquence. So that it was hard to know, whether the Concourse were greater to hear or see him: So mutually did his Aspect serve his words, and his words his Aspect. And therefore it is certain, that *Roscius* and *Aesopus*, the most skilful Actors in the world, would be always in Court when *Hortensius* pleaded, to carry away his postures to the Stage. (Valerius Maximus 8.10.3)

51. Valerius Maximus tells us that "none of the Men durst undertake to speak in their behalfs" (8.3.3).

52. Appian goes on,

On the following day [the triumvirs] reduced the number of women, who were to present a valuation of their property, from 1400 to 400, and decreed that all men who possessed more than 100,000 drachmas, both citizens and strangers, freedmen and priests, and men of all nationalities without a single exception, should . . . lend them at interest a fiftieth part of their property and contribute one year's income to the war expenses. (4.4.34)

53. A. J. Marshall tells us that the case of Maesia of Sentinum probably belongs to the period of Sulla's return, a period of lawlessness, when Italian communities were stripped of civil rights. As the men were often in hiding or transit, women were left to defend themselves and their property from physical or legal attack.

3. MEDIEVAL RHETORIC: PAGAN ROOTS, CHRISTIAN FLOWERING, OR VEILED VOICES IN THE MEDIEVAL RHETORICAL TRADITION

1. "Just as the Egyptians had not only idols and grave burdens which the people of Israel detested and avoided, so also they had vases and ornaments of gold and silver . . . which the Israelites took with them secretly when they fled, as if to put them to a better use" (Augustine, *On Christian* 2.40.60).

2. Early Christianity was a remarkably diverse and fractious religious movement, but the history of Christianity has, until recently, been told from a single point of view, often a view exclusionary of women's participation. In her *Gnostic Gospels*, for instance, Elaine Pagels explains the Gnostic God as embodying both masculine and feminine aspects, which naturally led to the powerful feminine imagery and ideology suffusing the Gnostic Gospels. Eventually outnumbered and overpowered by more mainstream Christians, the Gnostics were an early group of Christians who believed the Holy Spirit to be female and the Trinity to be Father, Son, and Mother.

3. English law forbade women fighting duels, appearing in court (except on behalf of their husbands or to testify on the birth order of twins), participating in any institution of government, or pressing criminal charges (except those connected with in-

stances of rape or murder). Of course, a woman could be sued in the same way as a man for nonpayment of debts, violation of contracts, illicit trade activities, adultery, and murder.

4. Then she could administer the estate (leasing land, collecting rents, maintaining buildings, managing the peasants, marketing crops and livestock, overseeing the budget), educate her children, and dispose of property or inheritance. Some women ran estates as large as towns that encompassed many varied tasks. In addition, some women presided over the court and took charge of the vassal services due the lord. She *was* the lord—albeit in his name rather than her own, unless, of course, she was a widow without male children.

5. As a "sister" of the guild, a wife could enjoy many of the religious, social, and charitable benefits of guild membership but at a second-rank and limited status.

6. Poor women, just like their male counterparts, had few legal rights beyond protection for their lives and limbs. And more often than the rich, of course, the poor bore the consequences of a savage and vindictive medieval law. The criminal who escaped hanging was liable to have a foot or a hand struck off or to be blinded and mutilated. Life was cheap and cruelty a matter of course, particularly for the disenfranchised, who could be exploited sexually, physically, and financially by any man above them in station. Since they were all illiterate, we have no records (no personal account books, let alone diaries or journals) that reveal their personal lives.

7. Unions between free women and unfree men were illegitimate. The woman in such a coupling stood to lose her property, freedom, and maybe even her life. Her children were reduced to servitude and could not inherit. On the other hand, no law prevented a free man from having sexual unions with his slaves, and resulting children could become legal heirs. Women could rise in social class through their marriages, particularly if they had property; men could not rise, so, in a way, women had a wider choice of mates.

8.

The Lord God formed man of dust from the ground, and breathed into his nostrils the breath of life; and man became a living being. . . . Then the Lord God said, "It is not good that the man should be alone; I will make him a helper fit for him." . . . So the Lord God caused a deep sleep to fall upon the man, and while he slept took one of his ribs and closed up its place with flesh; and the rib which the Lord God had taken from the man he made into a woman and brought her to man. (Gen. 2.7–22)

9. Aristotle believed that males are active and females passive: "the female always provides the material, the male that which fashions it, for this is the power we say they each possess, and *this is what is for them to be male and female*. . . . While the body is from the female, it is the soul that is from the male" (*Generation* 2.4.738.b.20–23).

10. Amount of heat determined whether a human would become male or female, for heat perfected the reproductive organs by forcing them to descend and externalize; heat also transformed menstrual blood into the more potent and important semen.

11. But even their tidy teleological interpretation of the female genitalia as the inverse of male genitalia fell short of explaining the significance of the female breasts. Except in obscure Arabic writings, the breasts were not considered to be erotic zones; most medieval writers described them as small and hard. Writing that breasts "attracted little attention from writers who commented on erotic foreplay," Claude Thomasset is one of many contemporary writers surprised by these "astonishingly unperceptive"

medieval accounts (47). Isabel Fonseca's recent essay, "Among the Gypsies," sheds light on medieval opinion:

> Breasts are associated with babies rather than with sex, and the upper body is not a source of shame. The lower body, by contrast, is considered highly dangerous from the point of view of pollution. . . .
>
> [After looking at the author's breasts, two Gypsy women] unself-consciously yanked their own breasts out of the tops of their dresses and presented them as proof of my freakishness. . . . [T]hey had breastfed for years, and their breasts hung in yamlike triangular flaps, with slightly discolored tips for nipples. Shyly earthbound, they were more tuber than sexual characteristic, strange and beautiful. (93)

Because "the purpose of menstrual blood is to nourish the embryo after conception," the only source of breast milk could have been "cooked menstrual blood," which ensured "a smooth transition from one form of nourishment to another" (Thomasset 54). Just as they miscorrelated menstrual blood with breast milk, medieval scientists provided a mistaken explanation for the placement of female breasts, an interpretation based on Plutarch, who had written that nature had placed the breasts of the human female high upon her body, so that she would embrace her baby as she nursed him, and so develop affection for him ("On Affection" 330–57).

12. I offer specifics about medieval religious practices below, when I discuss Julian of Norwich and Margery Kempe. This section serves only to frame the discussions of those two women.

13. In *Womanguides*, Rosemary Radford Ruether includes an illustration of a feminine Holy Spirit (taken from a fourteenth-century fresco in Urschalling Church, southwest of Munich, Germany), with this explanation: "This feminine Holy Spirit was thought of as mother and nurturer of the Christian. She was closely linked with baptism as the womb of rebirth and with regeneration imaged as breastfeeding of the reborn soul" (20). "This kind of imagery of the Holy Spirit as the female power of gestation, birth, and nurturing is evident in the Syriac Ode of Solomon, No. 19" (24).

14. However, women were exhorted to model themselves after biblical heroines. "Let her take pattern by Mary," wrote Jerome (Letter 107). Despite his call, the institutional clerical attitude toward women in monastic communities and as mother-educators remained ambivalent.

15. Stories of polygamy, divorce, murder, sacrifice, homosexuality, eroticism and sexuality, female leadership and daring, for example, were reinterpreted. With great ingenuity, Jerome explains away the marriage, even the polygamy, of the patriarchs but claims that the figures closest to God in the Bible were all virgins (Joshua, Elijah, John the Baptist, etc.). Solomon's case was harder to support, but Jerome manages, based on his own interpretation of the Songs of Solomon. Augustine ingeniously proved that the Old Testament patriarchs had sexual intercourse solely because they were obliged to procreate; Jacob, indeed, would have preferred to abstain from begetting children and only did so because his wives insisted.

16. With regard to Jesus's embodiment of both male and female parts of humanity and his relation to women, Dorothy Sayre writes:

> Perhaps it is no wonder that women were first at the Cradle and last at the Cross. They had never known a man like this Man—there never has been such another. A prophet and teacher who never nagged at them, never flattered or coaxed or patron-

ized. . . . There is no act, no sermon, no parable in the whole Gospel that borrows its pungency from female perversity; nobody could possibly guess from the words and deeds of Jesus that there was anything "funny" about woman's nature. (47)

In 1956, Charles Seltman wrote that "it is clear that Jesus was a feminist to a degree far beyond that of His fellows and followers" (184). And he goes on to catalog the many women in Jesus's scriptural life:

the widow seeking her mite, or giving it; the woman of Samaria with the outlook of a Greek girl-companion; a little girl, Jairus' daughter, brought back to health; the woman with a "bloody flux" who touched the hem of His garment; Mary and her sister Martha; the "woman taken in adultery"; another who bathed His feet in perfume and dried them with her hair; His Mother and the woman at the foot of the Cross; the opened tomb discovered by Mary of Magdala. . . . [T]he Messiah was ever concerned with females as much as with men. No other Western prophet, seer, or would-be redeemer of humanity was so devoted to the feminine half of mankind. (184)

17. "In my Father's house are many mansions: if it were not so, I would have told you. I go to prepare a place for you. And if I go and prepare a place for you, I will come again, and receive you unto myself; that where I am, there ye may be also" (John 14.2–3).

18. The Church Fathers had inherited the literary traditions of classical paganism, of ancient Israel, and of primitive Christianity, which were inconsistent in espousing equality and opportunity to women. Their sources—the Old Testament, Greek and Roman philosophy and law, and Aristotle's pseudoscientific tracts—took for granted women's inherent inferiority in body, mind, and spirit.

19. St. Jerome, who had an unusual gift for attracting the devotion of women, writes that "[A]s long as woman is for birth and children, she is different from man as body is from soul. But if she wishes to serve Christ more than the world, then she will cease to be a woman and will be called man" (qtd. in Bullough 498). Jerome prized his friendships with certain women, for theirs was the sex of Mary. Yet he exalted women at the expense of their sex, arguing that Mary was a perpetual virgin and that any other woman's pregnancy was revolting. St. Ambrose expresses a similar idea: "[S]he who does not believe is a woman and should be designated by the name of her bodily sex, whereas she who believes progresses to complete manhood, to the measure of the adulthood of Christ. She then does without worldly name, gender of body, youthful seductiveness, and garrulousness of old age" (qtd. in Bullough 498).

20. Mary remained in a category of her own.

21. Whether Christian perfection or perfect love, the goal remained unattainable; whether the Holy Mother or the exalted beloved, the woman was never a real human. Writers—and readers—may have seen through the superficiality (surely they saw through the oversimplification) of these concepts, but they, nonetheless, participated in the spirit of their culture, working to balance pre-Christian (Old Testament) and pagan tracts from religion, philosophy, and politics with contemporary Christian values and immutable patristic mores.

22. Rudolph C. Bambas, however, argues that the feminine inflections in the poem are the result of scribal error.

23. The poem was copied in the Exeter Book around AD 940.

24. The writings of first-century Jewish philosopher Philo were extremely influen-

tial in shaping medieval thought, particularly in the gendering of faculties and sensations. Like Plato, Philo associated woman with sense perception and man with the mind (*On the Virtues* 3.89.453). Philo also buttresses his argument with an interpretation of the second Creation story: "First [God] made mind, the man, for mind is most venerable in a human being, then bodily sense, the woman, then after them in the third place pleasure" (*Allegorical* 18.271).

25. "Judith," an early male-authored poem drawn from the deuterocanonical narrative of the Old Testament of the same name, was found at the beginning of the *Beowulf* manuscript, dating from the late ninth century.

26. Judith's success is read differently throughout the Middle Ages. Early on, this daring Jewish "noble maid" personifies an Anglo-Saxon fantasy: she is white, shining, and curly haired; she is noble, holy, courageous, and wise. Before she beheads Holofernes, she offers her petition to God:

> God, . . . I will pray for Thy mercy upon me
> Who need it. . . .
> Give to me, Lord of heaven, victory
> And true belief, that with this sword I may
> Hew at this giver of death. Grant me success,
> Strong Lord of men; never had I more need
> Of Thy compassion; now, O mighty Lord (Cook and Tinker 124)

In response to her prayer, "the highest Judge" encourages Judith "as doth he to each one / Of those here dwelling who seek Him for help / With reason and with true belief." God rewards Judith with wisdom and stamina; the Bethulians reward "the bright woman prompt of thought" with "all / Of treasure that the haughty chief possessed" (132). The Anglo-Saxon author and his audience could celebrate a "snare-devising maid, famed for her strength," a "holy woman the handmaid of God" (126, 129). Hers is a religious epic, recording the deeds of a female hero, who is protected by her proto-Christian belief and her trust in God.

27. *Juliana* tells the story of a Christian virgin, whose father promises her in marriage to a non-Christian. Juliana will marry only on the condition that he convert. He does not, and she is tortured to death. *Elena* is the story of St. Helena, mother of Emperor Constantine. Immediately following his victory over the Huns, Constantine sends his mother to the Holy Land to locate the True Cross of the Crucifixion. By means of a miracle, she is able to determine the actual cross. Both these stories are said to be the work of Cynewulf, ninth-century Northumbrian or Mercian poet.

28. Later medieval preachers read Judith's saga as a cautionary tale of feminine power, of how easily "muche pepull" are steered toward and "assententh to lechery by the nyse [foolish, nice] aray of women" (Roy. MS 18.B.xxiii, fols. 132b–3, qtd. in Owst 118). Even Holofernes, King Nebuchadnezzar's greatest lieutenant, could succumb, as the medieval sermon admonishes: "Loo sirs, here may ʒe see how that a prince, that wanne a grett parte of the world, myʒth not overcom, but was distrowed by the nyce aray and atyre of a woman" (qtd. in Owst 118). The preacher goes on to warn that "in thise days many men ben overcom spiritually and slayen in ther own soules" (qtd. in Owst 118). Judith's story, then, cautions all men regarding physical and spiritual temptation and the ease with which they can succumb, particularly to the wiles of fashionable women, no doubt a primary attraction.

29. Because this is a single episode in the Round Table saga, "Knight of the Cart"

is referred to as a *lai*. Lais were sometimes sung. Chrétien de Troyes opens his own story with

> Since my lady of Champagne wishes me to undertake to write a romance, I shall very gladly do so, being so devoted to her service as to do anything in the world for her, without any intention of flattery. But if one were to introduce any flattery upon such an occasion, he might say, and I would subscribe to it, that this lady surpasses all others who are alive, just as the south wind which blows in May or April is more lovely than any other wind. But upon my word, I am not one to wish to flatter my lady. I will simply say: "The Countess is worth as many qyeens as a gem is worth of pearls and sards." Nay I shall make no comparison, and yet it is true in spite of me; I will say, however, that her command has more to do with this work than any thought or pains that I may expend upon it. (Chrétien 270)

30. The spellings of Guinevere and Lancelot vary from version to version. *Morte D'Authur* was written by Malory and printed and edited by William Caxton.

31. A widow living on the edge of town evokes "witch" to fictional and historical medieval townspeople.

32. Because she is a "holy woman" who knows "nothing of witchcraft," Dame Sirith is able "with good men's alms and gifts / Each day [her] life to feed" (lines 204–6). Dame Sirith feeds her dog hot peppers and takes the weeping dog along to tell Margeri the "weeping bitch" tale:

> A proud cleric came with a tonsure
> To my daughter his love offered
> And she would not follow his advice.
> He could not his will have
> No matter how he begged
> Then went the clerk to witchcraft
> And transformed my daughter to a bitch.
> This is my daughter of whom I speak.   (lines 345–55)

33. In her prologue, Chaucer's Wife of Bath describes the pleasure her fifth husband took in reading such a collection: "When he had time and leisure / Or had no occupation . . . his pleasure, / . . . was to read this book of wicked wives" (lines 683–85). The Wife grabs his book and tears three pages out of it; he beats her. His apologies are not enough; she asks him to burn the book immediately, a request that he honors.

34. John Duns Scotus, thirteenth-century Scottish Franciscan, went further to argue that Mary was perpetually free of the taint of original sin, and he pronounced her own conception to be immaculate, her own childbearing to be virginal, and her assumption into heaven to be freedom from the putrescence of the flesh.

35. For example, Mary gives birth in the familiar way, but she does not dread the pain or fear the possibility of death. She is, after all, a virgin giving birth to God's own son. When the midwife checks her vagina to question the claim of virginity, she (according to medieval literature) finds that Mary is true and that her own doubt is suddenly figured by a withered hand that is eventually healed.

36. These cycles were named for the Feast of Corpus Christi, a holy day scheduled sixty days after Easter that celebrated the entire divine history of the world.

37. "Even the great cycle plays . . . though produced by civic guilds, were of clerical

authorship and were performed on religious festivals with the active cooperation of the Church" (Bevington 3).

38. One portion of the N-Town cycle centers on her life, as does an extant portion of the "Ludus Coventriae." Stanley J. Kahrl writes that the N-Town cycle manuscript is dated 1468 in the "hand of the scribe responsible for transcribing the bulk of the manuscript. [The date] appears at the end of a play on the Purification which represents a third stage of revision in the group of plays in this manuscript which deal with the life of the Virgin" (19). Although the only complete life of Mary is the "Ludus Coventriae," all the cycle plays highlight her life with both visiting angels and a measure of verisimilitude.

39. Naturally, the stories of her perfect womanhood fed the romantic tradition of courtly love and literature.

40. For the continued edification of those vessels, for the pleasure of medieval audiences, and for the glory of the Queen of Heaven, medieval literature is replete with would-be Virgin Marys. Mary served as handmaiden to the Church, just as these human reflections of the Virgin Mary would subordinate themselves to either the Church or their men. The *Pearl* poet in the late fourteenth century writes of his beautiful, flawless Pearl, his young daughter, recently deceased. Adorned as a queen of heaven, Pearl appears to her grieving father in a dream in which she comforts him and convinces him not to think of her but rather to think of his own soul and the Everlasting (*Pearl* 353–57, 412–15). Pearl's understanding and faith in her own earthly death emblematizes the expectations of other earthly women: they are to serve, with all their spirit, for "in God's kingdom . . . exists no uncertainty" (601–2). Over twelve hundred lines long, the only extant copy of *Pearl* is collected with *Patience*, *Cleanness*, and *Sir Gawain and the Green Knight* in the Cotton Nero Ax manuscript (c. late fourteenth century).

41. All translations of *Ancrene Wisse* are my own.

42. Héloïse of Paraclete and Hildegard von Bingen come readily to mind. They are, however, outside the scope of this study.

43. Vickers continues:

> [T]he medieval rhetorician's knowledge of classical rhetoric texts was largely confined to those introductory and extremely practical school texts, Cicero's *De Inventione* and the anonymous *Ad Herennium*, often found combined in manuscripts. . . . There were many commentaries on these works, . . . preserving other facets of the rhetorical tradition, but of course the circulation of manuscripts and commentaries was a haphazard affair, and many medieval writers had access to only a part of current knowledge. (*In Defense* 215–16)

44. See James J. Murphy's "Saint Augustine and the Debate about a Christian Rhetoric" for an elaboration of this topic.

45. "For since by means of the art of rhetoric both truth and falsehood are urged, who would dare to say that truth should stand in the person of its defenders unarmed against lying, so that they who wish to urge falsehoods may know how to make their listeners benevolent, or attentive, or docile in their presentation, while the defenders of truth are ignorant of that art?" (Augustine, *On Christian* 4.2.3).

46. Chapter 2 of Roxanne Mountford's unpublished dissertation, "The Feminization of the *Ars praedicandi*," offers a historical overview of the art of preaching, the only comprehensive overview that I know of. Her work on Augustine and the medieval Church has been especially helpful to me.

47. Besides supervising the copying and translating of the works of other nearby hermits, Jerome continued to build the linguistic and scholarly foundations of his permanent achievements as an ecclesiastical commentator: "No Christian writer before him (not even Origen) and no Christian-born writer for many centuries after him (possibly not until the seventeenth century) possessed a comparable command of Hebrew, and therefore of the Old Testament in its original language" (E. Rice 10).

48. Comprising the mathematical arts was the quadrivium of arithmetic, music, geometry, and astronomy; the verbal arts were the trivium of grammar, rhetoric, and logic.

49. In addition to Murphy's *Rhetoric in the Middle Ages*, Richard McKeon's "Rhetoric in the Middle Ages" remains an invaluable resource for the study of medieval rhetoric.

50. "Grammar was thought to discipline the mind and the soul at the same time, honing the intellectual and spiritual abilities that the future cleric would need to read and speak [and write] with discernment" (Huntsman 59).

51. Donatus's works are *De partibus orationis ars minor* ("the lesser art, concerning the parts of grammar") and the *Ars grammatica*, or *Ars major* ("the greater art").

52. In *Classical Rhetoric*, George Kennedy credits the eleventh-century Italian school of Monte Cassino and its first great teacher, Alberic, with systematizing the art of letter writing, linking it with rhetoric (185). Murphy writes that Alberic is a "pivotal figure in the history of medieval rhetoric. As a teacher in the oldest continuously operating Benedictine monastery in Europe, he inherited the ancient traditions of learning which went back to Benedict himself. It is not surprising then to find him quoting Cicero, Sallust, Lucan, Ovid, Terence, and of course Virgil in his own works" (203). Alberic's pupil John of Gaeta (who would become pope in AD 1118) emphasized the concept of *cursus*, or prose rhythm.

53. Besides, the "substantive consideration of law had moved into theology and had taken with it most of the appurtenances which might have made the law a learned profession, leaving only the verbal rhetoric of the *dictamen*" (McKeon 27).

54. "And God said, 'Let there be light'; and there was light. . . . And God said, 'Let there be a firmament in the midst of the waters, and let it separate the waters from the waters.' . . . And it was so. . . . And God said, 'Let the waters under the heavens be gathered together into one place, and let the dry land appear' " (Gen. 1.3–9).

55. Augustine argues,

[T]hose with acute and eager minds more readily learn eloquence by reading and hearing the eloquent than by following the rules of eloquence. There is no lack of ecclesiastical literature, . . . which, if read by a capable man, even though he is interested more in what is said than in the eloquence with which it is said, will imbue him with that eloquence while he is studying. And he will learn eloquence especially if he gains practice by writing, dictating, or speaking what he has learned according to the rule of piety and faith. But if capacity of this kind to learn eloquence is lacking, the rules of rhetoric will not be understood, nor will it help any if they are in some small measure understood after great labor. . . . [I]ndeed, I think that there is hardly a single eloquent man who can both speak well and think of the rules of eloquence while he is speaking. And we should beware lest what should be said escape us while we are thinking of the artistry of the discourse. Moreover, in the speeches and sayings of the eloquent, the precepts of eloquence are found to have been fulfilled, although the speakers did not think of them in order to be eloquent or while they were being eloquent, and they were eloquent whether they had learned the rules or never come in contact with them. They fulfilled them because they were eloquent; they did not apply them that they might be eloquent. (*On Christian* 4.3.4)

56. He writes that

in any of these three styles an eloquent man speaks in a manner suitable to persuasion, but if he does not persuade, he has not attained the end of eloquence. Thus in the subdued style he persuades his listener that what he says is true; he persuades in the grand style that those things which we know should be done are done, although they have not been done. He persuades in the moderate style that he himself speaks beautifully and with ornament. (*On Christian* 4.25.55)

57. Murphy goes on to write,

[M]ore than three hundred treatises still survive from this phase, which lasted into the Reformation. Early thirteenth-century writers like Thomas of Salisbury, Richard of Thetford, and Alexander of Ashby established a *modus* or *forma* for preaching based on divisions and amplifications. The *Forma praedicandi* (1322) of Robert of Basevorn is a typical manual which almost perfectly embodies the entire movement. (*Rhetoric* 275–76)

58. Rhetorical theorists were finally moving to a "formalism in which doctrine was left to theology and attention was centered on three problems: propriety of division of the subject stated in the theme of the sermon, brevity of distinction, and utility of expansion" (McKeon 27–28).

59. We know very little about Robert of Basevorn except that he was familiar with the university-style preaching of both Oxford and Paris and that his work informed some three hundred imitative handbooks and manuals of preaching. He dedicated his *Forma praedicandi* to a Cistercian abbot, though he does not appear to have belonged to a religious order.

60. For their ethical appeal, preachers need three qualities: "a good life, sufficient knowledge, and legal authority" (Robert 117). They can establish a pathetic appeal by following the examples set by the preaching greats before them (Jesus, Paul, Augustine, Gregory), who adjusted their methods to the theme of their sermon and to their audience, for whom they felt great charity and understanding.

61. Thus, even the most carefully prepared sermon must be delivered in the context of a favorable rhetorical situation (*quaestio*):

Let the preacher see to it above all that he have a good purpose for his sermon—such as the praise of God, or His saints, or the edification of his neighbor, or some such object deserving eternal life. If, secondarily, he also includes another purpose—that he be famous, or that he gain something temporal, or the like—he is an adulterer of the Word of God, and this is considered a mortal sin. But if such a subject occur to him that he cannot profit by his teaching unless he say something by which he shows himself learned and capable, he may have that intention not as an end and direct it to the purpose of edifying. (Robert 125)

62. As Kenneth Burke reminds us in *A Rhetoric of Motives*, "once you treat instruction as an aim of rhetoric, you introduce a principle that can widen the scope of rhetoric beyond persuasion" (77).

63. Regarding the communication theory of the Church Fathers:

[Their] whole congeries of ideas has enormous psychological and philosophical implications. It places a great stress upon individual judgment. It encourages private interpretation of messages received. It states flatly that rhetors do not persuade, but that hearers move themselves; that teachers do not teach, but instead that learners learn. (Murphy, *Rhetoric* 289)

64. There are two versions of her visionary experience, the shorter [S] Amherst text, formerly owned by Lord Amherst (British Library, MS 37790), and the longer [L] Sloane text (in duplicate, MS 2499 and MS 3701). I refer to them as S and L throughout.

65. The uncalibrated term *litterati* indicated those schooled in Latin, regardless of individual expertise or accomplishment. The only lexical provision for those who read or wrote or spoke only in the vernacular (in any number of languages or dialects other than Latin) was the apologetic and imprecise *illitterati*. No person, not even those *illitterati*, remained unaffected by literate practices and totemic texts.

66. Paul writes of his own mystical union with God: "The gospel which was preached of me is not after man. For I neither received it of man, neither was I taught it, but by the revelation of Jesus Christ. . . . When it pleased God, who . . . called me by his grace, to reveal his Son in me, that I might preach him among the heathen; immediately I conferred not with flesh and blood" (Gal. 1.11–12, 15–16).

67. Anyone who is

imbued with a very intense mystical experience will wish to communicate it to others, and will therefore make every effort to find a language which is capable of transmitting this intensity as far as is possible, so that the wish for a similar experience will be awakened in the reader. Here the mystics sometimes fall back on the tried and tested figures of . . . rhetoric, but above all they strive to make their mystical themes clear by means of sensual concrete metaphors and images . . . to produce concrete language. (Riehle 1–2)

68. "It is so clearly a matter of rhetoric to persuade a man by identifying your cause with his interests" (Burke, *Rhetoric* 24).

69. The modernizations from Kempe's *Book* are my own.

70. Vernacular verse was, of course, widely used.

71. Peter Rabinowitz provides a careful distinction of audiences (126–27).

72. Paul is usually faulted for his sexism, as evidenced in this biblical passage, but the beliefs of Augustine and Thomas Aquinas were just as pervasive: "woman has been made for man" (Augustine, *Confessions* 13.32); "whatever [woman] holds to, she holds to it weakly" and thus is more likely than man to sin (Thomas Aquinas 1.98.2).

4. INSCRIBED IN THE MARGINS:
RENAISSANCE WOMEN AND RHETORICAL CULTURE

1. See, for example, these lines from John Skelton's "Phyllyp Sparowe" (c. 1505):

> Our naturall tong is rude,
> And hard to be enneude
> With pullysshed termes lusty;
> Our language is so rusty,
> So cankered, and so full

Of frowardes, and so dull,
That if I wolde apply
To wryte ornatly,
I wot not where to fynd
Termes to serve my mynde.   (lines 774–83)

2. As translators, evangelists, poets, playwrights, pamphleteers, speechwriters, letter writers, and public speakers, the following Renaissance women all merit further study: Jane of Somerset, Jane and Mary of Arundel, Margaret How Ascham, Anne Askew, Anne Cooke Bacon, Elizabeth Faulkland Cary, Elizabeth Fane, Jane Fox, Lady Jane Grey, Mary Sidney Herbert, Jane Howard, Esther Inglis, Elizabeth Legge, Dorothy Leigh, Jane and Mary Maltravers, Margaret More Roper, Elizabeth Cooke Russell, Arabella Stuart Seymour, Mary Sidney, Marie Stuart, Catherine Tishem, Elizabeth Hane Weston, and Mary Sidney Wroth. Each of these women composed powerful English.

3. Compare this passage from *Lawes*:

In this consolidation which we call wedlock is a locking together. It is true, that man and wife are one person, but understand in what manner.

When a small brook or little river incorporateth with . . . the Thames, the poor rivulet loseth her name; it is carried and recarried with the new associate; it beareth no sway; it possesseth nothing during coverture. As woman as soon as she is married is called "covert" . . . ; she hath lost her stream. . . .

All [women] are understood either married, or to be married, and their desires are subject to their husbands. . . . the common law here shaketh hand with divinity.

4. Women's wages were always half those of men, regardless of the work. Besides their low pay, female employees offered another kind of financial advantage to their employers: employers expected to "hold" a young girl's wages for her, to be released, when needed, as a dowry. But in the case of a girl's losing her position or of the employer's losing his money, the girl had no guarantee of those wages, of her dowry.

5. Olwen Hufton tells us about the many girls who could not compete in the workforce, who were "chronically poor, undernourished, rickety, pockmarked, dirty, and lice-ridden. They lacked the training that fitted them for employment in even a modest household. . . . [They] were automatically excluded by the very poverty of their backgrounds from anything approaching a respectable situation" (22).

6. But these girls could threaten the male workers by working for less money and thereby undercutting journeymen's wages. "When work was plentiful and labor scarce, the guilds were relatively tolerant and turned a blind eye to women's activities in their sphere; but when times were harder, attitudes changed" (L. Stone 25).

7. Hufton estimates the number of female servants as "accounting for about 12 percent of the total population of any European town or city throughout the seventeenth and eighteenth centuries" (19).

8. In *The Diary of Lady Margaret Hoby*, Lady Hoby writes, "After I had prayed privately I dressed a poor boy's leg that came to me, and then brake my fast with Mr. Hoby: after, I dressed the hand of one of our servants that was very sore cut . . . after to supper, then to the lector: after that I dressed one of the men's hands that was hurt, lastly prayed, and so to bed" (qtd. in Otten 186–87).

9. Retha M. Warnicke writes that, since women

were also responsible for doctoring the farm's sick animals, the members of their household, and—if they were of the gentle classes—the entire population of the local village, they had to have salves, lotions, and other medicines replenished and available. Sometimes they had to assume control of the household in their husbands' absences and to protect the estate from violent attack by domestic and even foreign enemies. . . . [T]hey frequently had to see to the leasing of farms, to deal with attorneys about legal problems and to oversee the marketing of crops. . . . [Even a wife] who was childless remained an important part of the family's industry. (7)

10. Nancy Tuana writes that "scientists, like everyone, work within and through the worldview of their time. The theories they develop and the facts they accept must be coherent with this system of beliefs. Thus, it will come as no surprise that science has provided a biological explanation/justification of the image of woman as inferior" (147).

11. "The belief that female seed arose from the 'serious, salty, and acrid' blood of the left test[i]s was the only viable explanation of the perceived differences between women and men" (Tuana 161).

12. "Within the constraints of common sense, if not logical consistency, women cannot have a full-size penis within (the vagina) *and* a small homologue of the penis without (the clitoris)" (Laqueur 65).

13. In carrying the "gold out of Egypt," medieval scholars had extracted and modified already faulty classical texts in ways that substantiated Christian tenets.

14. Brian Vickers lists the early Renaissance discoveries of ancient texts as follows: papal secretary Poggio Bracciolini's 1416 discovery of a complete Quintilian in the abbey of St. Gall along with a manuscript of Asconius Pedianus's commentaries on Cicero's speeches; Poggio's earlier discoveries of eight Ciceronian speeches, including *Pro roscio*, *Pro murena*, and *Pro cluentio*; Bishop of Lodi Gerardo Landriani's 1421 discovery of complete Ciceronian *De oratore* and *Orator* as well as a totally unknown *Brutus* (*In Defense* 254–55). Poggio copied the entire Quintilian in great haste and took it back to Italy, where his version was copied and distributed among a large number of intellectuals, who arranged for additional copies to be made to meet the demand.

15. Their insistence upon and search for the "true" original led Renaissance scholars to the methods that would become modern "precise" scholarship.

16. Charles Trinkaus explains those five subjects of humanism:

grammar, including not only usage and sentence structure of the Latin language and of Greek, but philological and historical interpretation of all texts; rhetoric, the study of stylistic and literary aspects of all genres of texts by ancient authors as well as composition of orations and letters; history, increasingly separated from rhetoric and including both study of ancient historians and the writing of historical works about the classical and the recent past; poetry, study of Roman and Greek poets and composition of Latin verse; moral philosophy, including study, exposition, and interpretation of the moral thought of Cicero, Seneca, Aristotle, and other ancient writers and composition of numerous treatises on the ethical, domestic, and civic life of man. (19)

17. Perhaps the most famous work on Renaissance education is T. W. Baldwin's *William Shakspere's Small Latine and Lesse Greeke*. In an era of spectacular literary achievements in the vernacular, it seems astonishing that English was not taught in

schools: Latin was the thing, and "lesse Greeke." However, classic Latin, unadulterated, could not cope with the problems of the "new learning," as humanist studies were called. The modern world, science, and technology were compelled to seek utterance in the vernacular, and Latin, left unused, withered away. Learned terms expanded the vocabulary, as well as the capability, of English to handle the most complex and technical ideas of the then-current learning. *Conversion*, the use of one part of speech for another, was rampant, as was borrowing on a huge scale: many Latin words were taken in without alteration; others were altered slightly, including a host of Greek terms—literary, rhetorical, sporting, and scientific terminology. Originality and inventiveness were appreciated most in terms of felicity with language—so obvious now to readers of Renaissance literature. But at the time, Renaissance English was still struggling for full utterance, politically, socially, culturally, artistically, and religiously—until the Protestant Reformation, by abandoning Latin theology and liturgy, helped clinch the ultimate victory of English in every sphere. In the previous chapter, I demonstrate the ways both Julian of Norwich and Margery Kempe contribute to this linguistic trend of using the vernacular for religious purposes.

18. In *The Necessarie, Fit, and Convenient Education of a Yong Gentlewoman*, Giovanni Bruto writes that all learning should be directed toward chastity and purity, for once a woman knows how to read (whether in the vernacular or in a foreign language), nothing can prevent her from reading books of love (Ovid, Catullus, Homer, Virgil) and learning all about the loves and adulteries of humans and gods. Moreover, goodness and wisdom could not be derived from reading such tales: "A woman should beware of all these books, like as of serpents or snakes. And if there be any woman that hath such delight in these books, that she will not leave them out of her hands, she should . . . be kept from all reading, and so by disuse, forget learning, if that can be done" (Vives, qtd. in Watson 61–62).

19. Even if biblical texts were available to all social classes, a Christian humanist education would not be.

20. In *The Legacies of Literacy*, Harvey J. Graff writes: "It is necessary to distinguish Bible study as scholarly exegesis from Bible study as lay Bible reading. Protestantism [would support] both; Catholicism promoted only the former" (134).

21. "The doctrine of Christ casts aside no age, no sex, no fortune or position in life. . . . It keeps no one at a distance," wrote Erasmus in the preface to his *Paraclesis* (qtd. in Wyntjes 170). More, too, promoted this "new learning" for males and females alike, "since learning in women is a new thing . . . many will be ready to attack it. The harvest will not be affected whether it be a man or woman who sows the seed. Both are reasonable beings . . . ; both therefore are suited equally for those studies by which reason is cultivated" (qtd. in Rogers 121–22).

22. Between 1518 and 1540, seven important treatises dealing with the education of women were written or published by Christian humanists. In 1518, More, away from home in the royal service, sent a letter to his children's newest tutor, which defended liberal training for women. More made explicit suggestions on the personal character and learning he wished his daughters to have. Vives published *De institutione Christianae feminae* (*The Education of a Christian Woman*, 1523), *De ratione studii puerilis epistolae duae* (*Concerning a Plan of Study for Young People [Girls]*, 1523), and *Satellitum animi sive symbola* (*The Distinguishing Characteristics of Attendants [or Courtiers]*, 1524).

23. Castiglione's 1540 *Book of the Courtier* forwarded principles of temperance and prudence as paramount to the training of a perfect courtier, who could serve (i.e., ad-

vise) his prince "consummately in every reasonable matter" (1). We have only to re-place "prince" with "country" to have the identical philosophy of service that inspired Elyot.

24. Elyot writes,

> If there might once happen some man having an excellent wit to be brought up in such form as I have hitherto written, and may also be exactly or deeply learned in the art of an orator, and also in the laws of this realm, the prince so willing and thereto assisting, undoubtedly it should not be impossible for him to bring the pleading and reasoning of the law to the ancient form of noble orators. . . . [F]ew men in consultations should . . . compare with our lawyers, by this means being brought to be perfect orators, as in whom should then be found the sharp wits of logicians, the grave sentences of philosophers, the elegancy of poets, the memory of [civil law students], the voice and gesture of them that can pronounce come-dies—which is all that Tully [Cicero], in the person of the most eloquent man Marcus Antonius, could require to be in an orator. (125)

25. Only a small coterie of wellborn Tudor women enjoyed the luxury of quality home tutelage. In 1548, schoolmaster and playwright Nicholas Udall, in his preface to Princess Mary's translation of Erasmus, wrote,

> It was now no news in England to see young damsels in noble houses and in the courts of princes, instead of cards and other instruments of idle trifling, to have continually in their hands either psalms, homilies and other devout meditations, or else Paul's epistles, or some book of holy scripture matters, and as familiarly both to read or reason thereof in Greek, Latin, French or Italian, as in English. It was now a common thing to see young virgins so trained in the study of good letters, that they willingly set all other vain pastimes at naught, for learning sake. It was now no news at all, to see Queens and ladies of most high estate and progeny, in-stead of courtly dalliance, to embrace virtuous exercises of reading and writing, and with most earnest study both early and late, to apply themselves to the acquir-ing of knowledge, as well in all other liberal artes and disciplines, as also most es-pecially of God and his most holy word. (qtd. in Travitsky 90)

Coeducation offered equality in education, but the Church and most humanists frowned on such commingling; the tale of Héloïse and Abelard was cautionary.

26. Even though a number of highly educated noblewomen were emerging at this time, the least of educated men would always be more influential and more prestigious than the best of those women, except, of course, for Queen Elizabeth I.

27. In 1564, Puritan reformer Thomas Becon argued for extending education to the lower classes:

> [I]f it be thoughte conveniente . . . that scholes should be . . . set up for the right education and bringing up of the youthe of the male kynde: why should it not also be thought convenient, that scholes be built for the godly institucion and vertuous bringing up of the youth of the female kynde? Is not the woman the creature of God, so well as the man? . . . Can that woman govern her house godly, which knoweth not one poynt of godlynes? Who seeth not now then howe necessarye the vertuous education and bringinge up of the woman-kinde is? Which thinge canne

not be conveniently brought to passe except scholes for that purpose be appoynted. (qtd. in Travitsky 90)

28. "The education of girls was often intensive and produced effective managers of households . . . which were often sizable businesses, . . . but this education was not acquired in academic institutions, which taught rhetoric and all other subjects in Latin" (Ong, *Orality* 111).

29. The typical portrait of the Renaissance woman, whether literary or visual, celebrates her physical beauty with hyperbole: her complexion proverbially creamy, cheeks like damask roses, coral lips, teeth like ivory, golden curly hair, eyes like suns, breasts like globes, voice and breath like perfumed music. Typical of such poetic license is Thomas Campion's "There Is a Garden in Her Face":

> Where roses and white lilies grow;
> A heavenly paradise is that place,
> Wherein these pleasant fruits do flow.
> There cherries grow which none may buy,
> Till 'Cherry-ripe' themselves do cry.

> These cherries fairly do enclose
> Of orient pearl a double row,
> Which when her lovely laughter shows,
> They look like rose-buds filled with snow.

30. Although she neither founded universities nor established public colleges (as did her immediate successors on the throne), Queen Isabella accomplished so many humanist goals that the Spanish humanists placed her at their head. Besides sponsoring "a long line of truly famous women—teachers, writers, poets, scientists, artists, and musicians who flourished throughout the history of the Peninsular Revival," she hired a female tutor for herself and her daughters, Beatriz Galindo, also called La Latina (Cannon 52–53). She also tried to persuade Italian humanist Cassandra Fedele to join her court, but the Venetial Senate "issued a decree forbidding so great an asset to leave Venice" (M. King 199). Years before the Paris court had done so, Isabella established regius chairs of Hebrew and Greek in Aragon.

31. *Instruction of a Christian Woman* was translated by Englishman Richard Hyrde.

32. Renaissance scholars moved freely around Europe, often replenishing themselves at Italian universities and always staying in close (Latin) correspondence with one another. But these scholars were ready to go where their scholarship could support them, particularly in royal service.

33. All modernizations in this chapter are my own.

34. Travitsky catalogs the writings she has included in her 1981 *Paradise of Women*: "prose narratives, verses, prayers, essays, confessions, diaries, letters, and prefaces," explaining that these pieces, unlike the excluded, "derivative" translations, "provide a broad and representative selection of the[ir] writings . . . and show their range of interests and accomplishments in relation to the position of and limitations of women in Renaissance English society" (12). Thirty years earlier, Carroll Camden could account for only fifty Renaissance women who wrote some eighty-five compositions during the years from 1524 to 1640. Although Camden makes no reference to the source of these figures, I would imagine that he is referring to the pioneering work of Ruth Hughey, her 1932 dissertation, "Cultural Interests of Women in England, from 1524–1640."

Also, Camden is referring to published work only, which cannot accurately reflect the full scope of women's intellectual exhange.

35. Consider, for example, Edmund Spenser's *Faerie Queene*, George Peele's *Arraignment of Paris*, and John Davies's *Hymnes of Astraea in Acrosticke Verse*.

36. Shakespeare's plays bristle with strong-minded female characters, from Portia, Rosalind, Beatrice, Kate, and Viola to such historical figures as Joan of Arc, Queen Margaret, Lady Macbeth, and Catherine of Aragon, whose muscular personalities demand audience response. The same can be said for dozens of other women in Renaissance literature, from the heroine of *Appius and Virginia* to the heroine of *The Duchess of Malfi*.

37. The loss of virginity defines the *virgo* as *mulier*; therefore a "virgin queen" could be a "mother" (mater) to her nation without being a *mulier*.

38. See Mary R. Bowman's insightful work on Spenser's figuration of Queen Elizabeth. Bowman writes that "Britomart's actions can in part be explained in terms of the political and ideological constraints faced by the queen" (509).

39. In her most famous soliloquy, Lady Macbeth cries,

> Come, you spirits
> That tend on mortal thoughts, unsex me here,
> And fill me from the crown to the toe topful
> Of direst cruelty! Make thick my blood,
> Stop up th'access and passage to remorse,
> That no compunctious visitings of nature
> Shake my fell purpose, nor keep peace between
> Th' effect and [it]! (1.5.40–47)

40. The Renaissance audience had little fear that an actual woman would ever say

> What beast was 't then
> That made you break this enterprise to me?
> When you durst do it, then you were a man;
> And to be more than what you were, you would
> Be so much more the man. . . .
> I have given suck, and know
> how tender 'tis to love the babe that milks me—
> I would while it was smiling in my face,
> have pluck'd my nipple from his boneless gums,
> And dash'd the brains out, had I so sworn
> As you have done to this. (*Mac.* 1.7.48–58)

41. "Nurse, will you go with me into my closet / To help me sort such needful ornaments / As you think fit to furnish me to-morrow?" (*Rom.* 4.3.33–35).

42. Marilyn French argues that Shakespeare's tragedies are masculine because the female characters are always marginalized and often separated from any female support structure (32–34).

43. John Donne's woman, however, is often a partner to her man; she is not reduced to an object, either of spiritual contemplation or of sexual subservience, like his contemporary poets' women. His poetry celebrates the sexual union and recognizes woman's equal participation and credit—man and woman are "one another's best":

> Where, like a pillow on a bed,
>   A pregnant bank swelled up, to rest
> The violet's reclining head,
>   Sat we two, one another's best;
> Our hands were firmly cemented
>   With a fast balm, which thence did spring,
> Our eye-beams twisted, and did thread
>   Our eyes, upon one double string;
> . . . .
> As 'twixt two equal armies, Fate
>   Suspends uncertain victory,
> Our souls, (which to advance their state,
>   Were gone out), hung 'twixt her, and me.   (539–40)

Woman's power equals man's in the fleshly union, a religious mystical experience that, according to Donne, solves all earthly problems and confers limitless bliss. Donne's woman is a man's equal, but a man's *ideal* equal, his ideal sexual partner. Her "equality" is determined in the most private of domestic spheres—the bed. Once again, the female character is drawn by a man, and the portrait is idealized not real.

44. Rhetoric was not used to gain truth, which was unknowable, inexpressible.

45. In his 1516 *De tradendis disciplinis*, Vives wrote,

> Rhetoric is . . . necessary for all positions in life. For in man the highest law and government are at the disposal of will. To the will, reason and judgment are assigned as counsellors, and the emotions are its torches. Further, the emotions of the mind are enflamed by the sparks of speech. So, too, the reason is impelled and moved by speech. Hence it comes to pass that, in the whole kingdom of the activities of man, speech holds in its possession a mighty strength, which it continually manifests. (181)

46. The sustaining didactic curriculum behind the pursuit of public, practical eloquence was classical rhetorical theory, primarily the theory of public oratory advanced in pseudo-Cicero's *Rhetorica ad Caius Herennium*, as well as in Cicero's *Rhetorica* (it was still perfectly permissible to regard the *Herennium* as Cicero's). The Ciceronian ideal of using rhetoric for the public good, then, was translated into rhetorical theory, practice, pedagogy, and practicality.

47. Translating those second-century Ciceronian theories and practices into sixteenth-century ones was Erasmus, the most influential rhetorician in Renaissance England, whose enthusiastically received Latin rhetoric *De copia* (1512) became a staple of English schooling. What with its enthusiasm for classical literature and concomitant classical pedagogy, *De copia* set the pattern for English curricula and rhetorical training, one of thorough and intensive language training that would prepare young boys for a public life. *De copia* provided students with practical, nearly programmatic techniques for saying many things and saying them in many ways, in both Latin and English. Erasmus writes with Ciceronian authority, for "Cicero, the great father of all eloquence, was so dedicated to this kind of exercise that he used to vie with his friend, the actor Roscius, to see whether Roscius could express the same material more often using different gestures, or Cicero himself applying the resources of eloquence and using different languages" (2.27–32).

48. Since women were neither citizens nor public figures, Renaissance rhetors and teachers of rhetoric naturally carried forward another ancient practice: the exclusion of women from rhetorical study, as well as from the active and public intellectual life.

49. Briefly noted, French philosopher Petrus Ramus (Pierre de al Ramée) can perhaps be credited for this Renaissance rhetorical turn. In his 1543 *Dialecticae partitiones*, he began his program of redefining the trivium into systems of grammar, rhetoric, and logic so that they no longer overlapped in any way. He separated each of them so that grammar was restricted to matters of syntax and etymology, logic to invention and arrangement, and rhetoric to style and delivery.

50. Given the political, religious, and courtly enthusiasm toward the vernacular, the move toward Englishing literary works was already well under way. The aggressive nationalism emerging at the time was one reason for the competition of English as the dominant tongue. But that competition also resulted from the incessant demand of Englishmen (and some Englishwomen) in all walks of life to share in Renaissance accomplishment. Ideas and facts in Greek or Latin were a prize of the few; in English, they became a ready storehouse for all.

51. Alex L. Gordon talks about "Renaissance poetry with its strong rhetorical bent": "rhetorical poetry is concerned as much with audience as with poet: The rhetorical poet like the orator seeks to manipulate the passions of his listeners; their feelings, and the possibility of directing them, may be of more interest to him than his own. . . . The rhetorical poet is moved perhaps, but above all he wishes to move others" (378–79).

52. In 1589, George Puttenham would write: "So as the Poets were also from the beginning the best perswaders, and their eloquence the first Rethoricke of the world. Even so it became that the high mysteries of the gods should be revealed & taught, by a maner of utterance and language of extraordinarie phrase" (1.4).

53. In "The Sources of Euphuistic Rhetoric," Morris W. Croll identifies *wit* "with the wanton and secular curiosity of the Renaissance, . . . used in antithesis with *wisdom*, which stands for the indissoluble union of virtue, learning, and religion in the service of the national cause" (250–51).

54. Sidney writes:

> Marry, they that delight in poesie itself, should seek to know what they do, and how they do; and especially look themselves in an unflattering glass of reason, if they be inclinable unto it. For poesy must not be drawn by the ears, it must be gently led, or rather it must lead; which was partly the cause that made the ancient learned affirm it was a divine gift, and no human skill, since all other knowledges lie readie for any that hath strength of wit, a poet no industry can make if his own genius be not carried into it. (45)

55. Brian Vickers might well be referring to Sidney's theorizing when he writes,

> The English rhetorics belong firmly to the classical and continental traditions, not least in their fusion of rhetoric and poetics, granting the poet and the orator equal status, similar methods, identical goals—to move, to teach, to please—and distinguishing between them sometimes through the traditional dichotomy of media, prose against verse, sometimes through the presence or absence of fiction. ("Power" 412)

56. Caxton's *Mirrour of the World* might be the first work to mention the Ciceronian divisions.

57. Nelson uses an 1899 edition of Cox, edited by F. I. Carpenter (Chicago, 41–42).

58. The full title of Sherry's 1555 work is *Treatise of the Figures of Grammer and Rhetorike, Profitable for Al That Be Studious of Eloquence, and in Especiall for Suche as in Grammer Scholes Doe Reade Most Eloquente Poetes and Oratours.*

59. Vickers tells us that, since Latin was the official school language, rhetoric books in English were probably used by university students "unsure in Latin, who evidently used them as 'cribs' to the more demanding classical treatises. . . . Another class of readers may have been lawyers, who worked primarily with English . . . [which] was of daily relevance" ("Some" 89).

60. David Cressy writes that

aggregate figures for the sixteenth century are not readily available, but a reasonable guess might place male illiteracy around 80% and female illiteracy close to 95% at the time of the accession of Elizabeth. A projection back to the reign of Henry VII would find perhaps 90% of Englishmen illiterate at the turn of the century, with illiteracy claiming as many as 99% of the women. (176)

61. Douglas Bush writes that "more than two-fifths of the books printed in England from 1480 to 1640 were religious, and for the years 1600–40 the percentage is still higher." He goes on to quote first from William Jaggard's *Catalogue of Such English Books as Lately Haue Been, or Now Are, in Printing for Publication* of 1618 in which "nearly three-fourths of the books are religious and moral," and then from William London's *Catalogue of the Most Vendible Books in England* (1657–58), in which "the space given to works of divinity equals that occupied by all other kinds together" (Bush 310).

62. Patricia Gartenberg and Nadine Wittemore write that Renaissance women were participating in all the following genres: translations of religious works; meditations and prayers; admonitions for godly living and works on godly advice; lamentations; maternal advice manuals; and diverse poetic forms—songs, sonnets, dream visions, rhymed history; and narrative, descriptive, religious, and epistolary verse that used a variety of rhyme schemes and stanzaic patterns.

63. Otten tells us that this book, shaped by Catherine's Protestant readings, went into fifteen editions between 1545 and 1608: "Heavily doctrinal, the prayers or meditations . . . perhaps served a political purpose in directing women readers to the Reformed apprehension of the faith and away from Roman Catholic readings and modes of meditation in the disturbing religious climate of the time" (280).

64. Jones cited Leonardo Bruni's "Concerning the Study of Literature: A Letter Addressed to the Illustrious Lady, Baptista Malatesta" (Woodward 126).

65. Margaret and her father wrote in friendly competition about the Four Last Things (probably in 1522), though only her father's treatment, unfinished, remains. And she wrote in response to a declamation attributed to Quintilian in which the poor man's bees were killed by poison sprinkled on flowers in the rich man's garden. Quintilian defended the cause of the poor man; Margaret the rich, which, Stapleton points out, was the more difficult position to take and gave "greater scope for Margaret's eloquence and wit" (107).

66. Elizabeth McCutcheon reminds us that we know of Roper's literary productivity not through primary sources but through "incidental references in her father's letters or through [Thomas] Stapleton" (459). Furthermore, most of these lost works were either private letters or apprentice pieces written in Greek or Latin (double translations). So,

like the lives of so many other women, much of Roper's comes to us through the writings of others.

67. Anne Cooke Bacon, Mary Roper Basset, Elizabeth Falkland Cary, Mary Sidney Herbert (Countess of Pembroke), Elizabeth Cooke Russell, Margaret Beaufort Stanley (Countess of Richmond), Margaret Tyler—even Elizabeth and Mary Tudor—are some of the most celebrated of Renaissance Englishwomen noted for translations rather than for their original compositions. Their translations included tracts and sermons, as well as poetry (particularly Psalms) and narratives. The translators were often remarkably erudite, having had classical educations, and their translations were often remarkably skillful, revealing their rhetorical training. Often, their translations are underlined by deep religious commitment, especially those women facing the supposedly Pauline doctrine not to interpret the Scriptures for themselves.

68. Retha M. Warnicke tells us that only three women had preceded Margaret in print (Dame Juliana Berners, Margery Kempe, and the Countess of Richmond [30, n. 32]), putting the significance of Margaret's publication in context:

> By the customs of her day, even her one fortuitous publication should never have been permitted, for two decades had passed since the last Englishwoman . . . , the Countess of Richmond, mother to Henry VII, had been able to read her own work in print. After Margaret Roper's effort in 1524, more than twenty years elapsed before another Englishwoman, who, like the Countess, was a member of the royal family, again had her work published. (25)

69. In the original, compare, *Hocut indies magis ac magis praestare valeamus, adjuva, Pater coelestis, ut indies caro minus reluctetur spiritui nostro, ut spiritus noster magis ac magis unanimis fiat Spiritui tuo. Et quemadmodum nunc multis in locis parent voluntati tuae, qui obediunt Euangelio Filii tui: ita idem fiat per universum terrarum orbem, ut omnes intelligant, te solum esse rerum omnium Monarcham, tuisque divinis legibus volentes ac lubentes obediant in terris quemadmodum in coelis nullis est qui tuae voluntati repugnet.*

70. Margaret's daughter, Mary Roper Bassett, would eventually publish her own translations of Eusebius. Warnicke writes that "during the reign of Edward VI, she bound together in one volume her translations from Greek to Latin of the first book and into English of the first five books of Eusebius' *Ecclesiastical History*, for presentation to the King's sister, Mary" (107).

71. Charlotte F. Otten, in her introduction to part 2, "Women Describing Persecution and Life in Prison," mentions a list of reformist women who were punished: Anne Audland, Jane Waugh, Sarah Tims, Jane Whitehead, Lady Jane Grey, and, of course, Anne Askew (49–59).

72. The full titles known as the *Examinations* are *The First Examinacyon of Anne Askewe, Lately Martyred in Smythfelde, by the Romysh Popes Vpholders, wyth the Elucydacyon of Johan Bale* (1546); *The Lattre Examinacyon of Anne Askewe, Lately Martyred in Smythfelde, by the Wycked Synagoge of Antichrist, with the Elucydacyon of Johan Bale* (1547); *The Account of the Sufferings of Anne Askew, for Opposing the Gross Fictions of Transubstantiation: Written by Herself, and Re-printed by a Catholic* (1849).

73. Parr's associates were John Parkhurst, Lady Anne Parr Herbert (the queen's sister), Lady Elizabeth Tyrwhitt, Lady Lane Katherine Willoughby (Duchess of Suffolk), Lady Joan Denny, Lady Fitzwilliam, Philip Hoby, Robert Testwood, Henry Filmer, Anthony Parsons, Jon Lascelles, and Countess of Sussex (Beilin 36).

74. Three hundred years later, preaching on the proposed site of the Martyrs Memo-

rial Church, in London, Rev. Benjamin O. Sharp would remind his congregation that "Anne Askew was carried in a chair from Newgate to Smithfield, as a lamb to the slaughterhouse. . . . They tied her by the wrist with an iron chain, and then, ere they burned her they preached . . . *at* her. . . . With an angel's countenance and a smiling face, she said, 'I am not come here . . . to deny my Lord and Master' " (13).

75. Elizabeth received a broad humanist education at the hands of John Cheke, his favorite student, Roger Ascham, and Asham's own favorite pupil, William Grindall (Neale, *Queen* 11).

76. Benson quoted Aylmer's *Harborowe for Faithfull and Trewe Subjectes Agaynst the Late Blowne Blaste, Concerning the Gouernment of Women*, Strasbourg (J. Day, London, 1559, B3r).

77. Elizabeth's Italianate calligraphy is clear, strong, and beautiful, evidence of her artistic skills. Housed at Harvard's Houghton Library autograph collection, PfMS Typ 686 (c. 1552–53).

78. William Camden, Elizabeth's first biographer, revised, edited, and reconstructed the queen's speeches for publication, forever (re)shaping our assumptions and critical inheritance of her. In addition, the queen herself controlled the circulation of whatever speeches survive, however amended.

79. Axton quoted Edmund Plowden's 1779 *Commentaries and Reports of Edmund Plowden, Originally Written in French, and Now Faithfully Translated into English* (London, 217).

80. Heisch quoted from Stow MS 361, fol. 1., British Museum, London.

81. "Wherever there is persuasion, there is rhetoric. And wherever there is 'meaning' there is 'persuasion' " (Burke, *Rhetoric* 172).

WORKS CITED

Allestree, R. *The Whole Duty of Man*. 1663. London: Griffin, 1889.

"Ancrene Wisse." Bennett and Smithers 223–45.

Appian. *Roman History*. Trans. Horace White. 4 vols. Cambridge: Harvard–Heinemann, 1913.

Ardener, Edwin. "The Problem Revisited." *Perceiving Women*. Ed. Shirley Ardener. London: Malaby, 1975. 19–28.

Aristophanes. *Lysistrata, The Acharnians, The Congresswomen*. Trans. Douglass Parker. *The Frogs*. Trans. Richmond Lattimore. *Four Comedies*. Ed. William Arrowsmith. Ann Arbor: U of Michigan P, 1969.

Aristotle. *Generation of Animals*. Trans. A. L. Peck. Cambridge: Loeb-Harvard UP, 1963.

———. *Politics*. Trans. H. Rackham. Cambridge: Loeb-Harvard UP, 1977.

———. *The Rhetoric and the Poetics of Aristotle*. Trans. W. Rhys Roberts and Ingram Bywater. New York: Modern Library, 1984.

Arthur, Marylin. "Liberated Women: The Classical Era." *Becoming Visible: Women in European History*. Ed. Renate Bridenthal and Claudia Koontz. Boston: Houghton, 1977. 60–89.

Ascham, Roger. *English Works*. Ed. William Writing. Cambridge: Cambridge UP, 1970.

———. *The Scholemaster*. 1507. Boston: Small, 1888.

Askew, Anne. *The Lattre Examinacyon of A. Askewe. [A Reprint of the Wesel Editions.] The First Examinació of A. Askewe (the Lattre Examynacyon.)* 8°. Marpurg, 546–47.

Athenaeus. *The DeipnoSophists*. Trans. Charles Burton Gulick. Cambridge: Harvard UP, 1967.

Atwill, Janet. "Instituting the Art of Rhetoric: Theory, Practice, and Productive Knowledge in Interpretations of Aristotle's *Rhetoric*." T. Poulakos, *Rethinking* 91–118.

Augustine of Hippo. *Confessions*. Trans. R. S. Pine-Coffin. Middlesex, Gt. Brit.: Penguin, 1961.

———. *On Christian Doctrine*. Trans. D. W. Robertson, Jr. Indianapolis: Bobbs, 1958.

Axton, Marie. *The Queen's Two Bodies*. London: Royal Historical Society, 1977.

Babcock, Charles L. "The Early Career of Fulvia." *American Journal of Philology* 86 (1965): 1–32.

Baker, Denise Nowakowski. *Julian of Norwich's Showings; From Vision to Book*. Princeton: Princeton UP, 1994.

Bakhtin, M. M. *The Dialogic Imagination*. Trans. Caryl Emerson and Michael Holquist. Ed. Michael Holquist. Austin: U of Texas P, 1981.

Bald, R. C., ed. *Six Elizabethan Plays*. Boston: Houghton, 1963.

Baldwin, T. W. *William Shakspere's Small Latine and Less Greeke*. 2 vols. Urbana: U of Illinois P, 1944.

Ballif, Michelle. "Re/Dressing Histories; or, On Re/Covering Figures Who Have Been Laid Bare by Our Gaze." *Rhetoric Society Quarterly* 22 (1992): 91–97.

Works Cited

Bambas, Rudolph C. "Another View of the Old English *Wife's Lament*." *Journal of English and Germanic Philology* 62 (1963): 303–9.

Barilli, Renalto. *Rhetoric*. Trans. Giuliana Menozzi. Minneapolis: U of Minnesota P, 1989.

Baron, Hans. "Cicero and the Roman Civic Spirit in the Middle Ages and Early Renaissance." *Bulletin of the John Rylands Library* 22 (1938): 91–95.

Barrett, Harold. *The Sophists*. Novato: Chandler, 1987.

Beard, Mary. "The Classic Woman?" *History Today* 43.2 (1993): 29–35.

Beauvoir, Simone de. *The Second Sex*. 1952. New York: Vintage-Random, 1974.

Beer, Frances. "Julian of Norwich." *Women and Mystical Experience in the Middle Ages*. Woodbridge: Boydell, 1992. 130–57.

Beilin, Elaine V. *Redeeming Eve: Women Writers of the English Renaissance*. Princeton: Princeton UP, 1987.

Bell, Susan Groag. "Medieval Women Book Owners: Arbiters of Lay Piety and Ambassadors of Culture." *Sisters and Workers in the Middle Ages*. Ed. Judith M. Bennett, Elizabeth A. Clark, Jean F. O'Barr, B. Anne Vilen, and Sarah Westphal-Wihl. 1976. Chicago: U of Chicago P, 1989. 162–89.

———, ed. *Women: From the Greeks to the French Revolution*. Stanford: Stanford UP, 1973.

Belsey, Catherine. *The Subject of Tragedy: Identity and Difference in Renaissance Drama*. New York: Methuen, 1985.

Benedetti, Allesandro. *History of the Human Body*. 1497. Trans. L. R. Lind. *Studies in Pre-Vesalian Anatomy: Biography, Translations, Documents*. Ed. L. R. Lind. Philadelphia: American Philosophical Society, 1975.

Bennett, J. A. W., and G. V. Smithers, eds. *Early Middle English Verse and Prose*. 2nd ed. Oxford: Clarendon, 1968.

Benson, Pamela Joseph. *The Invention of the Renaissance Woman*. University Park: Pennsylvania State UP, 1992.

Berlin, James. "Revisionary Histories of Rhetoric: Politics, Power, and Plurality." Vitanza, *Writing* 112–27.

———. "Revisionary History: The Dialectical Method." *Pre/Text* 8 (1987): 47–62.

———. *Rhetoric and Reality: Writing Instruction in American Colleges 1900–1985*. Carbondale: Southern Illinois UP, 1987.

———. *Writing Instruction in Nineteenth-Century American Colleges*. Carbondale: Southern Illinois UP, 1984.

Best, Edward E., Jr. "Cicero, Livy, and Educated Roman Women." *Classical Journal* 65 (1970): 199–204.

Bevington, David. *Medieval Drama*. Boston: Houghton, 1975.

Biesecker, Barbara. "Coming to Terms with Recent Attempts to Write Women into the History of Rhetoric." *Philosophy and Rhetoric* 25 (1992): 140–61.

———. "Towards a Transactional View of Rhetorical and Feminist Theory: Rereading Hélène Cixous's *The Laugh of the Medusa*." *Southern Communication Journal* 57 (1992): 86–96.

Bizzell, Patricia. "Opportunities for Feminist Research in the History of Rhetoric." *Rhetoric Review* 11.3 (1992): 50–58.

———. "Praising Folly: Constructing a Postmodern Rhetorical Authority as a Woman." *Feminine Principles and Women's Experience in American Composition and Rhetoric*. Ed. Louise Wetherbee Phelps and Janet Emig. Pittsburgh: U of Pittsburgh P, 1995.

215

Works Cited

Bizzell, Patricia, and Bruce Herzberg. *The Rhetorical Tradition: Readings from Classical Times to the Present.* Boston: Bedford–St. Martin's, 1990.

Blair, Carole. "Contested Histories of Rhetoric: The Politics of Preservation, Progress, and Change." *Quarterly Journal of Speech* 78 (1992): 403–28.

———. "Refiguring Systems of Rhetoric." *Pre/Text* 12 (1991): 179–94.

Blair, Carole, and Mary L. Kahl. "Introduction: Revising the History of Rhetorical Theory." *Western Journal of Speech Communication* 54 (1990): 148–59.

Bloedow, Edmund F. "Aspasia and the 'Mystery' of the Menexenos." *Wiener Studien (Zeitschrift fur Klassiche Philologie und Patristic)* ns 9 (1975): 32–48.

Booth, Wayne C. *The Rhetoric of Fiction.* 2nd ed. Chicago: U of Chicago P, 1961.

Bordo, Susan. "Feminism, Postmodernism, and Gender-Scepticism." Nicholson 133–56.

Bowman, Mary R. " 'she there as Princess rained': Spenser's Figure of Elizabeth." *Renaissance Quarterly* 43 (1990): 509–28.

Bridenthal, Renate, and Claudia Koontz, ed. *Becoming Visible: Women in European History.* Boston: Houghton, 1977.

Brown, Peter. *The Body and Society.* New York: Columbia UP, 1988.

Bruto, Giovanni. *The Necessarie, Fit, and Convenient Education of a Yong Gentlewoman.* Anvers, 1553.

Bullough, Vern. "Medieval, Medical, and Scientific Views of Women." *Viator* 4 (1973): 484–501.

Burke, Kenneth. *Counter-Statement.* Berkeley: U of California P, 1931.

———. *Language as Symbolic Action.* Berkeley: U of California P, 1933.

———. *Perspectives by Incongruity.* Ed. Stanley Edgar Hyman. Bloomington: Indiana UP, 1964.

———. *A Rhetoric of Motives.* 1950. Berkeley: U of California P, 1969.

Burnett, Anne Pippen. *Three Archaic Poets: Archilochus, Alcaeus, Sappho.* Cambridge: Harvard UP, 1983.

Bush, Douglas, ed. *English Literature in the Earlier Seventeenth Century.* 2nd ed. Oxford: Oxford UP, 1966.

Butler-Bowdon, W., ed. *The Book of Margery Kempe.* New York: Devin-Adair, 1944.

Camden, Carroll. *The Elizabethan Woman.* New York: Elsevier, 1952.

Camden, William. *Annales; or, the History of the Most Renowned and Victorious Princesse Elizabeth, Late Queen of England.* 1625. Trans. R[obert] N[orton]. London: Benjamin Fisher, 1635.

Campbell, JoAnn, ed. *Towards a Feminist Rhetoric: The Writings of Gertrude Buck.* Pittsburgh: U of Pittsburgh P, 1996.

Campbell, Karlyn Kohrs. "Biesecker Cannot Speak for Her Either." *Philosophy and Rhetoric* 26 (1993): 153–59.

———. *Man Cannot Speak for Her: A Critical Study of Early Feminist Rhetoric.* 2 vols. New York: Greenwood, 1989.

Campion, Thomas. "There Is a Garden in Her Face." Hollander and Kermode 512–13.

Cannon, Mary Agnes. *The Education of Women During the Renaissance.* Washington: Catholic Education P, 1916.

Cantarella, Eve. *Pandora's Daughters.* 1981. Baltimore: John Hopkins UP, 1987.

Castiglione, Baldesar. *The Book of the Courtier.* Trans. and ed. Friench Simpson. New York: Ungar, 1959.

Certeau, Michel de. *The Writing of History.* 1975. Trans. Tom Conley. New York: Columbia UP, 1988.

Chambers, R. W. Introduction. Butler-Bowdon xv–xxiii.

Chance, Jane. *Woman as Hero in Old English Literature*. Syracuse: Syracuse UP, 1986.

Chaucer, Geoffrey. *The Riverside Chaucer*. Ed. Larry D. Benson. Boston: Houghton, 1987.

Chrétien de Troyes. "Knight of the Cart." *Arthurian Romances*. Trans. W. W. Comfort. London: Dutton, 1975. 270–359.

Cicero. *Brutus, On the Nature of the Gods, On Divination, On Duties*. Trans. Hubert M. Poteat. Chicago: U of Chicago P, 1950.

——. *Brutus, Orator*. Trans. G. L. Hendrickson. Cambridge: Loeb-Harvard UP, 1939.

——. *De finibus Bonorum et Malorum*. Trans. H. Rackan. Cambridge: Harvard-Heinemann, 1951.

——. *De inventione, De optimo genere, Oratorum, Topica*. Trans. H. M. Hubbell. Cambridge: Harvard UP, 1976.

——. *De oratore*. 2 vols. Trans. E. W. Sutton. Cambridge: Harvard UP, 1979.

Cixous, Hélène. "Laugh of the Medusa." ["*Le Rire de la Méduse*."] *L'Arc* (1975): 39–54. Rpt. in *The Signs Reader*. Ed. Elizabeth Abel and Emily K. Abel. Chicago: U of Chicago P, 1983. 279–97.

Cixous, Hélène, and Catherine Clément. "Sorties." *The Newly Born Woman*. 1975. Trans. Betsy Wing. Minneapolis: U of Minnesota P, 1986. 63–134.

Cole, Susan Guettel. "Could Greek Women Read and Write?" *Reflections of Women in Antiquity*. Helene P. Foley. New York: Gordon, 1981. 219–45.

Cole, Thomas. *The Origins of Rhetoric in Ancient Greece*. Baltimore: Johns Hopkins UP, 1991.

Collins, Vicki Tolar. "Walking in the Light, Walking in Darkness: The Story of Women's Changing Rhetorical Space in Early Methodism." *Rhetoric Review* 2 (1996): 336–54.

Conley, Tom. "Translator's Introduction: *For a* Literary *Historiography*." Certeau vii–xxiv.

Cook, Albert S., and Chauncey B. Tinker, eds. *Select Translations from Old English Poetry*. Cambridge: Harvard UP, 1935.

Corbett, Edward P. J. *Classical Rhetoric for the Modern Student*. 3rd ed. New York: Oxford UP, 1990.

Courtney, William. "Sappho and Aspasia." *Fortnightly Review* 97 (1912): 488–95.

Covino, William. *The Art of Wondering: A Revisionist Return to the History of Rhetoric*. Portsmouth: Boynton-Cook, 1988.

Crane, Mary Thomas. " 'Video et Taceo': Elizabeth I and the Rhetoric of Counsel." *Studies in English Literature* 28 (1987): 1–15.

Cressy, David. *Literacy and the Social Order: Reading and Writing in Tudor and Stuart England*. Cambridge: Cambridge UP, 1980.

Croll, Morris W. "The Sources of Euphuistic Rhetoric." Ed. R. J. Schoeck and J. Max Patrick. Croll, *Style* 241–98.

——. *Style, Rhetoric, and Rhythm*. Ed. J. Max Patrick and Robert O. Evans, with John M. Wallace and R. J. Schoeck. Woodbridge, CT: Ox Bow, 1989.

Crosby, Ruth. "Oral Delivery in the Middle Ages." *Speculum* 11 (1936): 88–110.

Crowley, Sharon. *The Methodical Memory: Invention in Current-Traditional Rhetoric*. Carbondale: Southern Illinois UP, 1990.

——. "A Plea for the Revival of Sophistry." *Rhetoric Review* 7 (1989): 318–34.

"Dame Sirith." Bennett and Smithers 77–95.

Davis, Natalie Zemon. "Women in Politics." *A History of Women in the West: Renais-*

sance and Enlightenment Paradoxes. Ed. Natalie Zemon Davis and Arlette Farge. Vol. 3. George Duby and Michelle Perrot, gen. eds. 1993. 5 vols. to date. Cambridge: Belknap-Harvard UP, 1992– . 167–83.

de Laurentis, Teresa, ed. *Feminist Studies/Critical Studies*. Bloomington: Indiana UP, 1986.

Delcourt, Marie. *Pericles*. N.p.: Gallemard, 1939.

Delia, Diana. "Fulvia Reconsidered." *Women's History and Ancient History*. Ed. Sarah Pomery. Chapel Hill: U of North Carolina P, 1991. 197–217.

Despres, Denise Louise. "Franciscan Spirituality: Vision and the Authority of Scripture." Diss. Indiana U, 1985.

Dionysius of Halicarnassus. *The Roman Antiquities*. Trans. Earnest Cary. Vol. 7. Cambridge: Harvard-Heinemann, 1950. 7 vols.

Donne, John. "The Ecstasy." Hollander and Kermode 539–40.

Ebert, Theresa. "The 'Difference' of Postmodern Feminism." *College English* 53 (1991): 886–904.

Ehninger, Douglas. "On Rhetoric and Rhetorics." *Western Speech* 31 (1967): 242–49.

———. "On Systems of Rhetoric." *Philosophy and Rhetoric* 1 (1968): 131–44.

Eisler, Riane. *The Chalice and the Blade*. San Francisco: Harper, 1987.

Elizabeth. *The Poems of Queen Elizabeth I*. Ed. Leicester Bradner. Providence: Brown UP, 1964.

Elshtain, Jean Bethke. *Public Man, Private Woman*. Princeton: Princeton UP, 1987.

Elyot, Thomas. *The Book Named the Governor*. 1531. Ed. John M. Major. New York: Teachers College P, 1969.

Enos, Richard Leo. *Greek Rhetoric Before Aristotle*. Prospect Heights, IL: Waveland, 1993.

———. *Roman Rhetoric: Revolution and the Greek Influence*. Prospect Heights, IL: Waveland, 1994.

Enos, Theresa. " 'A Brand New World': Using Our Professional and Personal Histories of Rhetoric." T. Enos, *Learning* 3–14.

———, ed. *Learning from the Histories of Rhetoric*. Carbondale: Southern Illinois UP, 1993.

Enos, Theresa, and Stuart Brown, eds. *Defining the New Rhetorics*. Newbury Park: Sage, 1993.

———, eds. *Professing the New Rhetorics*. Englewood Cliffs: Blair–Prentice Hall, 1994.

Epstein, Cynthia Fuchs. *Deceptive Distinctions: Sex, Gender, and the Social Order*. New Haven: Yale UP, 1988.

Erasmus, Desiderius. *De copia: Foundations of the Abundant Style*. Trans. Betty I. Knott. Toronto: U of Toronto P, 1978.

Ervin, Elizabeth. "Pederast: Rhetoric and Cultural Procreation in the Dialogues." *Pre/Text* 14 (1993): 73–100.

Euripides. *The Complete Greek Tragedies: Euripides I*. Ed. David Grene and Richmond Lattimore. Chicago: U of Chicago P, 1959.

Fantham, Elaine, Helene Peet Foley, Natalie Boymel Kampen, Sarah B. Pomeroy, and H. Alan Shapiro. *Women in the Classical World*. New York: Oxford UP, 1994.

Fausto-Sterling, Anne. "How Many Sexes Are There?" *New York Times*. 12 Mar. 1993, A29.

Ferguson, Margaret W., Maureen Quilligan, and Nancy Vickers, eds. *Rewriting the Renaissance*. Chicago: U of Chicago P, 1986.

218

Flaceliere, Robert. *Love in Ancient Greece*. 1960. Trans. James Cleugh. London: Frederick Muller, 1962.

Flax, Jane. "Postmodernism and Gender Relations." Nicholson 39–62.

Flynn, Elizabeth. "Composing as a Woman." *College Composition and Communication* 39 (1988): 423–35.

Fonseca, Isabel. "Among the Gypsies." *The New Yorker* 25 Sept. 1995, 84–97.

Foucault, Michel. *The History of Sexuality*. Vol. 1. 1978. New York: Vintage-Random, 1990. 3 vols.

Foxe, John. *Actes and Monuments*. 8 vols. New York: AMS, 1965.

French, Marilyn. *Shakespeare's Division of Experience*. London: Sphere, 1984.

Frey, Olivia. "Beyond Literary Darwinism: Women's Voices and Critical Discourse." *College English* 52 (1990): 507–26.

Frye, Ellen. *The Other Sappho*. Ithaca: Firebrand, 1989.

Galen of Pergamum. *On the Usefulness of the Parts of the Body*. Trans. Margaret Tallmadge May. 2 vols. Ithaca: Cornell UP, 1968.

Garner, Richard. *Law and Society in Classical Athens*. New York: St. Martin's, 1987.

Gartenberg, Patricia, and Nadine Wittemore. "A Checklist of English Women in Print, 1475–1640." *Bulletin of Bibliography and Magazine Notes* 34 (1977): 1–13.

Gee, John Archer. "Margaret Roper's English Version of Erasmus' *Precatio Dominica* and the Apprenticeship Behind Early Tudor Translation." *Review of English Studies* 13 (1937): 257–71.

Gilbert, Sandra M., and Susan Gubar. *The Norton Anthology of Literature by Women: The Tradition in English*. New York: Norton, 1985.

Gilmore, Perry. "Silence and Sulking: Emotional Displays in the Classroom." *Perspectives on Silence*. Ed. Deborah Tannen and Muriel Saville-Troike. Norwood, NJ: 1985. 139–64.

Glenn, Cheryl. "sex, lies, and manuscript: Refiguring Aspasia in the History of Rhetoric." *College Composition and Communication* 45 (1994): 180–99.

Gordon, Alex L. "The Ascendancy of Rhetoric and the Struggle for Poetic in Sixteenth-Century France." Murphy, *Renaissance* 376–84.

Gordon, Ann D., Mari Jo Buhle, and Nancy Schrom Dye. "The Problem of Women's History." *Liberating Women's History*. Ed. Berenice A. Carroll. Urbana: U of Illinois P, 1976. 75–92.

Gorman, Peter. *Pythagoras*. London: Routledge, 1979.

Graff, Harvey J. *The Legacies of Literacy: Continuities and Contradictions in Western Culture and Society*. Bloomington: Indiana UP, 1987.

Green [Wood], Mary Anne Everett, ed. *Letters of Royal and Illustrious Ladies of Great Britain, from the Commencement of the Twelfth Century to the Close of the Reign of Queen Mary*. 3 vols. London: Henry Colburn, 1846.

Greenblatt, Stephen. *Renaissance Self-Fashioning*. Chicago: U of Chicago P, 1980.

Grote, George. *Plato and the Other Companions of Socrates*. London: Murray, 1867.

Guinier, Lani. *The Tyranny of the Majority: Fundamental Fairness in Representative Democracy*. New York: Free, 1994.

Guthrie, Kenneth Sylvan. *The Pythagorean Sourcebook and Library*. Grand Rapids, MI: Phanes, 1987.

Guthrie, W. K. C. *A History of Greek Philosophy*. 6 vols. Cambridge: Cambridge UP, 1962.

Hallett, Judith P. *Fathers and Daughters in Roman Society*. Princeton: Princeton UP, 1984.

———. "Sappho and Her Social Context: Sense and Sensibility." *Signs* 4 (1979): 447–64.

Halperin, David M. *One Hundred Years of Homosexuality*. New York: Routledge, 1990.

———. "Why Is Diotima a Woman?" Halperin, *One Hundred* 113–52.

Hannay, Margaret Patterson, ed. *Silent but for the Word: Tudor Women as Patrons, Translators, and Writers of Religious Works*. Kent, OH: Kent State UP, 1985.

Harpsfield, Nicholas. *The Life and Death of Sir. Thomas More, Knight, Sometymes Lord High Chancellor of England*. 1558. Ed. Elsie Vaughan Hitchcock. Intro. R. W. Chambers. Early English Text Society, 1932. London: Oxford UP, 1963.

Harris, Thomas V. *Ancient Literacy*. Cambridge: Harvard UP, 1989.

Hedges, Elaine, and Shelley Fisher Fishkin, eds. *Listening to Silences*. New York: Oxford UP, 1994.

Heilbrun, Carolyn G. *Writing a Woman's Life*. New York: Norton, 1988.

Heisch, Allison. "Queen Elizabeth I: Parliamentary Rhetoric and the Exercise of Power." *Signs* 1 (1975): 31–55.

Hesiod. *Works and Days*. Trans. M. L. West. Oxford: Clarendon, 1978.

Heywood, Thomas. *A Woman Killed with Kindness. Elizabethan Plays*. Ed. Arthur H. Nethercot, Charles R. Baskerville, and Virgil B. Heltzel. New York: Holt, 1971. 801–45.

Hollander, John, and Frank Kermode, eds. *The Literature of Renaissance England*. New York: Oxford UP, 1973.

Homer. *The Iliad*. Trans. W. H. D. Rouse. New York: Mentor–New American Library, 1938.

———. *The Odyssey*. Trans. S. H. Butcher and A. Lang. Vol. 22. *The Harvard Classics*. New York: Collier, 1909. 50 vols.

Hooker, Richard. *Of the Laws of Ecclesiastical Polity*. 2 vols. 1593. London: Everyman's Library, 1965.

Howell, Martha C. "Citizenship and Gender: Women's Political Status in Northern Medieval Cities." *Women and Power in the Middle Ages*. Ed. Mary Erler and Maryanne Kowaleski. Athens: U of Georgia P, 1988. 37–60.

Hufton, Olwen. "Women, Work, and Family." *A History of Women in the West: Renaissance and Enlightenment Paradoxes*. Ed. Natalie Zemon Davis and Arlette Farge. Vol. 3. Georges Duby and Michelle Perrot, gen. eds. 1993. 5 vols. to date. Cambridge: Belknap-Harvard UP, 1992– . 15–45.

Hughey, Ruth Willard. "Cultural Interests of Women in England, 1524–1640, Indicated in the Writings of the Women." Diss. Cornell U, 1932.

Hull, Suzanne. *Chaste, Silent, and Obedient: English Books for Women, 1475–1640*. San Marino: Huntington Library, 1982.

Huntsman, Jeffrey F. "Grammar." *The Seven Liberal Arts in the Middle Ages*. Ed. David Wagner. Bloomington: Indiana UP, 1986. 58–95.

Inge, William Ralph. *Christian Mysticism*. London: Methuen, 1899.

Jaeger, Werner. *Paideia*. 2nd ed. 3 vols. 1939. Trans. Gilbert Highet. New York: Oxford UP, 1943.

Jameson, Fredric. *The Political Unconscious*. Ithaca: Cornell UP, 1981.

Janzen, Grace M. *Julian of Norwich, Mystic and Theologian*. London: Paulist, 1987.

Jarratt, Susan. *Rereading the Sophists*. Carbondale: Southern Illinois UP, 1991.

———, ed. *Rhetoric Society Quarterly* 22 (1992).

Jarratt, Susan, and Rory Ong. "Aspasia: Rhetoric, Gender, and Colonial Ideology." Lunsford 9–24.

Jarratt, Susan, and Nedra Reynolds. "The Splitting Image: Contemporary Feminisms and the Ethics of *êthos*." *Ethos: New Essays in Rhetorical and Critical Theory*. Ed. James S. Baumlin and Tita French Baumlin. Dallas: Southern Methodist UP, 1994.

Jehlen, Myra. "Archimedes and the Paradox of Feminist Criticism." *Feminisms*. Ed. Robyn R. Warhol and Diane Price Herndl. New Brunswick: Rutgers UP, 1991. 75–96.

Jerome. *Selected Letters*. London: Loeb-Putnam, 1933. 343–63.

Johnson, Nan. *Nineteenth-Century Rhetoric in North America*. Carbondale: Southern Illinois UP, 1991.

Jones, Ann Rosalind. "Surprising Fame: Renaissance Gender Ideologies and Women's Lyric." N. Miller 74–95.

Jonson, Benjamin. *Epicoene, or The Silent Woman*. Bald 207–96.

Julian of Norwich. *Julian of Norwich: Showings*. Trans. from the critical text by Edmund Colledge and James Walsh. New York: Paulist, 1978.

———. *Revelations of Divine Love*. Trans. Clifton Wolters. London: Penguin, 1966.

Just, Roger. *Women in Athenian Law and Life*. London: Routledge, 1989.

Juvenal. *The Satires*. Trans. Rolfe Humphries. Bloomington: Indiana UP, 1958.

Kahrl, Stanley J. *Traditions of Medieval English Drama*. Pittsburgh: U of Pittsburgh P, 1974.

Kellner, Hans. "After the Fall: Reflections on the History of Rhetoric." Vitanza, *Writing* 20–37.

———. "Afterword: Reading Rhetorical Redescriptions." T. Poulakos, *Rethinking* 224–56.

Kelly, Joan. "Did Women Have a Renaissance?" *Women, History, and Theory*. Joan Kelly. Chicago: U of Chicago P, 1984. 19–50.

Kempe, Margery. *The Book of Margery Kempe*. Ed. Sanford Brown Meech and Hope Emily Allen. London: Early English Text Society–Oxford UP, 1940.

Kennedy, George A. *The Art of Rhetoric in the Roman World*. Princeton: Princeton UP, 1972.

———. *Classical Rhetoric and Its Christian and Secular Tradition from Ancient to Modern Times*. Chapel Hill: U of North Carolina P, 1980.

Kerferd, G. B. *The Sophistic Movement*. Cambridge: Cambridge UP, 1981.

Keuls, Eva C. *The Reign of the Phallus*. New York: Harper, 1985.

King, John N. "Queen Elizabeth I: Representations of the Virgin Queen." *Renaissance Quarterly* 43 (1990): 30–74.

King, Margaret. *Women of the Renaissance*. Chicago: U of Chicago P, 1991.

Kinneavy, James L. *Greek Rhetorical Origins of Christian Faith*. New York: Oxford UP, 1987.

Kinney, Arthur F. "Rhetoric and Fiction in Elizabethan England." Murphy, *Renaissance* 385–93.

Kirk, G. S., and J. E. Raven. *The Presocratic Philosophers*. Cambridge: Cambridge UP, 1962.

Kitto, H. D. F. *The Greeks*. Middlesex, Gt. Brit.: Penguin, 1951.

Knowles, David. *English Mystical Tradition*. London: Burns, 1961.

Kristeller, Paul Oskar. *Renaissance Thought and Its Sources*. Ed. Michael Mooney. New York: Columbia UP, 1979.

Krontiris, Tina. *Oppositional Voices: Women as Writers and Translators of Literature in the English Renaissance*. London: Routledge, 1992.

Works Cited

Kuhn, Thomas. *The Structure of Scientific Revolutions*. 2nd ed. Chicago: U of Chicago P, 1970.

Laertius, Diogenes. *Lives of Eminent Philosophers*. 2 vols. London: Loeb-Heinemann, 1931.

Lakoff, Robin Tolmach. *Talking Power*. New York: Basic, 1989.

Lamb, Mary Ellen. "The Cooke Sisters: Attitudes Toward Learned Women in the Renaissance." Hannay 107–29.

Laqueur, Thomas. *Making Sex*. Cambridge: Harvard UP, 1990.

Laurence, Patricia. "Women's Silence as a Ritual of Truth: A Study of Literary Expressions in Austen, Brönte and Woolf." Hedges and Fishkin 156–67.

The Lawes Resolutions of Womens Rights. London, 1632.

Leuba, J. H. *The Psychology of Religious Mysticism*. London: Kegan Paul, 1925.

Levin, Carole, and Patricia A. Sullivan, eds. *Political Rhetoric, Power, and Renaissance Women*. Albany: State U of New York P, 1995.

Licht, Hans [Paul Brandt]. *Sexual Life in Ancient Greece*. London: Abbey Library, 1932.

Lipscomb, Drema. "Sojourner Truth: A Practical Public Discourse." Lunsford 227–46.

Livy, Titus. *Complete Works*. Trans. B. O. Foster. Vol. 2. Cambridge: Harvard-Heinemann, 1967. 14 vols.

——. *Rome and the Mediterranean*. Trans. Henry Bettenson. Harmondsworth, Gt. Brit.: Penguin, 1976.

Logan, Shirley Wilson, ed. *With Pen and Voice: A Critical Anthology of Nineteenth-Century African-American Women*. Carbondale: Southern Illinois UP, 1995.

Loraux, Nicole. *The Children of Athena*. Trans. Caroline Levine. 1984. Princeton: Princeton UP, 1993.

——. *The Invention of Athens*. Trans. Alan Sheridan. Cambridge: Harvard UP, 1990.

Lorde, Audre. "The Transformation of Silence into Action." *Zami / Sister Outsider / Undersong*. New York: Quality Paperback Club, 1993. 40–44.

Lunsford, Andrea A., ed. *Reclaiming Rhetorica*. Pittsburgh: U of Pittsburgh P, 1995.

Mackin, James A., Jr. "Schismogenesis and Community: Pericles' Funeral Oration." *Quarterly Journal of Speech* 77 (1991): 251–62.

Makin, Bathsua. "An Essay to Revive the Ancient Education of Gentlewom[e]n." 1693. *The Female Spectator: English Women Writers Before 1800*. Ed. Mary R. Mahl and Helene Koon. Bloomington: Indiana UP, 1977. 126–35.

Malory, Thomas. *Le Morte D'Arthur*. 2 vols. Middlesex, Gt. Brit.: Penguin, 1969.

Marcus, Leah S. "Shakespeare's Comic Heroines, Elizabeth I, and the Political Uses of Androgyny." *Women in the Middle Ages and the Renaissance*. Ed. Mary Beth Rose. Syracuse: Syracuse UP, 1986. 135–54.

Marrou, H. I. *A History of Education in Antiquity*. Trans. George Lamb. New York: Sheed, 1956.

Marshall, A. J. "Roman Ladies on Trial: The Case of Maesia of Sentinum." *Phoenix* 44 (1990): 46–59.

Mazzola, Elizabeth. "Expert Witnesses and Secret Subjects: Anne Askew's *Examinations* and Renaissance Self-Incrimination." Levin and Sullivan 157–72.

McComiskey, Bruce. "Disassembling Plato's Critique of Rhetoric in the *Gorgias* (447a–466a)." *Rhetoric Review* 11.3 (1992): 79–90.

McCutcheon, Elizabeth. "Margaret More Roper." K. Wilson, *Women Writers* 449–80.

McKeon, Richard. "Rhetoric in the Middle Ages." *Speculum* 17 (1942): 1–32.

Works Cited

Ménage, Gilles. *The History of Women Philosophers*. Trans. Beatrice H. Zedler. Lanham, MD: UP of America, 1984.

Merrill, Yvonne Day. *The Social Construction of Western Women's Rhetoric Before 1750*. New York: Mellen, 1996.

Middleton, Joyce Irene. *The Art of Memory in Toni Morrison's Song of Solomon*. In progress.

Miller, Nancy K., ed. *The Poetics of Gender*. New York: Columbia UP, 1986.

Miller, Susan. *Textual Carnivals: The Politics of Composition*. Carbondale: Southern Illinois UP, 1991.

Miller, Thomas P. "Reinventing Rhetorical Traditions." T. Enos, *Learning* 26–41.

———. "Teaching the Histories of Rhetoric as a Social Praxis." *Rhetoric Review* 12.3 (1993): 70–82.

Modleski, Tania. *Feminism Without Women*. Routledge: New York, 1991.

Mohrmann, Gerald P. "Problems in Current Scholarship." Murphy, *Renaissance* 56–83.

Molinari, Paul. *Julian of Norwich*. London: Longmans, 1958.

Moncrieff, C. K. *The Letters of Héloïse and Abelard*. New York: Knopf, 1942.

Montrose, Louis Adrian. "*A Midsummer Night's Dream* and the Shaping Fantasies of Elizabethan Culture." Ferguson, Quilligan, and Vickers 65–87.

Moss, Roger. "The Case for Sophistry." *Rhetoric Revalued*. Ed. Brian Vickers. Binghamton: Center for Medieval and Early Renaissance Studies, 1982. 207–24.

Mountford, Roxanne. "The Feminization of the *Ars praedicandi*." Diss. Ohio State U, 1991.

Mulvey, Laura. "Visual Pleasure and Narrative Cinema." *Screen* 16:3 (1975): 6–18.

Murphy, James J., ed. *Renaissance Eloquence*. Berkeley: U of California P, 1983.

———. *Rhetoric in the Middle Ages*. Berkeley: U of California P, 1974.

———. "Saint Augustine and the Debate about a Christian Rhetoric." *Quarterly Journal of Speech* 46 (1960): 400–10.

Neale, J. E. *Elizabeth and Her Parliaments*. 2 vols. New York: St. Martin's, 1958.

———. *Queen Elizabeth I*. 1934. Garden City: Anchor-Doubleday, 1957.

Neel, Jasper. *Aristotle's Voice*. Carbondale: Southern Illinois UP, 1994.

———. *Plato, Derrida, and Writing*. Carbondale: Southern Illinois UP, 1988.

Nelson, William. "The Teaching of English in Tudor Grammar Schools." *Studies in Philology* 49 (1952): 119–43.

Nepos, Cornelius. *Cornelius Nepos: A Selection*. Ed. N. Horsfall. Oxford: Oxford UP, 1989.

Nicholson, Linda J., ed. *Feminism/Postmodernism*. New York: Routledge, 1990.

Nye, Andrea. "A Woman's Thought or a Man's Discipline? The Letters of Abelard and Héloïse." *Hypatia* 7 (1992): 1–22.

Ober, Josiah. *Mass and Elite in Democratic Athens*. Princeton: Princeton UP, 1989.

O'Brien, Mary. *The Politics of Reproduction*. London: Routledge, 1981.

Ong, Walter. *Fighting for Life: Contest, Sexuality, and Consciousness*. Ithaca: Cornell UP, 1981.

———. *Orality and Literacy*. New York: Methuen, 1985.

———. "Tudor Writings on Rhetoric." *Studies on the Renaissance* 15 (1968): 36–69.

Orlin, Lena Cowen. "The Fictional Families of Elizabeth I." Levin and Sullivan 85–112.

Otten, Charlotte F., ed. *English Women's Voices, 1540–1700*. Miami: Florida International UP, 1992.

Owst, G. R. *Literature and Pulpit in Medieval England*. Oxford: Basil Blackwell, 1966.

Page, Denys. *Sappho and Alcaeus. An Introduction to the Study of Ancient Lesbian Poetry.* 1955. Oxford: Clarendon, 1959.

Pagels, Elaine. *The Gnostic Gospels.* New York: Random, 1979.

Paglia, Camille. *Sexual Personae.* New York: Vintage-Random, 1990.

Pantel, Pauline Schmitt, ed. *A History of Women: From Ancient Goddesses to Christian Saints.* Vol. 1. Georges Duby and Michelle Perrot, gen. eds. 1992. 5 vols. to date. Cambridge: Belknap-Harvard UP, 1992– .

Partner, Nancy F. "Making Up Lost Time: Writing on the Writing of History." *Speculum* 61 (1986): 90–117.

Pe[a]cham, Henry. *The Garden of Eloquence, Conteyning the Figures of Grammer and Rhetoric.* 1577. Menston, Gt. Brit: Scolar, 1971.

Peaden, Catherine Hobbs, ed. *Nineteenth-Century Women Learn to Write: Past Cultures and Practices of Literacy.* Charlottesville: U of Virginia P, 1994.

Pearl. Trans. and ed. Sister Mary Vincent Hillman. Notre Dame: U of Notre Dame P, 1961.

Petroff, Elizabeth. "Medieval Women Visionaries: Seven Stages to Power." *Frontiers* 3 (1978): 34–45.

Phelan, James. *Reading People, Reading Plots.* Chicago: U of Chicago P, 1989.

Philo. *Allegorical Interpretations of Genesis.* Trans. F. H. Colson and G. H. Whitaker. London: Loeb, 1929.

———. *On the Virtues.* Trans. F. H. Colson. Cambridge: Harvard UP, 1939.

Plato. *Euthyphro, Apology, Crito, Phaedo, Phaedrus.* Trans. H. N. Fowler. Cambridge: Harvard UP, 1977.

———. *Republic.* Trans. Paul Shorey. 2 vols. Cambridge: Harvard UP, 1982.

———. *Symposium, Lysis, Gorgias.* Trans. W. R. M. Lamb. Cambridge: Harvard-Heinemann, 1925.

———. *Timaeus, Critias, Cleitophon, Menexenus, Epistles.* Trans. R. G. Bury. 1929. London: Heinemann-Loeb, 1981.

Plett, Heinrich F. "The Place and Function of Style in Renaissance Poetics." Murphy, *Renaissance* 356–75.

Pliny the Younger. *Letters and Panegyrics.* Trans. Betty Radice. 2 vols. Cambridge: Harvard-Heinemann, 1969.

Plowden, Alison. *Tudor Women: Queens and Commoners.* New York: Atheneum, 1979.

Plutarch. *The Lives of the Noble Grecians and Romans.* Trans. John Dryden. Rev. Arthur Hugh Clough. New York: Modern Library, 1932.

———. "On Affection for Offspring." *Plutarch's Moralia in Sixteen Volumes.* Trans. W. C. Helmbold. Vol. 6. Cambridge: Loeb, 1920. 330–57.

Pomeroy, Sarah. *Goddesses, Whores, Wives, and Slaves.* New York: Schocken, 1975.

Poulakos, John. "Towards a Sophistic Definition of Rhetoric." *Philosophy and Rhetoric* 16 (1983): 35–48.

Poulakos, Takis. "Introduction: Alternative Approaches to the Rhetorical Tradition." T. Poulakos, *Rethinking* 1–10.

———, ed. *Rethinking the History of Rhetoric.* Boulder: Westview, 1983.

Pringle, Roger, ed. *A Portrait of Elizabeth I.* London: Ward Lock, n.d.

Puttenham, George. *The Arte of English Poesie.* 1589. Intro. Baxter Hathaway. Fac. rpt. of 1906 ed. Kent, OH: Kent State UP, 1970.

Quintilian. *Institutio oratoria.* Trans. H. E. Butler. 1920. 4 vols. London: Heinemann, 1969.

Rabinowitz, Peter. "Truth in Fiction: A Reexamination of Audiences." *Critical Inquiry* 4 (1977): 121–41.

Ratcliffe, Krista. *Anglo-American Challenges to the Rhetorical Tradition(s): Virginia Woolf, Mary Daly, and Adrienne Rich.* Carbondale: Southern Illinois UP, 1994.

Reynolds, E. E. *Margaret Roper.* New York: Kennedy, 1960.

Rice, Eugene F., Jr. *Saint Jerome in the Renaissance.* Baltimore: Johns Hopkins UP, 1985.

Rice, George P., Jr. *The Public Speaking of Queen Elizabeth.* New York: AMS, 1966.

Rich, Adrienne. "Cartographies of Silence." *This Dream of a Common Language: Poems 1974–1977.* New York: Norton, 1978. 16–20.

———. *On Lies, Secrets, and Silence.* New York: Norton, 1979.

Richards, Ann. "Keynote Address." *Vital Speeches* 54 (15 Aug. 1988): 647–49.

Riehle, Wolfgang. *The Middle English Mystics.* London: Routledge, 1981.

Robert of Basevorn. "*Forma praedicandi.*" *Three Medieval Rhetorical Arts.* Ed. James J. Murphy. Berkeley: U of California P, 1971. 109–215.

Robinson, David M. *Sappho and Her Influence.* New York: Cooper Square, 1963.

Rogers, Elizabeth Frances, ed. *Correspondence of Sir Thomas More.* Princeton: Princeton UP, 1947.

Roper, Margaret More. *A Devout Treatise Upon the Pater Noster, Tourned into English by a Young Gentyl Woman.* London: Berthelet, 1526.

Rorty, Richard. *Philosophy and the Mirror of Nature.* Princeton: Princeton UP, 1979.

Royster, Jacqueline Jones. "To Call a Thing by Its True Name: The Rhetoric of Ida B. Wells." Lunsford 167–84.

Ruether, Rosemary Radford, ed. *Religion and Sexism.* New York: Simon, 1974.

———. *Sexism and God-Talk: Toward a Feminist Theology.* Boston: Beacon, 1983.

———. *Womanguides: Readings Toward a Feminist Theology.* Boston: Beacon, 1985.

Rushing, Janice Hocker, ed. *Southern Communication Journal* 57 (1992).

Ryan, Lawrence V. Introduction. *The Schoolmaster (1570) by Roger Ascham.* Charlottesville: U of Virginia P, 1967.

Salzman, L. F. *English Life in the Middle Ages.* London: Oxford UP, 1926.

Sappho. *Sappho: A New Translation.* Trans. Mary Barnard. Berkeley: U of California P, 1958.

———. *Sappho: Poems & Fragments.* Trans. Josephine Balmer. Secaucus, NJ: Meadowland, 1984.

———. *Sappho's Lyre: Archaic Lyric and Women Poets of Ancient Greece.* Trans. Diane Raynor. Berkeley: U of California P, 1991.

Saxonhouse, Arlene W. "Eros and the Female in Greek Political Thought: An Interpretation of Plato's *Symposium.*" *Political Theory* 12.1 (1984): 5–27.

———. "The Philosopher and the Female in the Political Thought of Plato." *Political Theory* 4.2 (1976): 195–212.

Saylor, Steven. *Arms of Nemesis.* New York: Ivy, 1992.

———. *Catalina's Riddle.* New York: Ivy, 1993.

———. *Murder on the Appian Way.* New York: St. Martin's, 1996.

———. *Roman Blood.* New York: Ivy, 1991.

———. *Venus Throw.* New York: St. Martin's, 1995.

Sayre, Dorothy. *Are Women Human?* Grand Rapids, MI: Eerdmans, 1971.

Schaps, David M. "The Woman Least Mentioned: Etiquette and Women's Names." *Classical Quarterly* 27 (1977): 323–31.

Schiappa, Edward. "Neo-Sophistic Rhetorical Criticism or the Historical Reconstruction of Sophistic Doctrines?" *Philosophy and Rhetoric* 23 (1990): 192–217.

———. *Protagoras and Logos*. Columbia: U of South Carolina P, 1991.

———. "Sophistic Rhetoric: Oasis or Mirage?" *Rhetoric Review* 10 (1991): 5–18.

Scott, Joan Wallach. *Gender and the Politics of History*. New York: Columbia UP, 1988.

Scott, Robert L. "The Necessary Pluralism of Any Future History of Rhetoric." *Pre/Text* 12 (1991): 195–210.

Seltman, Charles. *Women in Antiquity*. London: Thames and Hudson, 1956.

Shakespeare, William. *The Riverside Shakespeare*. Boston: Houghton, 1974.

Sharp, Benjamin O. "Anne Askew—Martyr." 1896. *College Pamphlets* 1341. London, n.d.

Sidney, Philip. *An Apology for Poetry or The Defense of Poesy*. Ed. Charles W. Eliot. Vol. 27. *The Harvard Classics*. New York: Collier, 1910. 50 vols. 7–58.

Sissela, Guilia. "The Sexual Philosophies of Plato and Aristotle." Pantel 46–81.

Skelton, John. "Phyllyp Sparowe." *The Anchor Anthology of Sixteenth-Century Verse*. Ed. Richard Sylvester. New York: Anchor, 1974. 22–69.

Smith, Barbara Herrenstein. *Poetic Closure*. Chicago: U of Chicago P, 1968.

Smith-Rosenberg, Carroll. "Writing History: Language, Class, and Gender." de Laurentis 31–54.

Snyder, Jane McIntosh. *The Woman and the Lyre: Women Writers in Classical Greece and Rome*. Carbondale: Southern Illinois UP, 1989.

Spender, Dale. *Man Made Language*. London: Routledge, 1980.

Spenser, Edmund. *The Faerie Queene*. 2 vols. New York: Scolar, 1976.

Sprague, Rosamond Kent, ed. *The Older Sophists*. Columbia: U of South Carolina P, 1972.

Stallybrass, Peter. "Patriarchal Territories: The Body Enclosed." Ferguson, Quilligan, and Vickers 123–44.

Stapleton, Thomas. *The Life and Illustrious Martyrdom of Sir Thomas More*. 1588. Trans. Philip E. Hallett. Ed. E. E. Reynolds. New York: Fordham, 1966.

Stock, Brian. *Listening for the Text: On the Uses of the Past*. Baltimore: Johns Hopkins UP, 1990.

Stone, Lawrence. *The Family, Sex, and Marriage in England 1500–1800*. New York: Harper, 1977.

Stone, Robert Karl. *Middle English Prose Style*. The Hague: Mouton, 1970.

Swearingen, C. Jan. "A Lover's Discourse: Diotima, [Aspasia,] Logos, and Desire." Lunsford 25–52.

———. *Rhetoric and Irony*. New York: Oxford UP, 1991.

Szarmach, Paul, ed. *An Introduction to the Medieval Mystics of Europe*. Albany: State U of New York P, 1984.

Tacitus. *Dialogue on Oratory, Agricola, Germania*. Trans. William Peterson. Cambridge: Harvard-Heinemann, 1963.

Taylor, A. E. *Plato, the Man and his Work*. 7th ed. London: Methuen, 1960.

Teague, Frances. "Elizabeth I." K. Wilson, *Women Writers* 522–46.

Thesleff, Holger. *An Introduction to the Pythagorean Writings of the Hellenistic Period*. Abo, Finland: Abo Akademi, 1961.

Thomas, Keith. "Women and the Civil War Sects." *Past and Present* 13.2 (1958): 42–62.

Thomas, Yan. "The Division of the Sexes in Roman Law." Pantel 83–137.

Thomas Aquinas. *Summa Theologica*. Trans. Fathers of the English Dominican Province. Westminster, MD: Christian Classics, 1981.

Thomasset, Claude. "The Nature of Women." Trans. Arthur Goldhammer. *A History of Women in the West: Silences of the Middle Ages.* Ed. Christiane Klapisch-Zuber. Vol. 2. Georges Duby and Michelle Perrot, gen. eds. 1992. 5 vols. to date. Cambridge: Belknap-Harvard UP, 1992– . 43–69.

Thucydides. *History of the Peloponnesian War.* Trans. Rex Warner. London: Penguin, 1954.

Thurston, H. "Margery the Astonishing." *The Month* 2 (1936): 446–56.

Travitsky, Betty, ed. *The Paradise of Women: Writings by Englishwomen of the Renaissance.* Westport, CT: Greenwood, 1981.

Trinkaus, Charles. *The Scope of Renaissance Humanism.* Ann Arbor: U of Michigan P, 1983.

Tuana, Nancy. "The Weaker Seed, The Sexist Bias of Reproductive Theory." *Hypatia* 3 (1988). Rpt. in *Feminism and Science.* Ed. Nancy Tuana. Bloomington: Indiana UP, 1989. 147–71.

Valerius Maximus, Quintus. *His Collection of the Memorable Acts and Sayings of Orators, Philosophers, Statesmen, and Other Illustrious Persons of the Antient Romans, and Other Foreign Nations, Upon Various Subjects, Together with the Life of That Famous Historian.* London, 1684.

Verbrugge, Rita M. "Margaret More Roper's Personal Expression." Hannay 30–42.

Vernant, Jean-Pierre. *Myth and Society in Ancient Greece.* 1974. New York: Zone, 1980.

———. *Myth and Thought among the Greeks.* 1965. London: Routledge, 1983.

———. *The Origins of Greek Thought.* 1962. Ithaca: Cornell UP, 1982.

Vickers, Brian. *In Defense of Rhetoric.* Oxford: Clarendon-Oxford, 1988.

———. "The Power of Persuasion." Murphy, *Renaissance* 411–36.

———. "Some Reflections on the Rhetoric Textbook." *Renaissance Rhetoric.* Ed. Peter Mack. New York: St. Martin's, 1994. 81–102.

Vidal-Naquet, Pierre. *The Black Hunter.* Trans. Andrew Szegedy-Maszak. Baltimore: Johns Hopkins UP, 1986.

Vitanza, Victor. Editor's Preface, Dedication, and Acknowledgments. Vitanza, *Writing* vii–xii.

———, ed. *Writing Histories of Rhetoric.* Carbondale: Southern Illinois UP, 1994.

Vives, Juan Luis. *De tradendis disciplinis (The Transmission of Knowledge).* Trans. Foster Watson. Totowa, NJ: Rowman, 1971.

Vlastos, Gregory. "The Individual as an Object of Love in Plato." *Platonic Studies.* Princeton: Princeton UP, 1973.

Waithe, Mary Ellen, ed. *A History of Women Philosophers, Vol. 1. 600 BC–500 AD.* Dordrecht: Martinus Nijhoff, 1987. 4 vols.

———. "On Not Teaching the History of Philosophy." *Hypatia* 4 (1989): 133–38.

Ward, Julie K. "*Harmonia and Koinonia*: Moral Values for Pythagorean Women." *Explorations in Feminist Ethics.* Ed. Eve Cole and Susan Coultrap-McQuin. Bloomington: Indiana UP, 1992. 57–68.

Warnicke, Retha M. *Women of the English Renaissance and Reformation.* Westport, CT: Greenwood, 1983.

Watson, Foster, ed. *Vives and the Renascence Education of Women.* New York: Longmans, 1912.

Webster, John. *The Duchess of Malfi.* Bald 297–388.

Weissman, Hope Phyllis. "Margery Kempe in Jerusalem: *Hysterica compassio* in the Late Middle Ages." *Acts of Interpretation: The Text in Its Contexts, 700–1600: Essays on Me-*

dieval and Renaissance Literature. Ed. Mary J. Carruthers and Elizabeth D. Kirk. Norman, OK: Pilgrim, 1982. 201–17.

Welch, Kathleen. *The Contemporary Reception of Classical Rhetoric.* Hillsdale, NJ: Erlbaum, 1990.

———. "Plato, Diotima, and Teaching Discourse." Young Rhetoricians' Conference. Monterey, CA. July 1994.

Wertheimer, Molly Meijer, ed. *Listening to Their Voices: Essays on the Rhetorical Activities of Historical Women.* Columbia: U of South Carolina P, 1997.

West, Susan. "From Owning to Owning Up: 'Authorial' Rights and Rhetorical Responsibility." Diss. Ohio State U, 1997.

———. "Stolen Goods: Who 'Plagiarized' Lani Guinier?" Unpublished ms. 1996.

White, Hayden. *Tropics of Discourse.* Baltimore: Johns Hopkins UP, 1978.

Wider, Kathleen. "Women Philosophers in the Ancient Greek World: Donning the Mantle." *Hypatia* 1 (1986): 21–62.

Wilson, Katharina M., ed. *Medieval Women Writers.* Athens: U of Georgia P, 1984.

———. *Women Writers of the Renaissance and Reformation.* Athens: U of Georgia P, 1987.

Wilson, R. M. "Three Middle English Mystics." *Essays and Studies* ns 9 (1956): 85–112.

Wilson, Thomas. *The Arte of Rhetorique.* 1553. Intro. Robert Hood Bowers. Fac. rpt. Gainesville, FL: Scholars', 1962.

Winterowd, W. Ross. *Rhetoric: A Synthesis.* New York: Holt, 1968.

Wittig, Monique. "The Mark of Gender." N. Miller 63–73.

Woodbridge, Linda. *Women and the English Renaissance.* Urbana: U of Illinois P, 1986.

Woodward, William Harrison, ed. *Vittorino da Feltre and Other Humanist Educators.* New York: Columbia U, Teachers College P, 1963.

Wright, Frederick Adam. *Feminism in Greek Literature from Homer to Aristotle.* London: Routledge, 1923.

Wyntjes, Sherrin Marshall. "Women in the Reformation Era." *Becoming Visible: Women in European History.* Ed. Renate Bridenthal and Claudia Koontz. Boston: Houghton, 1977. 165–91.

Xenophon. *Memorabilia and Oeconomicus.* Trans. E. C. Marchant. Cambridge: Harvard UP, 1988.

INDEX

Cheryl Glenn is an associate professor of English at The Pennsylvania State University. Her historiographic work has earned her an NEH Fellowship and the Conference on College Composition and Communication Richard Braddock Award. With Robert J. Connors, she is the coauthor of the *St. Martin's Guide to Teaching Writing*.